Capitol

THE UNITED STATES CAPITOL

THE UNITED STATES CAPITOL
ITS ARCHITECTURE AND DECORATION

HENRY HOPE REED

PRINCIPAL PHOTOGRAPHY BY ANNE DAY

W. W. NORTON & COMPANY · NEW YORK · LONDON

TO CONSTANCE

Copyright © 2005 by Henry Hope Read

Composed in Perpetua, designed in 1929–30 by Eric Gill

Manufacturing by Mondadori Printing, Verona

Book design by Robert L. Wiser, Silver Spring, Maryland

Publication funded by the Arthur Ross Foundation

Endpapers: Detail of L'Enfant's plan of a future Capitol.
Universal Asylum and Columbia Magazine, *March 1792.*
Courtesy Library of Congress.

Page ii: West face of the United States Capitol. (Day)

Pages iv–v: The United States Capitol on the occasion of the Second Inauguration of President McKinley, March 1901. Courtesy Elliott Banfield.

Page vi: Freedom *by Thomas Crawford. (Day)*

Pages xxii–xxiii: Patent Corridor outside the Senate Committee on Foreign Relations Room. (Day)

Library of Congress Cataloging-in-Publication Data
Reed, Henry Hope.
    The United States Capitol ; its architecture and decoration /
Henry Hope Reed.
        p.   cm.
    Includes bibliographical references and index.
    ISBN 0-393-03831-9
    United States Capitol (Washington, D.C.) 2. Neoclassicism
(Architecture)—Washington (D.C.) 3. Interior architecture—
Washington (D.C.) 4. Washington (D.C.)—Buildings, structures,
etc. I. Title.
NA4411 .R44 2005
725'.11'09753—dc21
2001034509

W.W. Norton & Company, Inc.
500 Fifth Avenue, New York, N.Y. 10110
www.wwnorton.com

W.W. Norton & Company Ltd.
Castle House, 75/76 Wells Street, London W1T 3QT

1   2   3   4   5   6   7   8   9   0

CONTENTS

Foreword by Arthur Ross...*ix*

Preface...*x*

Acknowledgments...*xii*

INTRODUCTION

THE CAPITOL

The Siting of the Capital...2

Major Pierre Charles L'Enfant...4

William Thornton...5

Benjamin Henry Latrobe...8

Charles Bulfinch...10

THE CAPITOL EXTENSION AND THE DOME

Thomas Ustick Walter...13

Captain Montgomery Cunningham Meigs...21

Constantino Brumidi...24

The Dome...29

After the Dome...33

CODA

The Influence of the United States Capitol...36

OPEN TO THE PUBLIC

The Approach...44

The Dome...45

The East Front...51

The Great Rotunda...74

The Apotheosis of Washington...86

The Old House Chamber (Statuary Hall)...91

The Old Senate Chamber...98

The Old Supreme Court Chamber...105

The Crypt...108

The Brumidi Corridors...112

The Senate Reception Room...121

The Senate Chamber...128

The House Chamber...131

The Hall of Columns, the Hall of Capitols,
the Great Experiment Hall,
and the Westward Expansion Mural...134

The Facades, the Grounds, and the Terrace...138

CLOSED TO THE PUBLIC

THE SENATE COMMITTEE
ON APPROPRIATIONS

Room s-127...147

Room s-128...151

Room s-129...151

The President's Room (s-216)...153

The Lyndon Baines Johnson Room (s-211)
and the Office of the Vice President (s-212)...159

The Defense Subcommittee of the House Appropriations
Committee (Room h-144)...162

OTHER ROOMS
CLOSED TO THE PUBLIC

Three Architects' Rooms: The Senate Retiring Room,
the House Retiring Room, and the Sam Rayburn
or House Reception Room...165

The Speaker's Room...168

Some Mural Decorations of the 1900s...169

Stucco Enrichment: Its Role...171

APPENDIX

Identifications...174

Illustrated Glossary of Architectural
and Decorative Terms...183

Biographies...192

Notes...204

Index...207

The Classical America Series in Art and Architecture

Henry Hope Reed and H. Stafford Bryant, General Editors

IN PREPARATION

Architectural Rendering in Wash by H. Van Buren Magonigle

Motifs Historiques d'Architecture et Sculpture by César Daly

WITH W. W. NORTON & COMPANY, INC.

The Architecture of Humanism by Geoffrey Scott

The Classic Point of View by Kenyon Cox

What is Painting? and Other Essays by Kenyon Cox

Man As Hero: The Human Figure in Western Art by Pierce Rice

The Golden City by Henry Hope Reed

The New York Public Library: Its Architecture and Decoration by Henry Hope Reed

The United States Capitol: Its Architecture and Decoration by Henry Hope Reed

The Decoration of Houses by Edith Wharton and Ogden Codman, Jr.

The Elements of Classical Architecture by Georges Gromort;
H. Stafford Bryant, project editor, with translations and essays by J. François Gabriel,
Henry Hope Reed, Richard Franklin Sammons, and Steven W. Semes

WITH DA CAPO PRESS, INC.

Italian Villas and Their Gardens by Edith Wharton

WITH DOVER PUBLICATIONS, INC.

The American Vignola by William R. Ware

Greek and Roman Architecture in Classic Drawings by Hector d'Espouy

Monumental Classic Architecture in Great Britain and Ireland by Albert E. Richardson

WITH THE ARCHITECTURAL BOOK PUBLISHING COMPANY

Student's Edition of the *Monograph of the Work of McKim, Mead and White, 1879–1915*

Letarouilly on Renaissance Rome by John Barrington Bayley

Student's Edition of Paul Letarouilly's *Edifices de Rome Moderne et Le Vatican et la Basilique de Saint-Pierre*

Drawing of the Classical: A Videotape Series Devoted to the Five Orders by Alvin Holm, A.I.A.
Tape I: A Measured Approach to Architecture: The Moldings and the Baluster; Tape II: The Doric

The Institute of Classical Architecture and Classical America is the society devoted to the classical
tradition in the arts in the United States. Inquiries about the society should be addressed to:
Institute of Classical Architecture and Classical America, 20 West 44th Street, New York, N.Y. 10110.

FOREWORD

Each country has its symbol of national identity and ours is the U.S. Capitol. It is America's greatest building; it is in the monumental and classical tradition of Western art and is among the great symbols of Western civilization. The U.S. Capitol is regarded by the public and, one might say, universally, as the symbol of democracy. Within its walls are held the great debates that lead to the laws and policies that rule our country and extend its influence far beyond our shores.

In this fully illustrated volume, Henry Hope Reed, founder and former president of Classical America, and now honorary president and scholar in residence of the Institute of Classical Architecture and Classical America, presents an insightful and complete history of this great structure. It describes in particular those parts open to the public and explores this great display of architecture and interior artistic achievement. The magnificent illustrations combined with the author's stately prose, make this publication a significant historical document.

The construction of the Capitol commenced in 1790 on its present site at the center of America's premier classically planned city, Washington, D.C. The original structure was burned to the ground by the British in the War of 1812, and the present building was constructed on the same site and completed in 1855. Now viewed almost daily by millions on television, it has long been represented in engravings, woodcuts, and photographs. With its remarkable dome, designed by the Philadelphia architect, Thomas Ustick Walter, it has come to symbolize American aspirations.

The building, in the words of Mr. Reed, is one of the world's most splendid, comparable to St. Peter's in Rome, St. Paul's in London, and the Palace of Versailles. With its soaring cast-iron dome and elaborate interior decoration by Constantino Brumidi, the Capitol's unique aesthetic value was widely recognized and launched the monumental classical movement in this country. The building has more true fresco spread throughout its entire structure than is likely to be found in any comparable structure.

The House and Senate chambers, designed by Benjamin Henry Latrobe, reach a level of unsurpassed excellence. This set a standard, inspired our state capitols, courthouses, and city halls across the nation, and generally raised the country's level of taste.

The creation of this monumental, and now sacred, edifice as a symbol of America's greatness, received its sponsorship from our earliest illustrious leaders: George Washington, Alexander Hamilton, and Thomas Jefferson. In 1812, Thomas Jefferson said, "The Capitol is the first temple dedicated to the sovereignty of the people, embellishing with Athenian taste the course of a nation looking far beyond the range of Athenian destinies."

It is hoped that this book will heighten the awareness of this great structure in our country and abroad. The building and its interior decorations have had a major role in bringing the classical tradition to our shores and draws ever-greater attention to the functioning of our democracy.

Arthur Ross, Honorary Chairman
The Institute of Classical Architecture and Classical America
New York City, March 2004

PREFACE

No other parliament building in the world throws open its doors to the people as does the United States Capitol. This has been true from the beginning. In 1799, when the federal government moved from Philadelphia to the nascent city of Washington, President John Adams, the Congress, and the public were welcomed to a modest wing, the only portion then built. (It did not achieve its present silhouette until 1864.) The high point of the nation's quadrennial ceremony, which began in Washington with that of Thomas Jefferson in 1801, must be the second inauguration of President McKinley in 1901. An enthusiastic public, as might be expected, gathered in front of the inaugural stand at the central portico of the East Front. But what was astonishing, as shown in the photograph on pages iv–v, were the spectators on the roof. For a day the Capitol was a human anthill. Who then would have guessed that, a century later, there would be a construction site where the crowd once gathered? Begun in 1999, work on an underground visitor center had been well under way when the horror of September 11, 2001, underscored the importance of security.

An underground visitor center to a great building is a novelty. Such a restricted welcome was first adopted at the Louvre Museum in Paris where the center is identified aboveground by a glass pyramid. At the Capitol, there will be no pyramid but a standard skylight to permit a view from belowground of the familiar dome. The center will also serve the Jefferson Building of the Library of Congress nearby, to be reached by a long tunnel.

While the visitor center will rob both buildings of one of their spectacular wonders, that of stepping directly from the outside into a magnificent interior, much as is still possible at the Pantheon of ancient Rome, the loss will not discourage the endless daily stream of visitors. Other than the simple fact that one of the great buildings is our seat of government, the United States Capitol and the Jefferson Building are the two most embellished structures in Washington.

While we are accustomed to think of buildings primarily in terms of architecture, what distinguishes both is the presence of painted, carved, and modeled decoration. On this score, they are without rivals in the nation. The lessons here for all citizens is that all the decorative arts, not just architecture, make a great building. For that reason, the two are the best introduction for Americans to the classical tradition of sculpture and painting that is centered on the depiction of the human figure.

Visitors must be reminded that the role of the human figure is not confined to the two buildings but can be seen throughout the city of Washington. We think at once of the bronze cavalry, the equestrian statues that are so much a part of the city's vistas. Beyond the bronze cavalry are the domes. Washington is a city of domes. Then there are the sculpted masks, often on keystones, such as are found at the Mellon Auditorium on Constitution Avenue. Washington's fountains, while they may not rival the Mitchell Fountain in Detroit's Belle Isle Park, are among the nation's best. Consider the Neptune Fountain in front of the Jefferson Building and the cascade in Meridian Hill Park. Or there is the country's best classical column, that of the First Division Monument south of the Old Executive Office Building. There are balustrades at windows and rooftops. And there is the splendid arcade that fronts Union Station. Once the measure of the United States Capitol and the Jefferson Building is recognized, the city's wonders stand out. A new and radiant world comes into view.

To underscore the place of the Capitol and for that matter the Jefferson Building, in American art, one must point out that today's Modern art represents the total opposite of them both. The key reason that today's so-called Modern has such a grip on our outlook is the very word, "modern". For one thing, the label conveys the illusion of progress in human affairs, the inevitable superiority of all that is latest in human activity. But there is no such element as "progress" in the arts. For example, where is the progress after Raphael and Michaelangelo, or, for that matter, after the Venus de Milo? As for today's "progress in the arts," it is the product of notions a century and a half or two centuries old—hardly "modern." Whatever the source, the result with the label Modern is nothing less than an art of starvation—visual starvation, to mix a metaphor yet again. There is no attempt to respond to the sense of sight, the demands and the pleasure of just seeing.

For that reason, the word "modern" is not just useless; it is, to adopt a fashionable term, *counterproductive*. A new label will clear the air. I suggest the term Anorexic, taken from anorexia nervosa, a nervous ailment identified by an eating disorder, aversion to eating. It leads to starvation and even death. It strikes particularly girls and young women. Anorexic painting and sculpture would offer the equivalent of skeletons or, at best, fragments. The human figure is no longer distinguished by beauty but by ugliness, either by line or by repulsive colors.

In architecture, Anorexic is easily identified by a glass slab or a limestone building without any carved stone. In sculpture, it is bronze lumps 10 feet high with a hole or several holes. In painting, it may be tinted squares on lined canvas or a grotesquely depicted human form in bilious colors.

Ornament has been completely sacrificed. Streets, even whole communities are built without ornament, to the degree that they are termed inhuman. We have forgotten the apothegm of the philosopher George Santayana: a building without ornament is like the heavens without stars. And we can add that architecture without ornament is mere construction.

That the Western world should have rejected its glorious heritage for Anorexic art is bewildering. We can only echo another philosopher, Ernest Renan: The one element that gives us a sense of the infinite is the extent of human stupidity. The continuous destruction of the great Western tradition, above all the Classical, is dumbfounding.

Certainly the spectacle of great universities discarding collections of casts of classical and even Gothic architecture and sculpture is one of the extraordinary episodes in American cultural history. Columbia, Harvard, Yale, Pennsylvania, one after the other, emptied the halls of historic work. The University of Missouri, an exception, has kept its collection in storage. The University of Texas at Austin is a rare example where, in the administration of President Lorene Lane Rogers, the cast collection was restored and made accessible to students. Cornell University still has a collection, but much of it is on loan. Among major art museums, at least the Metropolitan Museum of Art has most of its large collection, if sadly neglected. Strangely enough Canada, which is restive in the shadow of the United States, went further: Nearly all casts have long vanished. (It should be remarked that several dozen casts, most from Cornell University, are on loan at the New York Academy of Art. There the mural painter Edward Schmidt insists that his students begin by learning how to draw the antique.) The disappearance of the casts from the major universities and art museums admittedly followed the shift from traditional to realism (naturalism). The Anorexic would turn up to replace realism, particularly the academic branch, with chaos, and, as for architecture, it would simply abolish ornament, once a domain shared with painting and sculpture.

Oddly enough, it is at small museums such as the Slater Memorial Museum in Norwich, Connecticut, the George Walter Vincent Smith Art Museum in Springfield, Massachusetts, and Mount Holyoke College in South Hadley, also in Massachusetts, where casts have survived. Of course, the Carnegie-Mellon Institute in Pittsburgh has always maintained its cast collection.

(The degree of the ruthlessness of the Anorexic can be seen in the dispersal of this country's greatest portrait collection, that of the Chamber of Commerce of the State of New York. Once housed in the Chamber's building at 85 Liberty Street, in New York City, the building is now the International Commercial Bank, owned by China. The Chamber has disappeared and the portraits have been sold.)

A curious aspect of the several shifts in the arts, often greeted as "revolt" or "revolution," was that they were part of the coming of a new social stratum, bohemianism or bohemia. Bohemianism was the domain of struggling artists and writers with a special rebellious code and manners, and oddly enough, bohemians, although basically middle-class, prided themselves in being anti–middle-class. After 1900 the Anorexic fitted nicely in the enclaves of bohemianism. It was only a matter of time before bohemianism spilled out of the enclaves among the well-to-do with the Anorexic as the chief message. Art history departments of the more prominent universities and the art museums joined the new band with the converts known as "Upper Bohemians." The anti–middle-class note was muted in a new snobbery. One of the most astonishing consequences can be seen in the simple fact that, with rare exception, new art museums and new wings of old art museums are Anorexic, as are the new structures of institutions of higher learning. Even the acanthus leaf, a supremely classical device, has disappeared from America's paper currency. Inevitably we return to the United States Capitol for some measure of guidance.

Henry Hope Reed
New York City, May 2004

ACKNOWLEDGMENTS

This book springs from Classical America. To Paul Hacker I would like to extend particular thanks as a first gesture for sustaining Classical America as its business manager for three decades.

The roots of Classical America go back almost two generations. Sparked by the enthusiasm of Wayne Andrews, several of us explored our country's historical and architectural heritage. For me this was supplemented by the privilege of exploring Rome with the architect John Barrington Bayley, then at the American Academy in Rome, on the G. I. Bill. Further good fortune came my way when Christopher Tunnard, professor of city planning at Yale University, employed me to do research for him when he was writing *The City of Man*, a groundbreaking study of our urban world. (This was supplemented by a joint venture—a survey of the various forces, with emphasis on civic design, which shaped the American community—entitled *American Skyline*.) Not to be overlooked was an exhibition, *Ars in Urbe*, at the Yale University Art Gallery in 1952. Organized by Christopher Tunnard and Lamont Moore, assistant director of the gallery, it proclaimed the triumph of the classical in the shaping of the city.

Two years later another exhibition, *Monuments of Manhattan*, sponsored by the University Club and the Municipal Art Society of New York, hailed the city's classical wonders, from a statue of Richard Morris Hunt with a stonecarver's mallet, a plaster cast of the one which once stood on a pinnacle of William K. Vanderbilt's mansion on Fifth Avenue, to a rendering of Horace Trumbauer's mansion for James Buchanan Duke, today the Fine Arts Institute of New York University. From this exhibition sprang the walking tours of the Municipal Art Society, initiated by the artist E. Powis Jones and the author in 1956. A book, *The Golden City*, foretelling the inevitable demise of Modern art (Anorexic art) and the triumph of the classical tradition, the dominant artistic current of Western civilization, appeared in 1959. (If the book has a hero, it is Arthur Brown, Jr., of Bakewell & Brown, who designed the San Francisco City Hall.)

In the late 1960s a few devotees of the classical gathered to found Classical America to initiate a renewal of the grand tradition. Interestingly enough, most of the founders and early board members were not architects. Among them were Professor Charles K. Warner (French history); John A. Day, a lawyer; Clark McLaine, a trucker and realtor; Professor William A. Coles (English literature); James T. Maher, author of *The Twilight of Splendor*; Pierce Rice, a painter;

Raymond Waldron, an interior decorator; David Garrard Lowe, magazine editor; H. Stafford (Stu) Bryant, journalist and an editor at the publishing firm of W. W. Norton & Company; and the architect John Barrington Bayley, who made palpable the glories of the classical.

Later board members would include Michael George, who worked in television; the muralist Hight Moore; Thomas S. Hayes, tour director; Nicholas King, journalist and travel writer; and the architects Allen Greenberg, John Blatteau, and Alvin Holm, but the architectural profession remained in the minority. The most important initial venture was the publication of a magazine, *Classical America*, with Professor Coles as editor. It was in its pages that were published the designs for country houses by Clay Lancaster. It was also in *Classical America* that Philip Trammel Shutze of Atlanta, a great classical architect hitherto neglected, gained national attention. The vernacular was not neglected, nor the work of Neel Reid, also of Atlanta, and William Lawrence Bottomley of Richmond, Virginia. And there was an article on American's greatest fountain, the little-known Scott Memorial Fountain on Belle Isle, Detroit.

A second venture, begun in 1977, was the offering of instruction in the classical and in perspective. The instructor was George Frederick Poehler, an associate of John Barrington Bayley in the designing of the new wing of the Frick Collection in New York, and the instruction was offered in a room made available at the Architectural School of University of Pennsylvania. Board member Pierce Rice later took over instruction, teaching it as well at the National Academy of Design in New York. His best student, Alvin Holm, would join him. At the time, Classical America was offering the only instruction in classical architecture in the country, to be underscored by the fact that the chief instructor was a painter, not an architect.

It could be that, at the time, the only other architectural course in the classical was offered by the International Correspondence School of Scranton, Pennsylvania. Classical America obtained the school's text, William H. Ware's *The American Vignola*, for distribution to members. (Beginning in the 1890s, *The American Vignola* had been a very popular text, Ware being the head of Columbia University's School of Architecture.)

When the International Correspondence School raised the price of what was little more than a brochure with plates, Stu Bryant suggested that he would try to interest W. W. Norton in publishing it. With a subvention promised by the Arthur Ross Foundation, his colleagues at the firm—George Brockway, Victor Schmalzer, James Mairs, and Diane O'Connor—accepted the project and, in 1970, the first volume of the *Classical America Series in Art and Architecture* was in print.

By then it was obvious that inexpensive texts had to be made available to an interested public. After all, New York's Museum of Modern Art had recognized the value of books in launching Modern (Anorexic) art; in fact, the noted museum was the largest publisher of art books in the world by 1939. And, of course, there was the simple fact that the invention of printing in the fifteenth century had made possible the spread of the Renaissance across Europe.

The year 1977 saw Classical America, with the help of the Arthur Ross Foundation, bring the wonderful models of the work of Andrea Palladio to New York, specifically to the Cooper-Hewitt Museum. Beautiful photographs of the master's work by Joseph Farber supplemented the models in the exhibition. A second exhibition, this time sponsored by Avery Library of Columbia University (Adolph Placzek, Librarian) Atlanta Historical Society, and Classical America, was devoted to the work of Philip Shutze. Held in the University's Low Library, twenty feet from the School of Architecture, the few students who ventured in hardly disturbed the peace. Shutze was probably the most distinguished graduate of the school.

In 1988 Classical America, with the assistance of George Parker, Jr., of San Antonio, Texas, held a conference on the classical at Southern Methodist University in Dallas. A year later Mr. Parker again had Classical America sponsor a second conference at the School of Architecture of the University of Texas in Austin. It was accompanied by an exhibition, *The Classical Tradition: The Wave of the Future*, at the University's Battle Hall, depicting recent classical buildings and decorative hardware.

In the 1980s, again with George Parker, Jr.'s support, Classical America sponsored student competitions in classical design. Then, in 1982, Classical America launched the Arthur Ross Awards, given to those in the arts who, today, have contributed to the great tradition. The key aspect of these awards is that they salute the humbler workers in the artistic vineyard, such as stucco workers, gardeners, wrought-iron artisans, as well as those in the fine arts. Notable examples are workers from Albany, Georgia, who worked on the classical Diplomatic Reception Rooms of the Department of State in Washington: Adolph Blaylock, wood-carver; George Peoples, ornamental plaster worker; as well as Clement Conger, in the category of patron, as curator responsible for the rooms.

What is of particular interest in these several ventures—instruction at the National Academy and at the University of Pennsylvania, and student competition—was that among the participants were the founders of the Institute of Classical Architecture. In fact, the institute's instructors have all been students of Pierce Rice and Alvin Holm.

In the 1980s the *Classical America Series* reached beyond architecture by notably adding to the list of titles Edith Wharton and Ogden Codman, Jr.'s *The Decoration of Houses*, Kenyon Cox's *The Classic Point of View* and *What is Painting?*, and Pierce Rice's *Man as Hero: The Human Figure in Western Art*, funded by the Oliver Grace Foundation. A most ambitious effort was the American edition of *The Elements of Classical Architecture* by Georges Gromort, with H. Stafford Bryant as project editor and translations and essays by Francois Gabriel, Steven W. Semes, Richard Franklin Sammons, and the author.

In addition to W. W. Norton & Company, other publishers have joined in the series: Dover Publications, Architectural Book Publishing Company, and Da Capo Press.

Ann Fairfax and Richard Sammons of Fairfax & Sammons Architects have been kind enough to provide the author desk space in their drafting room. Catesby Leigh, Elliott Banfield, Sophia Duckworth Schachter, and Seth Weine and Stu Bryant have made useful suggestions. Further, the author must thank Dr. Barbara Wolanin, curator of archives in the Office of the Architect of the United States Capitol, and members of her staff, notably Pamela McConnell and Eric Paff; and in the Architect's Office William Allen, architectural historian. Gratitude is extended to Ford Peatross of the Library of Congress for helping the author access the Library's Architecture Collection. Roger Moss, director, and Bruce Lafferty, curator, provided more than the customary welcome at the Athenaeum of Philadelphia. Anne Day with her camera underscored aspects of the Capitol too often overlooked, as she had done in the Jefferson Building of the Library of Congress. To say that this exploration of the great building was made possible by Pierce Rice's *Man As Hero: The Human Figure in Western Art*, as well as by his many newsletters for Classical America, would hardly be an exaggeration. And there is my debt to my wife, Constance, for her steadfast backing of Classical America.

FOREIGN RELATIONS

COMMITTEE ROOM

INTRODUCTION: THE CAPITOL

The Siting of the Capital

The story of the United States Capitol begins with the story of the nation's capital, Washington. Article 1, Section 8, Clause 17 of the Constitution of the United States reads:

To exercise exclusive Legislation in all Cases whatsoever, over such District (not exceeding ten Miles square) as may, by Cession of particular States, and the Acceptance of Congress, become the Seat of the Government of the United States.

The Constitution was forged in 1787, and it was accepted as the law of the land in 1788; and on April 30, 1789, George Washington became our first President in New York City, the nation's temporary capital. Finally, on July 16, 1790, the Residence Act, as it was known, was passed, creating the Federal City to be located on a sixty-five-mile stretch of the Potomac River.

It could be said that one consideration prompting the selec-

Site of the future city of Washington, 1793. Map by Don Alexander Hawkins, 1991.

tion of the Potomac site was that it would be near what was then the center of the population of the nation. As it turned out, the 1790 census numbered the country's souls at 3,929,214 with the population center twenty-three miles east of Baltimore across Chesapeake Bay. (By 1800 the center had shifted due west to a spot near Washington.)

Existing cities had contended for the honor. Philadelphia, the capital pro tem from 1790 to 1799 after New York, was the leading candidate, it being the country's largest city. The obstacle in its case—and this was true of other cities—was

the danger of having the government seat where a mob could gather. For example, when Congress met in Philadelphia in the 1780s, it was threatened by a demonstration of ex-soldiers demanding pay for past service.

Another obstacle for Philadelphia was that the Commonwealth of Pennsylvania was the first of the former Colonies, in 1780, to take steps to abolish slavery. Inevitably the Mason-Dixon Line, the boundary between Pennsylvania and Maryland, demarked the border between slave and free states. No state south of it was willing to be ruled from what was to be a free state.

The final choice actually sprang from an agreement between two members of Washington's cabinet, Thomas Jefferson, Secretary of State, and Alexander Hamilton, Secretary of the Treasury. They were attempting to resolve the question of whether the federal government should assume the revolutionary war debts of several states. Hamilton, from New York, saw this as an absolute necessity for the new federal government, and Jefferson, a Virginian, opposed the action. The emplacement of the Federal District was a bargaining point. In exchange for the assumption of the debts, those opposed, primarily the Southern states, accepted the Potomac solution. The choice of the actual site, as stated in the Residence Act, was left to the President.

In all this, Washington stood apart, but obviously nothing would have pleased him more than to have the capital city on the river flowing by his beloved Mount Vernon. The gesture gave visible form to the reverent esteem in which the nation held him. Having the responsibility to choose the actual site, he settled on the southernmost section of the prescribed sixty-five-mile stretch, at a point where the river was still navigable.

In selecting the site, he followed the examples of cities situated at the heads of navigation, i.e., the point on a river where ships could go no farther, such as Richmond, Virginia, on the James; Trenton, New Jersey, on the Delaware; and Albany, New York, on the Hudson.

(The ten-mile square chosen was divided between Maryland and Virginia, with its four corners oriented toward the

Topography of the future District of Columbia, 1791, by Andrew Ellicott. Courtesy Library of Congress.

cardinal points of the compass. The Virginia portion, what is now Arlington County south of the Potomac, was deeded back to the state in 1846.)

In the Federal District, first known as the Territory of Columbia and soon to be called the District of Columbia, would stand the capital city. The Congress had made provision for a District commission of three to be named by the President. They would take charge of development and, as it turned out, they were the ones who, in September 1791, named the projected city "Washington."

To our first President and his Secretary of State fell the responsibility for the city's plan and the design of the future capital. They were among the few who seemed to be aware of the boldness of even contemplating such a project. This is scarcely surprising since the nearest prototype was the distant St. Petersburg, which Peter the Great had decreed in 1703 for imperial Russia. That the proposed capital could be entirely new barely sparked the public imagination. Perhaps this was due to the fact that many of the suggested sites were in existing communities.

Still, one person, as early as September 1789, accepted the notion and even sent off a letter to Washington proposing himself as planner for the new capital. This was some ten months before the Residence Act was approved. He was a former major of engineers in the Continental army, wounded at the siege of Savannah, by the name of Pierre Charles L'Enfant.

What immediately appealed to Washington about the major was his vision. The city plan, L'Enfant wrote, "must leave to posterity a grand idea of the patriotic interest which promoted it."[1] Washington commented later that "I have received him not only as a scientific man but one who aded considerable taste to professional knowledge; and that, for such employment as he is now engaged in; he was better qualified than any one who had come within my knowledge in this country. . . ."[2]

In the spring of 1791, Washington sent him to Georgetown, one of the existing towns encompassed by the District and, today, one of the city's more fashionable residential quarters. In March, L'Enfant set to work. The painter John Trumbull, whose pictures adorn the Capitol's Great Rotunda, was in Georgetown not long after; in his autobiography he recalled, "I found Major L'Enfant drawing his plan of the city of Washington; rode with him over the ground on which the city has since been built—where the Capitol now stands was then (May, 1791) a thick wood."[3]

In going about his design, L'Enfant, as might be expected, turned to Thomas Jefferson for maps of major European cities. He himself was familiar with American cities, not least Annapolis with its circle and radiating avenues. Jefferson proposed a grid or orthogonal plan. L'Enfant considered Jefferson's scheme all very well for a flat site but lacking "a sense of the really grand and truly beautiful only to be met with where another contributed with art and diversified with objects."[4] The major did accept the grid in part but added circles, squares, wide radiating avenues found in French garden design, in French royal hunting forests, and in a number of city plans. For example, Sir Christopher

Wren, architect of St. Paul's Cathedral, produced a plan, never executed, to rebuild the city of London after the great fire of 1666 with squares, circles, and wide streets.

L'Enfant's most important contribution—and it was indubitably his own device—was the design of a main axis (what is now the famous Mall) running west from Jenkins Hill (as the site of the future federal legislature was called) to the Potomac River with a short north-south cross axis at the Mall's western end. What is more, he placed the "Capitol," as it was identified in the first plan, on the "Hill," and the "President's House" at the north end of the cross axis. Linking the two was a wide thoroughfare that got its name early on: Pennsylvania Avenue. The Mall and the avenue were L'Enfant's great contribution, the most important of their kind in the history of American city planning. With few equals in the world, they gave the Capitol its incomparable setting.

L'Enfant's famous plan, first published version. Universal Asylum and Columbia Magazine, *March 1792. Courtesy Library of Congress.*

We can only echo the architect Thomas Hastings, who, with John Merven Carrere, not only designed the New York Public Library but also the Cannon House and the Russell Senate Office Buildings. And he was thinking in the terms of our classical heritage. "Happy is the city," he wrote, "whose development in the cutting of new avenues and the building of new squares and parks have been governed by the rules of art."

On completing his plan—it was published in 1792—the major presumably turned to designing the principal government buildings. He had assumed that this was his prerogative, much as he had assumed that he would deal directly with the President instead of reporting to the District Commission. No doubt the major had visions of the buildings, for he was something of a fantasist, but no drawings survive. In fact, Jefferson was of the opinion that he never made any drawings. In any event, the major proved to be so difficult in implementing his city plan that the commissioners dismissed him.

Meanwhile, President Washington had decided on a competition for the Capitol. Jefferson wrote the announcement and had it published in March 1792.

The results received by the deadline proved disappointing to the extent that the District commissioners invited additional submissions. With this delay, one Dr. William Thornton, living on the island of Tortola in the distant British Virgin Islands, was prompted to send in what turned out to be the winning design.

Thornton, born in 1760, was educated in England and Scotland, obtaining a degree in medicine in 1784. Independent means allowed him to travel on the European continent; eventually he divided his time between Tortola and this country. Upon winning the competition, he moved to Washington, and in 1794 he became one of the three District commissioners.

His interests lay outside medicine, which he never practiced. He experimented, for example, with steamboats in partnership with John Fitch. He organized a society to help African-Americans settle in Africa. He had a modest skill in portraiture, which he occasionally indulged, but in the arts, it was architecture that held his interest. Beyond his work for the Capitol, he is best known for having designed the Octagon, a house that is today the headquarters of the American Institute of Architects, and Tulip Hill, a large residence in Georgetown. He remained a District commissioner until 1802, when he was named superintendent of patents, a post he held until his death in 1828.

Washington, on seeing his Capitol design, declared "grandeur, simplicity and convenience appear to be so well combined in this plan of Dr. Thornton's" that he commended it to the District commissioners.[5] In this he was joined by Jefferson. Both were pleased, above all, by his treatment of the exterior, which we see today at the center. To Thornton we owe the columned porch (without the steps in his design), the walls to either side of the portico, and the concept of a rotunda.

As this last element is a most important part of the building, it is worth mentioning one comment of John Trumbull's. As noted earlier, he had seen L'Enfant at work, and he emphasized that the major was the first to suggest a rotunda with a high dome. The earliest plan of the Capitol appears in the first printed version of the L'Enfant Plan, and it shows, at the center, a large circular room.

The concept of a rotunda appealed to Washington because, like so many Americans of his day, he was steeped in the world of ancient Rome. It was easy for his fellow countrymen to compare him to Cincinnatus, the Roman patriot of the fifth century B.C. called from the plow to lead his people to victory. The inspiration for the Rotunda was the Pantheon in Rome, the best preserved of ancient buildings; its round interior covered by a dome symbolized the wonders of those ancient times.

The choice of Thornton's design in April 1793 was but the first step in the ambitious project. Washington himself admitted that he favored it because of its exterior elevation, as well as for the Rotunda. Work had to be done on the plan; to that end, a Frenchman, Stephen Hallet, who had come in second in the competition, was retained. Later, an Englishman, George Hadfield, and even James Hoban, the Irish architect of the White House, were invited to provide solutions. As if there had not been enough confusion surrounding the competition, calling on other architects inevitably made for more.

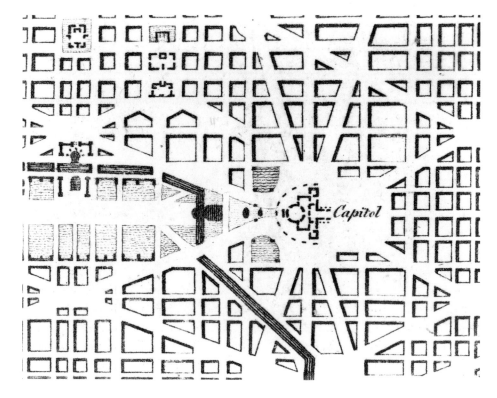

Plan of a future Capitol, as seen in L'Enfant's plan. Universal Asylum and Columbia Magazine, *March 1792. Courtesy Library of Congress.*

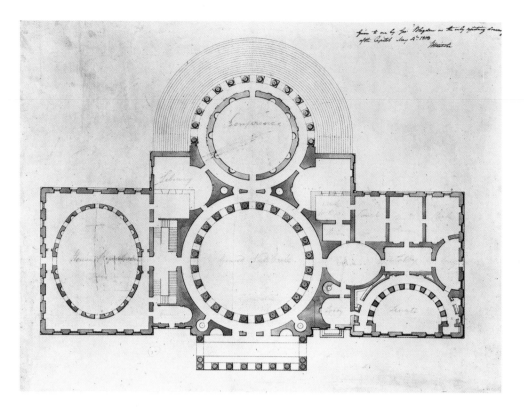

Thornton's plan for the Capitol with two round rooms, 1796. Plan of wings by Stephen Hallet. Courtesy Library of Congress.

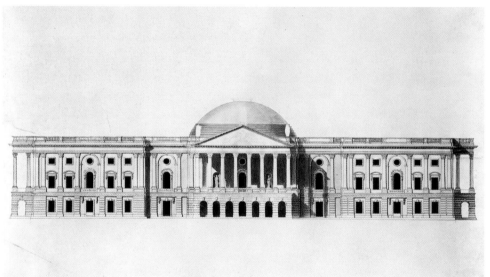

Oldest known elevation, ca. 1796, of the East Front by William Thornton. Courtesy Library of Congress.

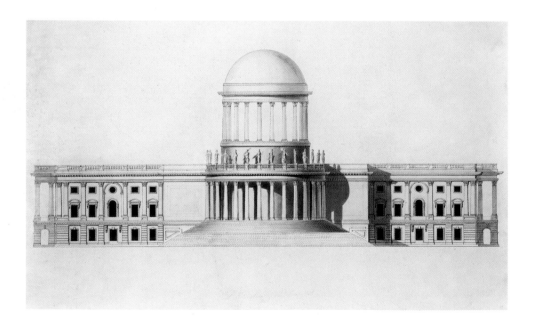

Thornton's elevation of the West Front with two round rooms, 1796, the rear one with a high dome. Courtesy Library of Congress.

Despite the changes in the building's plan, construction began on the Capitol on August 1, 1793, with the acceptance of Thornton's design. On September 18 George Washington laid the cornerstone with appropriate ceremony, military and Masonic.[6] (Where the cornerstone is no one today knows.) Construction advanced slowly, as might be expected, with the different architects being consulted as the work progressed.

One cause of delay was the constant shortage of skilled workmen, who had to be brought into the nascent city. Many of the masons were of Scottish origin, men who also worked at the White House then being built. A few Irish were among them. "The masons and workers are paid from a dollar up to two per day," recorded a Polish traveler in the 1790s. "They work from 6 in the morning to 8 o'clock; they then breakfast up to 9, work then up to one o'clock, eat dinner up to two, returning to work until six o'clock in the evening. Besides their times of rest I have seen them often quit their work, come in a little dramshop in order to talk while drinking a glass of *grog*."[7]

Among the laborers were slaves who dug the foundations and did the unskilled work. Their wages were paid to their masters. After 1808 nonresident slaveholders were taxed on the income derived from this kind of labor, with the result that the practice of contracting slaves stopped at the Capitol. (The buying and selling of slaves in the District, however, was not ended until 1850, and slavery itself continued to 1862.)[8]

It is hardly surprising that construction at the Capitol was slow. When President John Adams left Philadelphia for Washington in September 1800 to settle in the White House, only the Senate wing on the north side had been completed. It housed both legislative houses and the Supreme Court. A year later a temporary brick shelter, nicknamed "The Oven," was built to serve the House of Representatives. A major step had to be taken, and the decision fell to Thomas Jefferson. In 1803 he asked the country's first professional architect, Benjamin Henry Latrobe, to take charge.[9]

Thornton's north wing of the Capitol, completed in 1800 in time for President John Adams's move to Washington from Philadelphia. Watercolor by William Russell Birch. Courtesy Library of Congress.

Benjamin Henry Latrobe

Born in 1764 in Yorkshire to an English father and an American mother and educated on the European continent, Benjamin Latrobe turned to engineering and architecture in London. By the 1790s he had his own practice. For family and financial reasons, this tall, six-foot-two individual of thirty-one left England to come to this country in 1796. Practicing first a year or so in Richmond, he then made his way to Philadelphia, the nation's largest city as well as its capital pro tem. (In 1800 it had a population of 69,000 compared to New York's 60,000.)

There were commissions, the most important being the Philadelphia Water Works in 1801. Another was designing a bank, no longer standing, modeled on a Greek temple, the first example of what was to be called the Greek Revival, the main architectural fashion prior to the Civil War.

Latrobe, who had been left a widower with two children in England, now was successful enough to remarry in 1800. But the nature of the profession, especially in those days, with its ups and downs, left him financially strapped by 1803. So, when President Jefferson offered him the post of "Surveyor of the Buildings of the United States at Washington," he rejoiced in accepting it.

His first duty was to produce a detailed report on the Capitol for the President. Among its parts was a review of the condition of the Senate wing that told of dry rot attacking structural timbers. He also considered making changes in the plans that he believed to be necessary. The President told him that he had to abide by the original design approved by Washington. In attempting to locate it, he learned that it had been lost, and realized that the version Thornton had offered him was one incorporating changes by Hallet and Hadfield. One result of his quest was that he ran afoul of Thornton and found himself in a long-standing quarrel with the doctor, who was jealous of anyone who tampered with what he considered his particular domain. So heated was the conflict that Latrobe sued Thornton for libel. The case dragged on for five years; Latrobe won it, obtaining a reward of a penny.

As "Surveyor of the Buildings," he had extensive work in the new city. Among these were structures in the Navy Yard. Jefferson called on him to execute additions for the White House. Its furnishings in the first Madison administration were under his aegis; most of the objects were purchased, but the furniture was specially built to his designs. All was lost in the burning of the White House in 1814. Along with the White House, Latrobe's work at the Capitol was destroyed, left a charred ruin by the English invaders.

Outside of Latrobe's government commission, his most important was the Roman Catholic Cathedral of Baltimore. Beginning in 1804, Bishop Carroll asked him for a design; he was to do seven altogether before construction began. As usual with cathedrals, work went slowly; it was not completed until after his death in 1821.

Latrobe had been making $3,000 a year as surveyor when appropriations stopped. By 1811 even the private commissions were limited, and there was the threat of war. Trying to find alternative sources of income, he engaged in ventures outside the field of architecture, such as building steamboats in Pittsburgh in partnership with no less a figure than Robert Fulton. (We are reminded that Latrobe's competitor, William Thornton, was a close associate of another steamboat inventor, John Fitch.) In September 1813 the family moved to Pittsburgh.

The project turned into a disaster, leaving the architect seriously in debt with no income. Fulton, who was largely responsible for the failure, died. Latrobe lapsed into a seemingly hopeless depression. Fortunately, he regained his old job in 1815 and, fully recovered, returned to work in Washington.

Back in Washington, Latrobe was at work on the Hill. What he accomplished in the next few years was a triumphant product of his talent. First, he had to remove all the charred damage to the building. Then followed new plans, for both the south and the north wings, the latter with a larger Senate Chamber. There were also plans for the Great Rotunda and the Library of Congress west of the Rotunda. As to the east portico, he had already greatly improved the design of Thornton's portico by enlarging it with more columns and by providing a flight of steps, with cheekblocks, to the principal floor. He also designed an elaborate West Front that was never executed. For all intents and purposes, cued by Thornton's initial scheme, he had created the Capitol and, in doing so, had produced two of the country's most opulent interiors, pre-1850, in his House and Senate chambers. These were only to be surpassed in the late 1850s by the work of Thomas Ustick Walter and of Constantino Brumidi in the Capitol extension, and by the magnificent interior of the Cathedral of St. Peter and St. Paul in Philadelphia.

One aspect of Latrobe's skill has to be underscored: his command of vaulting. He was the first American architect to

View of the proposed Capitol from the east, 1806, by Benjamin H. Latrobe. Latrobe's wash rendering given to Thomas Jefferson.
Courtesy Library of Congress.

incorporate extensive vaulting in his buildings. We have to remind ourselves that, before cast iron and, later, steel, the only method of covering a room other than with wood beams was by means of vaulting. A vault is an arched construction of masonry—that is, of stone or brick. The ancient Romans were the first to make extensive use of the method, and, significantly, they made it a visual as well as a structural device. It can take many forms. In the Capitol, it is seen in the barrel vault, the groined vault, the saucer-dome vault, and the intersecting vault. Latrobe had even intended, in 1816, to have masonry domes in the House and Senate chambers but had to substitute wood. (The House Chamber semidome was replaced with a steel one in the early 1900s.) Fortunately, Latrobe had an expert in vaulting at hand. George Blagden, trained in England, had been on the Capitol staff as master mason since the 1790s, and he had the technical competence to construct the sophisticated vault of the Old Supreme Court Chamber.[10]

Despite the obvious quality of his work, Latrobe had conflicts with his immediate superior. In 1817 he resigned; his career at the Capitol was at an end. He was to die four years later in New Orleans.

Sketch of the ruined Capitol in 1814 by Chittenden. Courtesy Library of Congress.

As Latrobe's successor President James Monroe chose Charles Bulfinch of Boston. Born in 1763 to a wealthy family, he went to Boston Latin School and Harvard College and, on graduating, became an architect. For a while he was very successful in designing, among other buildings, the Connecticut State Capitol, the Massachusetts State Capitol (the "State House"), and Harvard's University Hall. In January 1818 President Monroe named him Architect of the Capitol, a position he held until President Andrew Jackson shut down the office in 1829.

Something of the man is indicated by his assessment of the Latrobe drawings given to him when he came to the Capitol. He wrote to his wife:

At first view of these drawings, my courage almost failed me—they are beautifully executed, and the design is in the boldest style. . . . I feel the responsibility resting on me and should have no resolution to proceed if the work was not so far commenced as to make it necessary to follow the plans already prepared for the wings; as to the center building, a general conformity to the other parts must be maintained. I shall not have credit for invention, but must be content to follow in a prescribed path."[11]

Bulfinch's appreciation is refreshing, and it is to his credit that he evidently disarmed William Thornton, who left him alone. Bulfinch abided generally by Latrobe's designs, except at the West Front, where he had a colonnade of single and paired columns much like those at his Massachusetts State House and an attic with a balustrade instead of a pediment.

With the plans in hand, Bulfinch pushed forward on construction. In March 1819 the Supreme Court was meeting in its new chamber; in December the Senate and House were in theirs. In the Crypt, where he was ably seconded by the master mason George Blagden, Bulfinch devised circular barrel vaults joined by intersecting vaults that, like those in Latrobe's Supreme Court Chamber, are models of their kind, although they have never received the

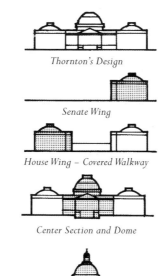

Thornton's Design

Senate Wing

House Wing – Covered Walkway

Center Section and Dome

New House Wing – New Dome – New Senate Wing

East Front Extension

*The expanding Capitol.
Diagrams showing the east elevation
and the plan of the Capitol indicating
the five stages of its expansion.
Courtesy Architect of the Capitol.*

attention paid to Latrobe's ceiling. In the Crypt, Bulfinch sustained the tradition of masonry vaulting.

In the Great Rotunda where Latrobe had intended niches, Bulfinch had plain walls set off by pilasters. John Trumbull thus had the large spaces needed for his canvases. Bulfinch also added the reliefs to the upper parts of the walls, installed in 1829. He went so far as to have a well placed in the Rotunda floor to permit a view of the Crypt below, where a statue of Washington was to stand above the tomb intended for his remains. However, when Trumbull complained that the cold air from the Crypt led to dampness in the Rotunda and damage to his canvases, the well was filled, leaving the floor as it is today. At the request of President Monroe and Secretary of State John Quincy Adams, Bulfinch placed the dome some 145 feet above the Rotunda floor and roofed it with wood and copper. Today the most conspicuous part of the building, which is identified with Bulfinch, remains the center of the West Front with its colonnade and entablature without a pediment.

In keeping with Latrobe's plan for the East Front, with its columned porch and flight of steps, Bulfinch made it the building's main facade. As a consequence, the West Front became the equivalent of a garden facade overlooking the Mall.

Work on the Capitol depended on appropriations. When it proceeded, it did so briefly, even lightheartedly. The monolithic columns of the East Front were of Aquia Creek sandstone from a quarry forty miles down the Potomac. Long blocks of the stone were brought up the river to a canal that then ran to the foot of the hill. "Two hundred workmen labored toward its completion. Setting up the columns for the east portico was 'quite a frolic,'" runs one description. "They are brought by water from a quarry of freestone [Aquia Creek sandstone] thirty miles below the city and weigh eighteen tons each. [The workers] drink scute (as they call whiskey) on the job.”[12] The blocks would be carved into column shafts on site. (These same columns were removed in the 1960s, when the East Front was extended and replaced with marble ones. They were reerected in the National Arboretum.)

From Andrew Jackson in 1829 to Dwight D. Eisenhower in 1953, the presidential inaugurations, with a few exceptions, were held at the old sandstone portico of the East Front. John F. Kennedy held his in the present marble portico. In 1981 the ceremony was moved by President Ronald Reagan to the West Front, a custom continued by President George W. Bush.

In following the history of the Capitol in the 1820s, it is impossible not to be saddened by one curious fact. As far as we know, Jefferson never returned to Washington after his retirement in 1809.[13] The President with the passion for architecture, who had done so much to shape the city and the Capitol, was never to record impressions or pen a few notes of comment on what he had helped to bring about.

In 1829, three years after Jefferson's death, Andrew Jackson abolished the office of Architect of the Capitol and Bulfinch returned to Boston.

The building was finished. Still, with its heavy and growing use, there was always some work for an architect. The House Chamber was one part that needed attention. From the beginning, it suffered from poor acoustics. Numerous attempts to correct the flaw were made, but only in 1830, on the advice of the architect Robert Mills, was the floor raised and a screen placed behind the columns.[14] Despite these efforts, the nuisance remained. In the 1830s, the Capitol was placed in the care of the Commission of Public Buildings, no architect having been named.

We have mentioned the sculptors who joined the architects in embellishing the building. Their earliest work, commissioned by Latrobe, vanished in the fire of 1814, with the exception of the corncob capitals. When the sculptors returned, they were promptly retained. In 1815 we find Giovanni Andrei being sent to Italy to have the Corinthian capitals of the House Chamber and the Ionic capitals of the Senate Chamber carved

The East Front, ca. 1846. Photo John Plumber. Courtesy Library of Congress.

The West Front, 1848. Lithograph by August Koellner. Courtesy Library of Congress.

at Carrara. He came back with two colleagues, one of whom, Francisco Iardella, executed the tobacco-leaf capitals of the Senate Rotunda; the other, Carlo Franzoni, did *The Car of History* of the Old House Chamber and *Justice* in the Old Supreme Court Chamber. Bulfinch, on becoming architect, put the following sculptors to work in the Great Rotunda: Enrico Causici, Nicolas Gevelot, Andrea Capellano, and Francesco Iardella. Causici was the one who did the colossal *Liberty* and the *Eagle* in the Old House Chamber. Luigi Persico carved the *Genius of America* in the pediment of the center portico, along with *War* and *Peace* in the portico niches.[15]

Interior of the Pantheon, Rome. Photo Roger Viollet.

the *Pilgrims* (1843), John Vanderlyn's *Landing of Columbus* (1847), and William H. Powell's *Discovery of the Mississippi* (1855).

It is easy enough to identify the painters and sculptors by their contributions. With the architects of the Capitol, it is a more complicated undertaking. To William Thornton belong the entrance portico (without steps), the two wings set off by pilasters, and the plan of the Great Rotunda. Latrobe has the credit for the two legislative chambers, the Supreme Court Chamber with its vestibule, the small rotundas, the enlarged portico with its steps and cheek-blocks, and the initial design for the Great Rotunda—changes that made for a more imposing building. Bulfinch did the final design of the Great Rotunda, which is there today, and the Crypt as well as the West Front and the first dome. Altogether the result was a handsome, if modest, structure worthy of a young nation.

To convey some idea of the importance of the Capitol, a table comparing the cost of the ten most expensive American buildings constructed prior to 1850 is offered below. (*See* page 12, Introduction by Bruce Laverty in Bruce Laverty, Michael J. Lewis, Michele Taillon Taylor, *Monument to Philanthropy, The Design and Building of Girard College 1832–1848*.)

Trumbull's four canvases were placed on the walls of the Rotunda in 1826. These were followed by John Chapman's *Baptism of Pocahontas* (1840), Robert W. Weir's *Embarkation of*

Building	City	Architect	Date	Cost
United States Capitol	*Washington*	*Various*	*1792–1849*	*$2,660,000*
Girard College	*Philadelphia*	*Thomas U. Walter*	*1833*	*$1,933,821*
New York Custom House (*Federal Hall Memorial on Wall Street*)	*New York*	*Town & Davis*	*1833*	*$ 960,000*
Boston Custom House (*Custom House Tower*)	*Boston*	*Ammi B. Young*	*1825*	*$ 776,000*
U.S. General Post Office (*under development*)	*Washington*	*Robert Mills*	*1840*	*$ 776,000*
U.S. Treasury Building	*Washington*	*Robert Mills*	*1836*	*$ 700,000*
Eastern State Penitentiary (*now part museum*)	*Philadelphia*	*John Haviland*	*1821*	*$ 670,000*
U.S. Patent Office (*National Portrait Gallery and Museum of American Art*)	*Washington*	*Robert Mills*	*1839*	*$ 448,000*
U.S. Naval Asylum	*Philadelphia*	*William Strickland*	*1827*	*$ 276,000*
Second Bank of the United States (*now property of National Park Service*)	*Philadelphia*	*William Strickland*	*1818*	*$ 257,000*
Smithsonian Institution (*"The Castle"*)	*Washington*	*James Renwick*	*1848*	*$ 250,000*

THE CAPITOL EXTENSION AND THE DOME

Thomas Ustick Walter

In the 1840s it became apparent that the ever-growing nation required an enlarged Capitol. Robert Mills, self-styled "architect of public buildings," was consulted, and in 1846 he drew up a plan for an eastern extension. Four years later, he presented a report and another design to the Senate Committee on Public Buildings, one of whose three members was the senator from Mississippi, Jefferson Davis.[16] Instead of accepting the design of Mills, the committee opted for a competition. None of the submissions proved satisfactory. Instead, five were given awards, and Mills was called on to produce the final design, which presumably would include the best features of the five. At this juncture, Congress stepped in and, on September 30, 1850, voted a $100,000 appropriation for the Capitol extension and left the responsibility for the design to President Millard Fillmore with the proviso that he choose the architect. This he did on June 10, 1851, and he named one of the five competition finalists, Thomas Ustick Walter of Philadelphia, "Architect of the United States Capitol Extension."[17]

Walter was to be the first of three men who created the Capitol we see today; the other two were the army engineer Montgomery Cunningham Meigs and the painter Constantino Brumidi. If, in the course of this introduction, we dwell on these three, the reasons are several. There is the obvious fact that they took full advantage of a small pleasing structure on a splendid site and made it worthy of its name and purpose. What had been a handsome but modest building with two beautiful main rooms (the House and Senate chambers) and the Great Rotunda became the nation's grandest building. On another count, they have been neglected. Strange as it may seem, the building they made has found no place in our literature. American writers, for whatever reason, have been incapable, with rare exception, of describing man-made splendor. Or perhaps it is not so much inability as total unawareness, because the Capitol has not been the only victim. As it is one of the objectives of this book to underscore the role of art in shaping the Capitol, an art with a certain opulence, the three men deserve more than passing attention.

Thomas Ustick Walter was born in Philadelphia in 1804.[18] His German grandfather, who landed in Philadelphia an orphan after his parents had died aboard ship, became a bricklayer; and so did his son, Walter's father, who fought in the Revolution. Walter himself started out as a bricklayer and became a master in the craft. While still a youth, he found time for school, concentrating on mathematics. At fifteen, he was in the office of William Strickland, a Philadelphia architect best known for the Tennessee State Capitol in Nashville, and there he learned linear drawing and architecture. He left the firm to devote full time to the sciences, mechanical construction, drawing, and painting, and then returned to Strickland's office, where he remained from 1828 to 1830. On leaving it, he began his own practice and soon had abundant commissions extending as far as Virginia. The work ranged from some row houses in 1834 for Michel Bouvier, ancestor of Jacqueline Kennedy Onassis, to the city hall of Norfolk, Virginia, now the MacArthur Memorial.[19]

The most important commission by far came when he won the competition in 1833 for Girard College in Philadelphia.

Founder's Hall, Girard College, 1833–48, by Thomas U. Walter.
Photo © Wayne Andrews/ESTO.

*"Andalusia," 1833, summer residence of Nicholas Biddle,
by Thomas U. Walter. Courtesy James Biddle.*

*The MacArthur Memorial, formerly City Hall, 1847,
Norfolk, Virginia, by Thomas U. Walter. Photo Edward Boone, Jr.
Courtesy MacArthur Memorial.*

Guided by Nicholas Biddle, the famous banker and Philhellene on the college's board of trustees, Walter produced in the Founder's Hall what was considered the most beautiful Greek Revival building of its day, and which in our time is accepted as the finest example of the Greek Revival style in America. Even now, the beholder cannot help but be awed by the splendid proportions of the columns and the design of the Corinthian capitals. Obviously, Girard College is the work of a superior architect.

One significant feature of the building is the presence of cast iron. The ceiling inside the colonnade of the peristyle is of the metal, made to resemble marble. Walter was to do the same with the ceiling of the Hall of Columns in the present House wing of the Capitol.

Of the same high caliber as the college is Walter's conversion of "Andalusia," Nicholas Biddle's country place on the Delaware, from a modest summerhouse by Latrobe to a Doric temple still much admired. It was only one of many commissions. In 1850, for example, he was to design seventeen houses, four stores, twelve churches, five schools, and two hotels, plus other work. No other architect of the day had so solid a practice, and few could boast of a building to rival Girard College. Admittedly, he was working in the nation's largest manufacturing city. (In the middle of the century, Philadelphia, with a population of 409,000, ranked second to New York, with a population of 516,000.) Walter stood among the best in his profession.

His practice was by no means confined to Philadelphia, and extended particularly to the South. A good example is to be found in Norfolk, Virginia. There he designed the city hall in 1849. We know it today as the MacArthur Memorial since it houses the tomb of General Douglas MacArthur.

Walter was very much the family man. He married twice. By his first wife, who died in 1847, he had eleven children, two of whom died young. A year later he remarried and then had two more. By the time the family moved to Washington, only the younger members of the brood were with him. Outside family and profession, there was the church. Named for his parents' Baptist minister, he was baptized in the Schuylkill River, a tributary of the Delaware. (Baptisms in rivers, lakes, and ponds on the part of the Baptist Church are commonly done in the South.) In Washington the family joined the E Street Baptist Church off Sixth Street, Northwest, a few blocks from the Capitol. Walter was more than a regular communicant, even attending church twice on Sundays, if not always his own. He taught a young men's Bible class, so much a part of the Baptist Church, with as many as fifty in the weekly classes. That he should have been called on to design as many as seven churches in a year, however modest they may have been, seems only fitting.

Beyond family, church, and profession, he had an acknowledged position in the intellectual world of Philadelphia.

Recognition came to him in the form of membership in the American Philosophical Society and the Franklin Institute. At the latter, founded to promote the useful arts, he did some teaching and, important for us, contributed to its *Journal.* Thanks to his articles, we know how he regarded our classical heritage and how he analyzed classical architecture. Certainly his general cultivation and his grasp of this heritage, as well as his professional ability, prompted the trustees of Girard College to send him in 1838 to England, France, Italy, and Ireland to study what improvements, if any, he could make in his buildings for the college.[20]

In four months, he went from London to Rome and back to London, with a dash to Dublin, before returning home. Quite obviously, like the architectural students of the 1890s and 1900s who went abroad, he carefully studied beforehand the great buildings and monuments he would be viewing for the first time; they were old friends. Equally fascinating is the fact that he took such pains to see the great domed buildings that had nothing to do with the college. Did he have a premonition that he would one day raise the nation's greatest dome? Or was it an instance of his compulsion to seek out the most imposing structures that form the basis of the study of architecture?

What is more, Walter's report to the trustees was not limited to descriptions and opinions; these were accompanied by measurements! Of course, he could easily have kept a notebook where he collected essential information prior to sailing or he could have added the data on his return. For example, of St. Paul's Cathedral in London, Sir Christopher Wren's magnum opus, he wrote it had a dome 105 feet in diameter and that the dome's brick walls were 18 inches thick.

On the other hand, if such care with dimensions showed obvious deference, his brief notes contain reservations. "As respects the architectural taste of St. Paul's," he wrote, "I can say little in its favor;—its general proportions are however graceful, and when seen from a distance it is certainly a beautiful object, but upon close inspection the multiplicity of breaks and incongruous forms with which the whole composition abounds (excepting only the Dome) is found to destroy all repose and harmony, and to produce a confused effect that interferes with every idea of beauty."[21]

In Paris one building commanded his full attention: the Panthéon. "This is undoubtedly the most beautiful specimen of architecture," he noted, and of all the buildings he saw on his galloping tour, it was the only one to receive such praise.[22] While he studied the whole structure, it was the dome that made the greatest impression; he even illustrated his report with a small sketch of its elevated cross section. At the Panthéon, there is an inner dome with a wide oculus and, over it, a second dome with a large mural, and both are enclosed by the third, or exterior, dome. The second and third are linked by the base of a lantern at the top of the third. It was

The dome of St. Paul's Cathedral, London. Photo Joseph Farber.

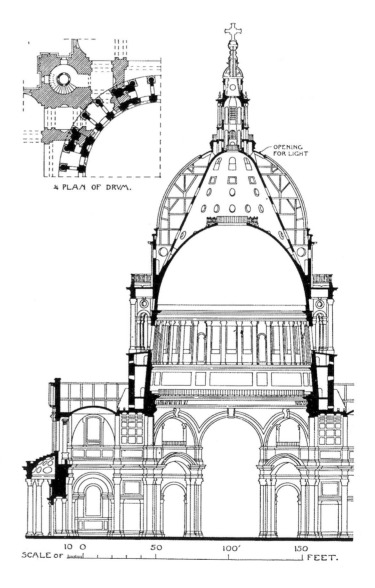

Section elevation of transept and dome, St. Paul's Cathedral, London, from Frederick Moore Simpson, A History of Architectural Development, *vol. 3 (London, 1911).*

Walter's sketch of the section elevation of the dome of the Panthéon, Paris. From Thomas Ustick Walter, "Report to the Building Committee of Girard College for Orphans, 1838." ourtesy Athenaeum of Philadelphia.

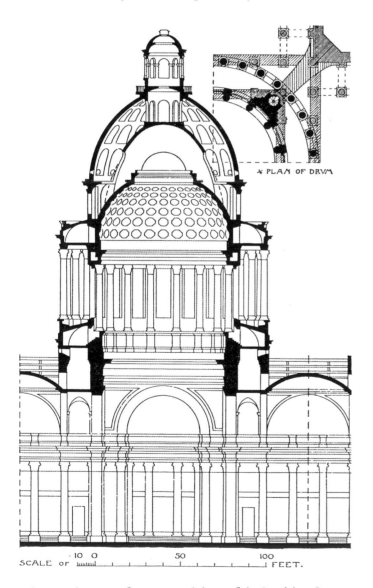

SCALE OF ‒10 0   50   100 FEET.

Section elevation of transept and dome of the Panthéon, Paris, from Frederick Moore Simpson, A History of Architectural Development, *vol. 3 (London, 1911).*

The dome of the Panthéon, Paris, from the northwest. Photo Roger Viollet.

this general scheme that Walter was to adopt at the Capitol; only he substituted a canopy for the second, or inner, dome.

Curiously, he makes no mention of the Invalides, where Napoleon lies buried. In some ways, it is the building most closely resembling the central part of the Capitol. As with the Capitol, the dome rises just behind a pedimented front, and not behind a long nave, as in the other great churches. Also of interest are the consoles with single volutes at the attic. They might well have inspired the more numerous double-voluted consoles at the Capitol's secondary attic that are so distinctive a part of the decoration.

In contrast, Walter's reactions to the wonders of Rome come as something of a surprise. For example, if he admired the Farnese Palace, the work of Michelangelo and Antonio da Sangallo, he was not above criticizing the facade: "The windows are overcharged with ornament and there are far too many of them, and the great space over the upper range produces a heavy and disagreeable effect." In the same way, he has reservations about St. Peter's: "Notwithstanding the magnitude and costliness of St. Peter's it possesses very little architecture of merit." And he writes, "The magnitude of St. Peter's being all that it possesses of interest I shall say nothing of its exterior architecture, which is beneath criticism."[23]

Nor is he more generous in his assessment of the interior: "On entering St. Peter's one's taste seems almost paralyzed for a moment and the spectator is forced to exclaim how grand! how beautiful!—After a little consideration however, his sensations change and the mind begins to revolt at the want of harmony and proportion that everywhere prevail. The vast magnitude of the structure is lost amid the profusion of incongruous embellishments with which the whole is charged." He complained especially of the extraordinary 7-foot cherubs supporting the holy water fonts that, he felt, destroyed the concept of magnitude. Enlarging on the theme of the ornament, and noting especially that the figures seemed too large, he observed that "the Italians seem to have been prone in all their architecture to exaggerate their details for the purpose of giving them importance but, in all the fine arts, nothing has a worse effect; if figures be executed in reference to a distant view, they will only look well from that point, but if executed true to nature, and not exaggerated they nowhere look bad; but upon closer inspection they gratify the mind and from every point of view they set the imagination right, as regards surrounding objects and again, when the spectator once discovers an exaggeration [as the above-mentioned babies in St. Peter's], it recurs and offends the mind even when surveying the object from the point of sight that represents it most favorably." (Walter actually did not have that much faith in being "true to nature," at least in the realm of architecture. Two years later, in a lecture entitled "Architecture Considered as a Fine Art," he announced "that architectural beauty can never be attained by closely imitating nature.")

Other comments follow; he even cites St. Peter's as "the worst Italian taste as regards design, but much of its execution is highly creditable." St. Peter's wins out in the end. Standing on the basilica's roof, he salutes "the immense dome, the outside diameter of which is 160 feet, 'swells vast to heaven' with a majesty and grandeur that atones for many a fault in the minutiae of its design."[24]

Did his strictures arise out of fear that he would be overwhelmed by Europe's splendor? In any event, they made no difference, as he absorbed all he studied. Evidence of this may be found in a series of lectures he gave at the Franklin Institute in 1840. Unlike many architects, Walter was articulate about his art, but he was not one of those writing architects who dwell on some social mission of the profession or the importance of democracy. Rather, he thought of the basic nature of architecture in terms of artistic principles. Admittedly, others before and after him have attempted to do the same, but few have succeeded in prose that all can grasp. It is refreshing to turn to a cultivated professional who was prepared and, more, willing to define the essentials. Some of his explanations will be cited as we explore the building.

In the particularly interesting lecture "Architecture Con-

The dome of the Invalides, Paris, from the southwest. Photo Roger Viollet.

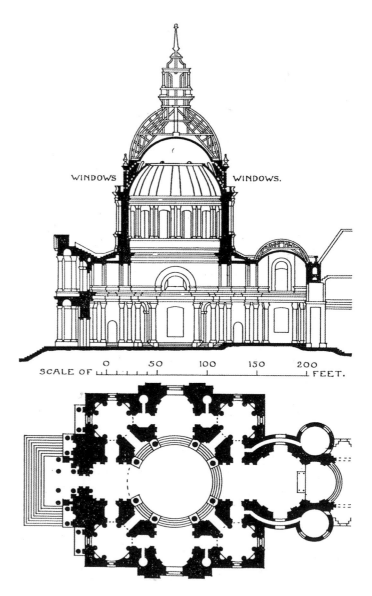

Section elevation of the Invalides, Paris, from Frederick Moore Simpson, A History of Architectural Development, *vol. 3 (London, 1911).*

sidered as a Fine Art," Walter points out that architecture embraces "*utility*, *durability*, and *beauty* [his emphasis]."[25] Speaking of the first two, he tells us: "Being entirely of a practical or mechanical nature, we shall pass over them and limit ourselves to the consideration of architectural composition, with reference alone to the production of beauty.

"The first principle in all compositions to have any claims to beauty is that of producing a combination of harmonious forms so as to present a *unity of design*." Having presented the unity of the whole and the contiguity of parts as essential, he examines the nature and properties of effect or expression, effect in architecture being that quality which gives luster to all other qualities. It attracts and retains the attention

The dome of St. Peter's, Rome, seen from the south.
Photo Anderson, Roger Viollet.

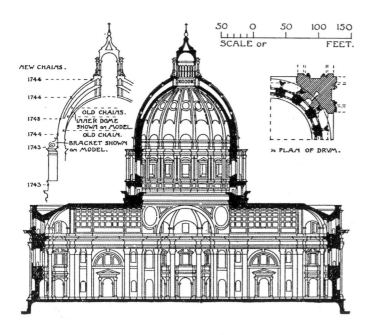

Section elevation of St. Peter's, Rome, from Frederick Moore Simpson, A History of Architectural Development, *vol. 3 (London, 1911).*

of the beholder to the object, and renders the whole composition agreeable. This quality may be considered as arising from a judicious combination of projecting and flat surfaces, relieved by graceful moldings, and harmonized by symmetry of form and appropriateness of color. The most pleasing and brilliant contrasts of light and shade spring from these varied combinations and produce a striking and beautiful expression.

As to variety in art, he sees it as important in producing the architectural effect. "This quality, therefore, when introduced without interfering with the principles of unity, is always found to enhance the beauty of the composition." In making use of "*variety*, under any circumstances, the strictest regard should be had to *symmetry*;—this quality harmonizes all other qualities and, without it, every attempt to produce an architectural whole would fail."

He also includes under "variety" the need for intricacy and harmony. "The chief property of intricacy is to engage the eye and the mind by exciting the curiosity."

As an example of intricacy and harmony, he cites the column: "A combination of these two qualities is strikingly evident in the form of a column. Notwithstanding the beholder can see but one half of the circumference at the same time, his imagination fills up with certainty the entire column, and he realizes its circular form as satisfactorily as though he had examined it all around; thus the harmonious form of the column renders its intricacy an agreeable quality."

And he adds: "In *harmony*—in *intricacy*—and in every modification of *variety*—or in all architectural compositions, the beauty of which depends chiefly on *forms*, the essential principle will be found to be *contrast* [his emphasis]."

In his analysis of his art, Walter, we must remember, was always thinking primarily in classical terms, the main artistic current of Western civilization. In this tradition, and in other traditional styles for that matter, ornament has an essential place, as do certain rules of proportion seen, for example, in the ratios of the Corinthian column where the height is ten times the diameter at the base of the column shaft. His comprehension of classical principles helped Walter to achieve his greatest work, the United States Capitol.

Walter's first efforts on being named Architect of the Capitol Extension—at the time there was no question of a new dome—were devoted to revising one of his prize-winning designs. He had submitted two in the competition, one with the new chambers in an addition to the east wing of the Old Capitol and the other with them placed at the north and south wings, separated from the Old Capitol by courtyards. In his new design, with the aged Daniel Webster advising, he had the intended north and south wings joined to the old building by corridors.[26] This plan, substantially reflecting what is there today, was the one approved by President Fillmore when he named Walter architect on June 10, 1851.

Walter's design of the Capitol extension, with the old dome and without pediments on the wing porches.
As approved by President Fillmore in 1851. Courtesy Athenaeum of Philadelphia.

Construction began at once, and on the Fourth of July the President laid the cornerstone and Webster gave the address.

In his design—and here we are concerned only with the exterior—Walter took his cue from the Thornton/Latrobe/Bulfinch facade. At the end of each wing, he had a portico of Corinthian columns with steps between cheekblocks. Beneath the portico were a driveway and a pedestrian way, the latter repeated at other colonnades on the north, south, and west sides of the wings. More columns were placed on either side of the connecting corridors. In all, the architect had *one hundred* columns of Maryland marble gracing wings and corridors.

On the interior, there were, of course, additional columns, but here what is important is that Walter continued the tradition of masonry vaulting begun by Latrobe and Bulfinch. It takes several forms: groined, barrel, intersecting, and saucer-domal with pendentives. What is astonishing is that they are found on all floors; there are no "shell" vaults as in the main floor halls of the Jefferson Building of the Library

Walter's design, 1855, with the extension, the new dome, and the wing pediments. Courtesy Athenaeum of Philadelphia.

Hoisting a column shaft at the connecting corridor of the House wing, November 28, 1860. The white-haired man with his hand on his hip is the architect, Thomas U. Walter, and to the left, beyond the column shaft, is Senator Jefferson Davis of Mississippi. Courtesy Athenaeum of Philadelphia.

The Senate wing and, beyond, the center with the unfinished dome. Note the cast-iron volutes with enrichment in the foreground. They are intended for the base of the yet unbuilt cupola. November 1860. Courtesy Athenaeum of Philadelphia.

of Congress. (By "shell" vaulting, I mean vaulting of stucco and lath suspended on trusses.)

Work was, in part, interrupted in December 1851, when the Library of Congress, inside the Capitol west of the Great Rotunda, caught fire on Christmas Eve. A good part of the collection was destroyed, a severe loss, and its monumental hall gutted. Walter at once designed a new library, which would last until 1897. This interior was a very rare example of a large room to be built entirely of cast iron. It established him at once as obviously at the top of his profession, at the same time signaling the role the metal would have in the extension of the Capitol.

Walter pursued the initial construction as well as drafted his constantly changing design. His office was part of the Department of the Interior, but it was President Fillmore, rather than his Secretary of the Interior, who took an active interest in the project. It will be remembered that Fillmore

had called on Andrew Jackson Downing, the country's outstanding landscape architect of the time, to provide plans for the Mall and the President's Park, as well as the five public parks around the White House, including Lafayette Park and the Ellipse. (Downing also served on the committee, along with Professor Joseph Henry, secretary of the Smithsonian Institution, and Professor Alexander Dallas Bache of the Coastal Survey, which conducted the testing of the marble that would go into the extensions.)

Fillmore's interest was not limited to consulting or even informing members of Congress about the project. As long as he was President, Walter was sole authority when it came to the Capitol. This was undoubtedly why construction moved rapidly, but it also meant that Walter faced accusations from disgruntled contractors and congressmen. A House committee investigated Walter, only to clear him as a result of pressure from the President.

The outcome did not allay congressional dissatisfaction. As a consequence, the incoming administration of Franklin Pierce in 1853 had an excuse to shift the project to the War Department, where Jefferson Davis was named Secretary. Davis could now assume authority over the construction of the extension, denied him when he was senator from Mississippi and member of the Senate Building Committee. His first move, on taking office, was to appoint Captain Montgomery Cunningham Meigs superintendent of the extension; with that, the second major figure in the enterprise made his appearance.

It may seem extraordinary that the first man to be part of the history of the United States Capitol, Major L'Enfant, was an army officer. Now, here was a second army officer, Captain Meigs, who, as much as the architect Thomas Ustick Walter, was to help shape the enlarged Capitol.

Once again, as in the case of Thomas Ustick Walter, we shall be following the career of an extraordinary American. Montgomery Cunningham Meigs was born in 1816 in Augusta, Georgia, where his father, a physician, practiced for a short time.[27] Soon after the family moved to Philadelphia, the elder Meigs, who had obtained his medical degree from the University of Pennsylvania, became one of the city's leading doctors. The young Meigs attended local schools and was briefly enrolled at the University of Pennsylvania. Then, at the age of sixteen, he transferred to the United States Military Academy at West Point, class of 1836.

In the histories of the nation's educational system, West Point hardly receives any attention. They tend to focus on liberal arts colleges and universities. When the young Meigs arrived at the celebrated site overlooking the Hudson River in 1832, the school had been transformed by Colonel Sylvanus Thayer, the "Father of the Military Academy." Thayer, who had been named superintendent by John C. Calhoun, who served as Secretary of War in President Monroe's cabinet, instituted much-needed discipline and appointed a strong faculty. One consequence was that the Academy, then the nation's only school to teach engineering, civil as well as military, became a school for engineers as the industrial revolution was overtaking the country.

Inevitably many of the fledgling army officers, after brief service on graduating, opted for civilian careers, with the result that they were at work building canals, improving harbors and rivers, and, above all, constructing the new railroads.

The academy was to remain the chief source of engineers even after they began to graduate in the 1830s from the new Rensselaer Polytechnic Institute (RPI) near Albany, New York. Mathematics, physics, chemistry, and geology were among the subjects taught, but as we can gather from Meigs's notebooks, topography, dredging, carpentry, masonry, and even "concrete or beton [the French word for concrete]" were also included in the curriculum.

One special subject was a course in drawing. Such courses were found in European military schools of the time. One of Meigs's instructors was Seth Eastman, a future brigadier general; some of his pictures of Indians and of forts are in the Capitol. Robert W. Weir, painter of *The Embarkation of the Pilgrims* in the Great Rotunda, became the drawing instructor in Meigs's second year. Here is a list of the subjects taught: delineation of topography; freehand drawing of the figure; and landscape drawing, which included measuring and aerial perspective. Meigs responded to the teaching because he had a knack for drawing; this we know from the pencil and watercolor sketches found among his papers. Throughout his career, he kept at it, as busy as he often was; among his drawing companions when in Washington was his former instructor Seth Eastman.

(Colonel Thayer was to remain superintendent only for Meigs's first year, as a result of a curious episode in the Jacksonian presidency. Jackson saw West Point as fostering a military elite, and there were those around him who even wanted to do away with it altogether. A factor in this was a disgruntled nephew of Jackson's who, when a cadet, had been disciplined by Thayer and wanted revenge. The academy survived, one good reason being its role in training engineers, but Jackson made Thayer's position so difficult that the colonel resigned and never returned to the Point.)

Meigs's interests also extended to architecture. Among the books recommended to him by Colonel Thayer were several French works on architecture, one being Jean-Baptiste Rondelet's *Traité théorique et pratique de l'art de bâtir*; Rondelet was one of the architects of the Panthéon, the building so admired by Walter. On Meigs's graduation in 1836, he stood fifth in a class of forty-nine.

At first given a commission in the artillery, Meigs obtained a brevet of second lieutenant in the Corps of Engineers a year later. Then began tours of duty that led him around the country. Early on, he briefly served under Lieutenant Robert E. Lee in surveying the Mississippi. There was a short stay in Washington, where he met and married in 1841 the daughter of a commodore in the navy. He was now part of an extended service family. (That tradition has continued in the Meigs family. In the recent Gulf War, a Colonel Montgomery Cunningham Meigs was in an armored brigade, as was his father, who was killed at Bastogne in World War II.)

The tours of duty continued. For nine years he was, with his family, in Detroit, then little more than a frontier town. Washington followed again, and a stint on the northern shores of Lake Champlain. Finally, in November 1852, he was called back to Washington, where he remained for the rest of his life.

When the family came to the nation's capital, it found itself in a community of dusty or muddy streets, brick and wooden houses scattered among empty lots, virtually no sanitation, indifferent streetlighting, and, of course, no municipal water supply. What set it apart from other growing American cities was that instead of factories, warehouses, and other evidence of industry and commerce, there were government buildings of white marble or of white-painted stone concentrated near the White House, with one, the Capitol, off by itself.

At least the Congress, in the year of Meigs's arrival, tackled one key need: that of potable water. It called on the army for a report, with recommendations, on a possible aqueduct. The job fell to Lieutenant Meigs. He produced a survey and offered three solutions, each one carefully analyzed as to cost and gallons obtainable. The report ended with a coda that told something of the man. Not for him the example of Latrobe's pumping station and pipes (1800) in Philadelphia nor the extension of the system (1822), nor New York's great Croton Aqueduct (1842), nor Boston's water system (1848). Only Rome would serve as model. "Let our aqueduct be worthy of the nation," he almost cried out. "And, emulous as we are of the ancient Roman republic, let us show that the rulers chosen by the people are not less careful of the safety, health and beauty of their capital than the emperors who, after enslaving their nation, by their great works conferred benefits upon their city which, their treason almost forgotten, cause their names to be remembered with respect and affection by those who still drink the water supplied by their magnificent aqueducts."[28] The result was a modest appropriation, and the project was soon under way.

The year 1853 signaled a new administration. The incoming President Franklin Pierce named Senator Jefferson Davis of Mississippi Secretary of War and transferred the construction of the Capitol to the War Department from the Department of the Interior. Shortly after assuming office, Davis appointed Meigs, now a captain, superintendent in charge of the Capitol extension, a position he held until the late fall of 1859, when President James Buchanan's Secretary of War would dismiss him.

It is quite extraordinary that a little-known army captain would be the dominant figure in shaping Washington in the decade before the Civil War. His responsibilities extended well beyond the Aqueduct and the Capitol to the Patent Office and the General Post Office. He became part of a small band of scientists and men of learning that included Alexander Dallas Bache of the Coastal Survey and Joseph Henry of the Smithsonian Institution. In 1854 he, like Walter, was elected a member of the American Philosophical Society, and he was to become a member of the new National Academy of Science and a regent of the Smithsonian.

Despite the important position Meigs held, he remained on an officer's pay. "It is a trial to have the habit of paying and handling thousands, to be buying with costs of thousands daily, and yet to have the constant feeling of necessity in my own affairs with such rigid economy," he wrote in his journal in 1854.[29] What sustained him and his wife was religion. A communicant of St. John's Church on Lafayette Square, he was active in the parish to the extent of serving two terms on the vestry. While religion did not play the role that it did with Walter, it was very much a part of Meigs's family life.

Of course, there was his work. His officer's salary, as might be expected, was ridiculous compared to what he might have received in the private sector.[30] Above all, he rejoiced in his work in designing the Washington Aqueduct and in his responsibility in supervising the extension of the nation's greatest building, the United States Capitol.

In all his projects, his high sense of mission was joined to technical knowledge, skill, and ingenuity, not to mention administrative talent. Typically, he designed the derrick built in the Great Rotunda to raise the metal parts of the dome and, more, he had John Augustus Roebling, who was to design the Brooklyn Bridge, furnish the wire cabling.

Such was the man whom Walter welcomed as his superior at the Capitol. "The Captain is as noble a man as the country can produce," he wrote in 1854, "and he is better fitted for the post than anyone they could find whether *soldier* or *civilian*, and I most sincerely desire that he may not be removed; such a thing would be a disaster to the country in general and me in particular. You have no idea what a luxury it has been to me, during the past year, to be able to devote myself to my legitimate professional duties, and be freed from the annoyances of contractors, appointments, disbursements, and the like, all of which take time, unhinge the mind, and create an army of enemies. I have enough to do without such troubles, and my ardent desire is that they may allow things to remain as they are." Meigs, in his opinion, "is composed of good stuff, and I shall stand by him through thick and thin."[31]

As superintendent of the Capitol extension, Meigs was to have a key role in the construction. Walter, in his design, had specified wood throughout, as per instructions and budget requirements. Meigs ordered that it be replaced by cast iron, where possible, such as at doorframes, window embrasures, and some ceilings. The Library of Congress fire and Walter's use of the metal in its replacement had indicated the value of such a substitute as well as his ability to make use of it. Where Walter had specified drums for the shafts of the exterior columns, Meigs called for monoliths. If there is scagliola—that is, plaster work in imitation of marble—found on the walls of both new wings, it is due to Meigs. The captain also called for the flooring of Minton tile, the encaustic tile manufactured by Minton, Hollins and Company of Stoke-on-Trent, England. If the rooms and corridors have vaulting, again it is the captain who asked for it in abundance. Admittedly, Walter had every intention of making use of it, but not in such variety. Meigs insisted on many forms, as he wanted to avoid the tedium of undecorated ceilings overhead and, also, to provide a pleasing form for any decoration. (In this connection, the fact is that the undecorated ceiling is too often the weakest part of any American room. Yet this ever-present bare space remains a persistent blight in American architecture.)

Meigs commissioned the bronze doors of Thomas Crawford and Randolph Rogers, as well as Crawford's statue, *Freedom*, on the top of the dome. He had plate glass, of French manufacture, installed in the windows.[32] Not only did he have Walter place the legislative chambers in the center of the wings instead of at their west sides, he had the architect give pediments to the porticoes of the wings, much like those found in the old center pediment designed by Latrobe and Bulfinch.

It was Meigs who suggested that the Old House Chamber be set aside for statues of leading Americans. In February 1854 he received a letter from an acquaintance, Gouverneur Kemble. A close friend of Washington Irving's, Kemble, who, like the author of *Rip Van Winkle*, lived on the banks of the Hudson River, where he had a cannon foundry across from West Point. "I have proposed that, after the removal of Congress to the new buildings, this hall shall be set apart for the reception of busts and statues, actual likenesses of the great men of our country," he suggested.[33] To this Meigs replied that from the start, he had desired the Old House Chamber to be set aside for just such a purpose. "It is on this principle," he wrote, "that I have put so many niches in the wings."[34] (Note that he does not say that he asked the architect to do so.) For the same reason he set aside the Old House Chamber as Statuary Hall, with the support of Congressman Justin S. Morrill of Vermont of the Morrill Land Grant Act of 1862.

From the start, Meigs saw the necessity of sculpture. Besides niches he called for pediments on the porticoes of the new wings, additional settings for statues. In 1854 he proposed commissions not just to Crawford but also to Hiram Powers, another fellow citizen, this one living in Florence. Crawford was the one who acted promptly and was called on to do the figures for the Senate pediment.[34] Other orders followed: two marble figures for the inside of the Senate

porch, the bronze doors both for the Senate and the House wings, and, last, the statue of Freedom for the dome.

Thomas Crawford, a New Yorker, had decided early on that as a sculptor he would do best to settle in Rome. The city had many advantages, not least its artistic heritage. In terms of sculpture and of instructors, it was the center of Europe. There was also the presence of skilled journeyman sculptors, assistants who could duplicate in marble what the young American executed in clay and plaster. And it is worth remembering that visiting countrymen of means on a European tour would often commission portraits; some would even become true patrons. One such was the senator from Massachusetts William Sumner. However, what drew Meigs to Crawford was the fact that he had won the competition to execute the equestrian statue of Washington in Richmond in 1854; Crawford was now the outstanding American sculptor.

Meigs and Kemble also discussed the need for mural decoration in the extensions and what form that decoration should take. Here Kemble advised, "For your frescoes and arabesques you must get an artist who has studied more in Rome."[36] Meigs fully agreed. His awareness of the necessity of having painted decoration as well as sculpture was astonishing for the time. What is very revealing of the man was that he sought books on ornament done by ancient Romans and Renaissance Italians. Not easily located, such books could be found in the library of the National Academy of Design in New York. One was Lewis Gruner's *Specimens of Oriental Art Selected from the Best Models of the Classical Epochs* (London, 1850), a giant folio of illustrations in full scale or close to it. Another was a three-volume work on Raphael's decoration in the Vatican, which Meigs came upon in the Astor Library, also in New York.[37] (The building of the Astor Library is still standing on New York's Lafayette Street. It is now the Public Theater. The Astor Library is one of the three constituent parts of the New York Public Library.) In this way, he gained a very clear idea of what was required.

To be sure, the old center building had the most elaborately decorated rooms in the country in the Old House and Old Senate chambers, but far more was needed for what was to be, in truth, a public palace for the people. The essential ingredient, other than sculpture, was mural decoration in the grand tradition.

Only a year after Meigs's exchange of letters with Gouverneur Kemble, there walked into his office one Constantino Brumidi, an immigrant from Rome. He was a master decorator with a command of fresco technique. Would Captain Meigs be able to make use of him? As it turned out, the captain could and did, giving him the commission (to be sure, only as a test) to decorate Room H-144, then that of the House Agricultural Committee. Thus began a career of epic proportions, for Brumidi would devote the rest of his life, over a quarter of a century, to decorating the United States Capitol.

Constantino Brumidi

Constantino Brumidi was born in Rome in 1805, to a Greek father and a Roman mother. When quite young, he revealed a talent for drawing, which led to his enrolling in the school of the Accademia di San Luca.[38] (Named for the patron saint of the arts, it is the oldest organization of painters and sculptors and, as such, served as a model for similar organizations, including the National Academy of Design in New York and the Pennsylvania Academy of Art in Philadelphia.) His training was far removed from that of today's artists. Rather, it bears comparison to that of athletes; we think at once of tennis players, gymnasts, and swimmers. It began early, it was strict, and it lasted longer, being based on the view of the fine arts as crafts. The objective in Rome was to produce a corps of artists to execute work for churches, palaces, and public buildings generally. The training was thorough, focusing on drawing ancient statues and copying the work of great masters—Michelangelo and the Carracci brothers. At the head of the Accademia was Vincenzo Camuccini, 1771–1844. He, according to the authority Jon L. Seydl, upheld "the 18th century Roman authority of draftsmanship, the unswerving commitment to the High Renaissance, and the notion of the artist as an engaged public servant. . . ." We must remind ourselves that painting and sculpture were seen in part as crafts, which accounts for the rigorous training. Proof of Brumidi's apprenticeship is found in his standing in student competitions, the records of which give some notion of the training. At sixteen he stood fifth in the modeling of a copy of the Apollo Belvedere. A year later he was second with a copy of a picture of a cherub, there being a special class in the drawing of babies. In addition students were taught geometry, history, mythology, engraving, and painting and received special instruction in drawing and painting cloth. Of course, there was the city outside the school with its unrivaled artistic wonders.[39]

On leaving school he undoubtedly served as assistant in artists' studios. His first known work, obtained in 1836,

Kneeling angel, 1837, by Brumidi, Weld Chapel, San Marcello al Corso, Rome. Photo Vasari Studio Fotografico.

was for the Torlonia family, the great patron of nineteenth-century Rome. A year later he designed sculpture for a crypt chapel. Commissions then came from the Holy See, a portrait of Pope Pius IX in 1847 and subsequently portraits of eleven popes, long dead, which were careful studies for the portraits in mosaic which decorate the restored Basilica of St. Paul's-Outside-the-Walls.

The modest career was shattered by the Revolution of 1848 that swept through Europe, driving Pope IX into exile and launching the Roman Republic. Brumidi participated in the new order, becoming a member of the Civic Guard of the Republic. His role would have passed unnoticed had he not participated in a raid on a monastery. The result was that, on the return of Pope Pius and the reestablishment of the Papal States, he was sent to prison. But it was not until after he had time to execute his most important Roman commission, figurative panels for the Chapel of Santa Maria dell'Archetto.

Brumidi would have remained in prison had not the monks of several orders, declaring him innocent, petitioned for his release. Two American clergymen, Archbishop John Hughes of New York and a young Jesuit, John Norris, who had befriended the hapless artist, must have had some influence; they held out the promise that if Brumidi were permitted to immigrate to the United States he could devote himself to decorating churches. In September 1852 he arrived in New York.

Portraits and some church work occupied him on arrival, and he even worked for a while in Mexico City. Shortly after his return from Mexico in December 1854 he called on Captain Meigs and, after submitting a design for a lunette in the House Committee for Agriculture, he embarked on what was to be the career of a lifetime, the decoration of the Capitol. He was ready for the job. He drew and painted in the grand tradition, that is, in a generalized and idealized interpretation of nature, begun by the Greeks and the Romans and given new life in the Italian Renaissance. (The definition I owe to the painter Pierce Rice.) The tradition enabled him to paint on a vast scale, as in *The Apotheosis of Washington* in the Great Rotunda. He worked for a quarter of a century in the building in more than one medium. He and his assistants used fresco, fresco a secco, oil on plaster, and tempera. The Capitol work did not prevent him from executing murals elsewhere if he was free. A few blocks north of the Capitol in the Church of St. Aloysius Gonzaga, he did a reredos, *St. Aloysius receiving the Host from St. Charles Borromeo*, and in Philadelphia he did a large *Crucifixion* in the Cathedral of St. Peter and St. Paul in one of America's great monumental interiors. (Unfortunately, the *Crucifixion* no longer exists.)

Admittedly, the work in the Capitol is uneven, with the decorative portions often surpassing the figurative panels, the latter's quality diminishing toward the end of Brumidi's career. But how many artists can have their lifework assembled under one roof without it revealing some change, and not always for the best?

No other building in the country—including the many state capitols—surpasses the Capitol both in the amount of true fresco and the sheer quantity of mural work. Even the Jefferson Building of the Library of Congress is rivaled in quantity of painted ornament. Looking elsewhere, to legislative palaces beyond our borders, there is the Palace of Westminster, rebuilt in the 1840s in the Gothic style. Nor should the interested overlook the Parliament House of the Republic of Hungary. This extraordinary building, too little known, was constructed in the last decade of the nineteenth century, its Gothic design inspired by the Palace of Westminster. In the center of Budapest, with a dome 315 feet high, it stretches along the Pesth side, on the right bank of the Danube. These three buildings are the most lavishly decorated parliament buildings on the globe; beside them, those of other nations seem very plain indeed.

Of course, Brumidi did not work alone. He had assistants, among them Louis Franze, Joseph Rakeman, and George W. Strieby, as well as an associate, James Leslie. And what was he paid? The salary of a congressman. In 1855 and 1856 he worked 329 days at $8.00 a day, (one assistant for 156 days was paid $4.00 a day, and a laborer 240 days at $1.25 a day.) In 1857 his daily wage climbed to $10.00 a day, where it remained for the rest of his life.

His career at the Capitol did not go unquestioned or unresented. In 1859 a group of artists, including Rembrandt Peale, Henry Kirke Brown, Albert Bierstadt, and others, peti-

Pope Sixtus I. Oil painting for mosaic in St. Paul's Outside-the-Walls, Rome. Photo Vasari Studio Fotografico.

tioned Congress to create an art commission to supervise the Capitol decoration, with members to be named by the President. Commissioners were duly appointed; they met and submitted a report to Congress. After a year, the commission was abolished.

More serious than the artists' questioning of his work was Walter's opposition to the very need for mural decoration. In a letter to the Secretary of War in 1859, the architect wrote:

First, *I recommend that the very ornate and inappropriate decoration of the walls and ceilings of the committee rooms be dispensed with. These rooms, being intended for the transactions of the business of the committees, can be seen only by a very few, unless they should be kept open for exhibition, which, of course, cannot be contemplated, as it would interfere with an important branch of legislation.*

If these rooms are painted at all, the walls and ceilings should be laid off in panels and painted light and harmonious tints; in each room some single appropriate device, of small dimensions, may be introduced in fresco; this would be far more effective than the tawdry ornament with which the rooms that have been finished are crowded. Some of these rooms are so extravagantly decorated with crude and inharmonious colors that it is painful to remain in them, and when they are overshadowed by the projecting arcades of the porticos yet to be built, they will be dark and gloomy. Even though these rooms are unobjectionable in point of taste, it would seem that so large an expenditure as it has required to put them in their present condition would demand that they should be kept open for

Dome of Chapel of Santa Maria dell'Archetto. Photo Vasari Studio Fotografico.

figures in the center pediment of the East Front. And we have seen Walter's reaction to St. Peter's, where he condemned what he called "Italian taste."

At one point, Brumidi went so far as to remove Walter's decoration in one room, whereupon Walter, in turn, ripped out Brumidi's preparation for a mural. The dispute between painter and architect is a fascinating story of conflict between top professionals.

Walter's attitude toward painted decoration is perhaps not so startling today, such is the disdain of contemporary architects for all decoration. What has now become endemic in the architectural profession is just as widespread among intellectuals—that is, those who write. The Capitol's interior, even the Great Rotunda, has no place in American literature; no major American writer has described the ornament, inside and out. What is more, the disdain, for it is beyond indifference, goes back to the first years of the expanded Capitol.

Yet one exception does exist. Walt Whitman, in Washington as a hospital volunteer during the Civil War, wrote to his brother Jeff (Thomas Jefferson Whitman) in February 1863 on a visit to the building:

I spent several hours in the Capitol the other day—the incredible gorgeousness of some of the rooms, (interior decorations &c.)—rooms used perhaps but for merely three or four Committee meetings in the course of the whole year, is beyond one's flightiest dreams. Costly frescoes of the style of Taylor's Saloon in Broadway [in New York], only really the best and choicest of their sort, done by imported French & Italian artists, are the prevailing sorts (imagine the work you see on the fine China vases, in Tiffany's—the paintings of Cupids & goddesses &c. spread recklessly over the arched ceiling and broad panels of a big room—the whole floor underneath paved with tessellated pavement, which is a sort of cross between marble & china, with little figures drab, blue, cream color &c.).

These things, with heavy, elaborately wrought balustrades, columns, & steps—all of the most beautiful marbles I ever saw, some white as milk, others of all colors, green, spotted, lined, or of our old chocolate color— all these marbles used as freely as if they were common blue flags [Hudson River bluestone or graywacke, which was the pavement of New York's sidewalks]—with rich door-frames and window-casings of bronze and gold—heavy chandeliers and mantels, and clocks in every room—indeed by far the richest and gayest, and most un-American and inappropriate ornamenting and finest interior workmanship I ever conceived possible, spread in profusion through scores, hundreds, (and almost thousands) of

exhibition, and not as the private apartments of the committees, where they may retire for the transaction of the business connected with legislation.

Secondly, I object to the dark and heavy, and excessively ornate painting that has been commenced in the entries and passages of the north wing [the Brumidi Corridor] and I respectfully recommend that it be stopped immediately, and that all the passages and entries be finished in light and harmonious tints, with a very sparing application of foliated ornament and gold leaf, and the introduction of a few frescoes where the lights are favorable.

The passages and entries, particularly in the basement [first floor] have but little light, hence it is injudicious to paint them in dark colors, and useless to waste upon them expensive decorations; a better effect may be produced in such places by harmonious coloring in flat tints, than by any foliated or gilded ornamentation. Such a system of painting, besides greatly reducing the cost, would be more in accordance with the purposes of the building.[40]

Walter went on to detail the cost of Brumidi's decoration in one room and to protest the use of scagliola.

As his comments indicate, Walter held to opinions common among architects of his day and since. The architects of the Greek Revival era were very cautious in their use of any kind of ornament. For example, sculpture is seldom found on Greek Revival buildings; one never sees a figure in a pediment. Indeed, the Capitol was a rarity at the time in having *rooms—such are what I find, or rather would find to interest me, if I devoted time to it—But a few of the rooms are enough for me—the style is without grandeur, and without simplicity—These days, the state our country is in, and especially filled as I am from top to toe, of late with scenes and thoughts of the* hospitals*, (America seems to me now, though only in her youth, but brought* already here *feeble, bandaged and bloody in* hospital*)—these days I say, Jeff, all the poppy-show goddesses and all the pretty blue & gold in which the interior Capitol is got up, seem to me out of place beyond any thing I could tell—and I get away from it as quick as I can when that kind of thought comes over me. I suppose it is to be described throughout—those interiors—as all of them got up in the French style—well enough for a New York [incomplete]."*[41]

Beyond the fact that the poet had a cloudy notion of what the "French style" was, it was hardly a time, with the Virginia front so close to Washington, to pause to reflect on the Capitol's wonders.

To Walter's credit, he came to appreciate Brumidi and his work. In fact, he gave Brumidi the order to paint *The Apotheosis of Washington*. At around the same time, he commissioned the artist to do some decoration for his house in Philadelphia, where Brumidi was at work on the *Crucifixion* for the Cathedral of St. Peter and St. Paul.

If Walter and Brumidi were eventually reconciled, there was no reconciliation between Walter and Meigs. The engineer, unable to eliminate the architect, would at least have his name permanently registered in the building. Walter accepted that Meigs was to design those portions of the building where engineering expertise was paramount, as in the case of the roofs of the new wings. (Had not Walter in his Franklin Institute lecture said of utility and durability that, "Being entirely of a practical or mechanical nature, we shall pass over them and limit ourselves to the consideration of architectural composition, with reference alone to the production of beauty"?) To make sure his presence would not be forgotten, the captain had each beam of the new House and Senate chambers cast with the inscription "CAP^t M.C. MEIGS, INV. A.D. 1854" ("inv." stands for the Latin *invenit*, meaning "designed").[42] The irony was that the beams—they are no longer there—were invisible to the public. It should be added that Walter's name is still there, and visible to those who know where it is. To be seen from the third floor of the Senate wing, the inscription is carved on a lintel in the Senate portico (*see* "The Senate Chamber" on pages 128–30).

We may smile at the two men's determination to have their names stamped, as it were, on the building, but we do so with a sad shake of the head. The conflict was serious. With the arrival of the Buchanan administration and a new Secretary of War in 1857, it became more and more bitter. At one point, in an argument over control of the architectural drawings, Walter even transferred his drafting room and drawings to the part of the Capitol under the jurisdiction of

*The Virgin in the center of the dome.
Photo Vasari Studio Fotografico.*

Cherub in panel in the dome. Photo Vasari Studio Fotografico.

Reredos mural, 1864, by Brumidi in the Cathedral of St. Peter and St. Paul, Philadelphia. (Mural no longer there.) Photo Robert S. Halvey.

the Speaker of the House. There Meigs could not touch his work. With good reason, Walter was one of the founders of the American Institute of Architects, determined to obtain recognition for the profession, and in the last years of his life, he was to be its president.

To grasp the roles of the two men we must look on Meigs, first of all, as a brilliant and knowledgeable patron; one who fully accepted the Renaissance view of the classical. Nor was he above turning to the best authorities such as Raphael, even if it meant going to the Astor Library in New York and the National Academy of Design to study books of plates. Where the captain, in his pride at being in charge of the extension of the United States, overstepped the role of patron was seeking to have his name on Walter's drawings as a designer. Yet, when Brumidi had his portrait in *The Apotheosis of Washington* in the group *Commerce* next to that of Robert Morris, Meigs, now General, had the artist remove it. Walter, on the other hand, is portrayed in the group *Science* as the portrait of Samuel F. B. Morse (*see* pages 86–87).

By the fall of 1859 the outcome of the struggle was that the

Secretary of War ordered Meigs into virtual exile by sending him to a distant island fort off the Florida coast. Meigs was now out of the picture, although he did return to the Capitol briefly in 1861 when he, again, tried to remove Walter. Then, in a most extraordinary series of events, the consequence of the outbreak of war, the captain, now colonel, was introduced to President Lincoln by his Secretary of State, William Seward. Very impressed, Lincoln told the commanding general Winfield Scott: "I very much wish to appoint Colonel Meigs Quartermaster General. . . . I have come to know Colonel Meigs quite well for a short acquaintance and, so far as I am capable of judging, I do not know one who combines the qualities of masculine intellect, learning and experience of the right sort, and physical power of labor and endurance as he."[43]

Promoted to brigadier general, Meigs assumed the title of quartermaster general, and in that position he furnished materiel, forage, transportation, etc. to a Union army that, in April 1861, counted 16,000 men and four years later numbered 1 million.

The Dome

When the war broke out, the Capitol extensions were still unfinished. To be sure, the representatives and senators were already in their new chambers, but the wing porches of the East Front were without colonnades, steps, and cheekblocks. Rooms awaited decoration. The most conspicuous part of the building, the dome, had risen to the attic above the columned peristyle (*see* illustration on page 20, right).

The reason for the delay was simple: Obtaining approval for a new dome and achieving a final design had taken a long time. Walter's first design for the enlarged building, approved by President Fillmore in June 1851, preserved the old dome of Bulfinch. That November the architect was at work on a high new one. This he was not to complete until four years later. Submitted to Congress, his plan was enthusiastically received, and on March 3, 1855, the dome was approved for construction.

Then began the drafting and redrafting, which led to the final design four years later. Walter and Meigs, for all their

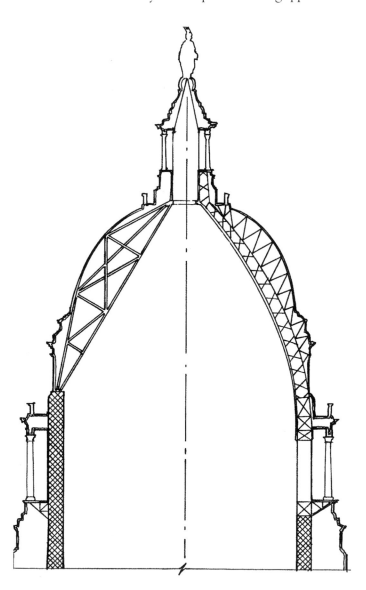

Section elevation of the dome, showing the structural solutions of Thomas U. Walter (left) and August Schoenborn (right). Drawing by Richard Sammons based on a drawing by Turpin C. Bannister, "The Genealogy of the Dome of the United States Capitol," plate 2. Society of Architectural Historians, Journal, *vol. 7.*

The dome of the Capitol with half cut away to show the structure of the canopy and the interior dome as well as the exterior dome, 1859, wash rendering by Thomas U. Walter. Courtesy Athenaeum of Philadelphia.

growing differences, worked together, and they had substantial assistance from Walter's chief draftsman, August Schoenborn.[44] The basic parts of the approved dome remained the same: a stylobate, or platform, a drum with a peristyle of columns, an attic of high windows separated by pilasters with recessed panels, a secondary attic, a cupola, a lantern in the shape of a tholos, or round temple, and, at the top, a statue. Changes were made—for example, the number of peristyle columns was reduced from forty to thirty-six—but two significant parts remained the same. The cupola was held to its elliptical shape, and on the interior there was no interior dome on the inside of the cupola.

The use of cast iron permitted certain structural innovations. One, devised by Meigs, was placing the peristyle columns on iron brackets extending from the masonry wall of the Rotunda, thus permitting the drum to have a bigger diameter than the Rotunda below. The brackets were concealed by a cast-iron apron that made for a false stylobate, so shaped that it resembled a stone one. It is a perfect example of a structural instrument making possible a visual element demanded by the architect.

Only the design of the lower dome was final. This allowed construction of the drum and even the attic. The upper part was open to change pending the arrival of the plaster model of *Freedom*, the statue destined for the top of the dome. Four years before, the captain had asked the sculptor Thomas Crawford for sketches of a giant statue. Already at work in Rome on figures for the Senate portico and bronze doors for the House and Senate wings, the sculptor sent the drawings to Meigs, who, on obtaining the approval of the Secretary of War, Jefferson Davis, commissioned a full-scale model. What with Crawford being ill (he died in 1857) and the vicissitudes of transportation, the plaster model did not reach Washington until the spring of 1859. Its size, 19 feet 16 inches, astonished all, not least the architect. He had to change his design, this time lowering the cupola height by 17 feet and transforming what had been an elliptical silhouette into the round one of a hemisphere. In this way, he also provided a wide base for a larger lantern to support the statue.

At this point, St. Isaac's Cathedral in St. Petersburg seems to have had some influence. Both the architect and the captain knew of the building, which was completed in 1842. In its dome, its French architect, Auguste Ricard de Montferrand, had made use of cast iron in the structural parts. While the quantity used in St. Isaac's was negligible compared to the amount in the Capitol dome, its presence there strengthened Walter's and Meigs's case in favor of using the metal in the Capitol. Interestingly enough, when Walter designed the armature of the cupola, he followed Ricard's pattern. The design chosen by Meigs turned out to be one by Schoenborn. The nearby illustrations offer a comparison.

Recently the authority William C. Allen has shown that the influence of St. Isaac's might have been greater than first recognized. Here is a table giving some dimensions that show that Walter took a good hard look at the cathedral when working on his final dome design. Allen, in his book *The Dome of the United States Capitol*, sees Walter as following the St. Petersburg model closely, even to the point of specifying close or identical dimensions.

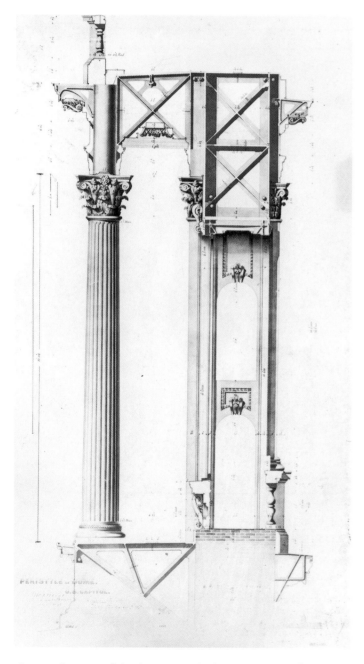

Section elevation of the drum peristyle showing the use of cast iron.

	CAPITOL		ST. ISAAC'S
	1855 Design	1859 Design	1818–1858
Height of dome	230'6"	218'	218'
Height of cupola	56'	39'¼"	40'
Diameter of tholos base	20'5"	24'4"	25'3"
Diameter of tholos	14'10"	18'3"	18'

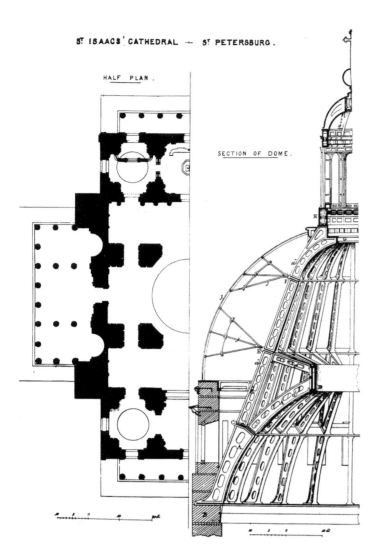

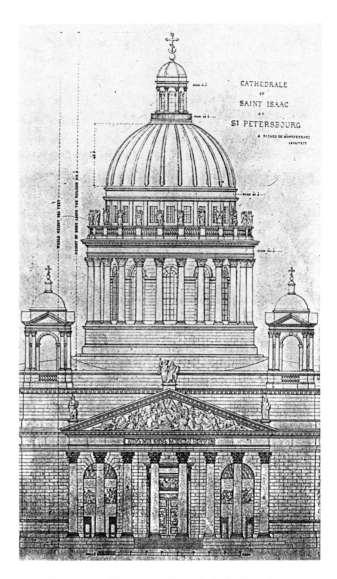

Section of dome of St. Isaac's Cathedral, St. Petersburg, by Auguste Ricard de Montferran. Civil Engineer's and Architect's Journal, vol. 12, 1849, pages 9–12, plate 2. Courtesy New York Public Library.

Elevation of St. Isaac's Cathedral, St. Petersburg. Courtesy Architect of the Capitol.

The similarities are astonishing, but it must be underscored that the two buildings are altogether different. St. Isaac's, other than being a cathedral, is square in plan with four equal sides. While cast iron is found in its structure, granite, marble, bronze, as well as gold on its dome, make for a polychrome building as against one all white marble and white-painted cast iron. Further, St. Isaac's has no secondary attic, and its primary attic, while a columnade, is lower than that of the Capitol. (Further differences are discussed in "The Dome" on pages 45–50.)

If the influence of St. Isaac's was late in coming, what of that of the Panthéon, with its interior parts consisting of an interior cupola with a large oculus and a canopy over the oculus absent from the first designs? Walter had singled out the Panthéon for praise in his 1838 report to the Girard College trustees and had accompanied his description with a sketch. Also, what can we make of the fact that all of the models he saw in 1838 have spherical cupolas, not one being elliptical? Did he really want the latter shape, until he was

forced to accept the hemisphere with the arrival of the Crawford statue?

War broke out in April 1861, and a month later work on the dome stopped. Federal moneys now went to prosecuting the war, and even the Capitol itself was pressed into use as temporary barracks as the regiments from the North came to the defense of Washington. The stop order left the contractors, Janes, Fowler, Kirtland & Company of New York and Brooklyn, with 1,300,000 pounds of iron at the Capitol site. They decided to go ahead for financial reasons, certainly, but also because of their pride in the commission. Lincoln shrewdly took credit for pursuing the construction as a symbolic gesture in the war to save the Union.

The dome was completed in 1863 and Crawford's *Freedom* placed atop the columned lantern on December 2. In 1865 Brumidi painted *The Apotheosis of Washington* on the canopy. In May of that same year, Thomas U. Walter resigned as architect. The drama of what was virtually the making of a new Capitol was over.

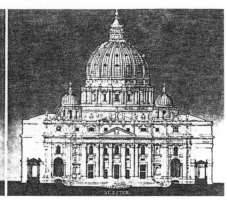

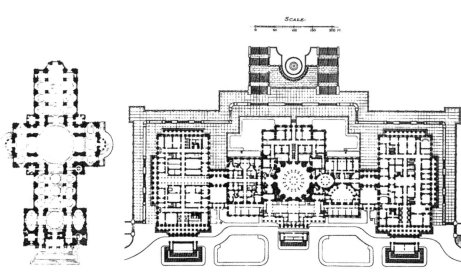
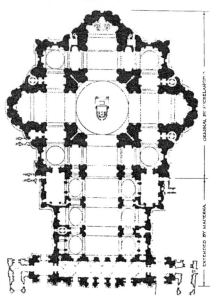

Front elevations and ground-floor plans of St. Paul's in London, the Capitol, and St. Peter's in Rome, drawn to the same scale. Courtesy Architect of the Capitol.

Diagram comparing the elevation of the Capitol (black), St. Paul's in London (crosshatch), and St. Peter's in Rome (hatch). Courtesy Architect of the Capitol.

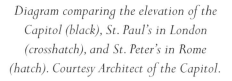

Silhouette of the Old Capitol set against the East Front of today's Capitol. Courtesy Architect of the Capitol.

What follows down to our own time is something of an anticlimax. Brumidi was to work away until his death in 1880. His most important mural during this period was his frieze in the Great Rotunda, left unfinished at his death. An assistant, Filippo Costaggini, took over and executed a portion, guided by Brumidi's sketches. The third and last section was completed between 1950 and 1954 by Allyn Cox.

Why did Walter resign in 1865? He had been Architect of the Capitol for fourteen years and had worked on other buildings in Washington, admittedly under great stress. With *Freedom* in place, his part seemed to be over. He faced the threat of working for an officious superior (who was the uncle of the sculptor Daniel Chester French). In the back of his mind was the expectation that his offer of resignation would be turned down and that he would be pressed to stay on. Instead it was accepted, and, worse, he suffered the humiliation of being replaced by his office assistant, Edward Clark, who had been cultivating the right people behind his back.

One important part of the Capitol had been left to the future: the landscaping, particularly the construction of the great marble staircase of the West Front. What was there in the 1860s was Bulfinch's work, ca. 1826, consisting of a landing just at his center front. From it descended two flights of steps to the sides of a second landing; here a third flight, in the middle, dropped to the foot of the hill. In 1864, with the completion of the House and Senate wings, Walter had extended the grassy slopes on either side of the small terrace and steps. Had Walter remained in office, he no doubt would have seen to some change. As it was, in his retirement, he repeatedly proposed a western expansion of the center of the building. Among those who opposed his project was Brigadier General Meigs. Finally, in 1874, Senator Justin Morrill of Vermont, who, as representative, had taken so much interest in Statuary Hall, persuaded Congress in 1874 to retain Frederick Law Olmsted to design the grounds.

Olmsted, thanks to his work with Calvert Vaux on New York's Central Park and Brooklyn's Prospect Park, then stood at the head of his profession. He proposed the scheme we see today: three landings joined by two flights of steps at the sides, with a wide short flight linking the third to a fourth landing, or bottom, landing. Completed in 1891, the design was successful. The terrace serves as a visual foundation or buttress to the Capitol above. There is also the nice touch in the arch windows of the landing walls and the fact

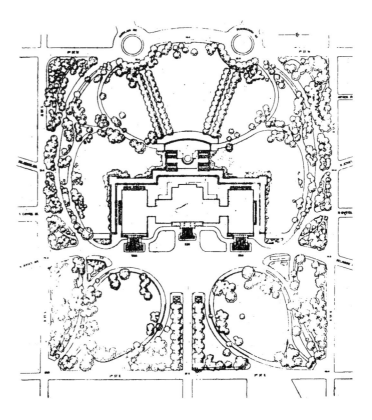

Design of the Capitol grounds and terrace by Frederick Law Olmsted in 1874, completed in 1892. Courtesy Library of Congress.

that the walls are contrasting, the upper being straight and the lower curved.

The architect responsible for the details of the terrace at the Capitol and the minor structures on the nearby lawn was Thomas Wisedell. He chose to work in the Romanesque Revival style, which provided something of a contrast to the classical architecture of the building above. It is most evident in the fountain and lanterns at the foot of the hill as well as the brick grotto in the northwest quadrant of the slope. Wisedell also designed the bench walls, lanterns, fountain, and wrought-iron shelters along the plaza on the east side of the Capitol.

A major step was taken in the 1890s with the construction of a separate building for the Library of Congress. Today called the Jefferson Building, it was the first of more than ten built over a century, the last being the Judiciary Office Building, which serves the United States Supreme Court. The Jefferson Building was the start of the ever-expanding domain of the Architect of the Capitol to its present 273.7 acres.

Of national importance was the decoration of the Jefferson Building. Over fifty painters and sculptors were employed in its decoration, producing a quantity rivaled only by the amount of it in the Capitol. Embellishment on such a scale was part of the triumph of the classical tradition signaled by the World's Columbian Exposition of 1893, held in Chicago on the shores of Lake Michigan. Many of the artists at the Chicago Fair also worked in the new Library. Inevitably there was also a small wave of mural decoration in the Capitol in the rooms that replaced Walter's old Library of Congress. Among the Library's artists was George W. Maynard, who repeated, in a smaller version of his Library work, panels with floating figures. Another was Elmer Ellsworth Garnsey, who decorated one of the new rooms. Interestingly enough, when a band of the Library artists visited the Capitol, they were overheard to say of Brumidi's decoration: "We have nothing equal to this in the Library. There is no one who can do such work today."[45]

The Congress may not have known it, but the adornment of their new Library was just one of its contributions to the beginning of what became the City Beautiful movement. Equally important was the creation in 1901 of the McMillan Commission, named for Senator James McMillan of Michigan, to plan Washington. It meant that L'Enfant was at last discovered. In fact, his remains, after lying in state in the Great Rotunda in 1904, were reinterred at Arlington Cemetery.

Among the members advising the senator were Frederick Law Olmsted, Jr., a landscape architect like his father, the sculptor Augustus Saint-Gaudens, and the architects Charles Follen McKim and Daniel H. Burnham. Their starting point was the Capitol and the Mall. They cleared the Mall of a leafy picturesque glade directly north of the Smithsonian Institution's "Castle," thus opening the vista to the Washington Monument and carrying the vista beyond to the site now occupied by the Lincoln Memorial. They persuaded the Pennsylvania Railroad to take out the southbound tracks at the foot of the Hill and place them underground, and to join with other railroads, including the Baltimore & Ohio, which had its station on the Mall's edge, in the construction of Union Station—not just an ordinary station but also a grand one by Daniel H. Burnham of Chicago that would complement the Capitol. By bringing life to the Mall, they gave the Capitol the setting that Major L'Enfant had planned—that is, a climax at the east end of a giant allée. When the Lincoln Memorial was inaugurated in 1922, the American people acquired the nation's greatest man-made vista.

Additional changes had occurred on the periphery of the Capitol. The navy's Civil War Peace Monument, dated 1877, and the splendid Garfield Monument, 1887, by J. Q. A. Ward, were already in place at the foot of the Hill. In 1922 the Grant Monument by Henry Merwin Shrady and the architect Edward Pearce Casey was unveiled. This is a glorious bronze ensemble with the great general on his charger, Cincinnatus, above two groups: the cavalry (north) and the artillery (south). Several years later, the United States Botanic Garden was built

nearby on the designs of Parsons, Bennett & Frost of Chicago. A charming building in the French classical manner, it has a garden in back with a beautiful fountain by Frédéric Auguste Bartholdi, the sculptor of the Statue of Liberty. In the early 1930s Bennett, Parsons & Frost was to design the approach to the Capitol from North Capitol Street with an underground garage, fountains, and pools. Farther west, off Constitution Avenue, the Robert A. Taft Memorial, a bell tower with a statue of the senator from Ohio, was built in 1959.

The east periphery of the Capitol has seen more change than the west. There the Supreme Court in 1935 joined the Library of Congress, and the Library itself has added two more buildings. The Supreme Court also has a new annex, an office building next to Union Station. The Senate and House now have three office buildings each.

If the domain around the Capitol has been transformed, as was inevitable with the expansion of government offices, the Capitol itself would seem at first glance to have changed very little. Yet how many millions who go through the building know that the interiors of the two legislative chambers over which Walter and Meigs labored vanished to give way to wholly new ones between 1949 and 1950? The two had to be reroofed; this led to the decision to redo them completely. Instead of cast-iron paneling and detail came marble and wood following the designs of John Harbeson of Harbeson, Hough, Livingston & Larson of Philadelphia.

Similarly, very few visitors realize that the center of the East Front dates from 1959–62. There is no reason why they should, so carefully were the new facade, steps, portico, and all duplicated by the architectural partnership of Poor, Shelton & Swanke. Where the stone of the facade had been painted sandstone, it is now white marble, much like that of Walter's House and Senate wings. True, the new front is 32½ feet forward from the old, but the mighty dome rules the setting as before.

On the interior, the change, if it can be called change, is the careful restoration in 1975 of the Old House and Old Senate chambers and the Old United States Supreme Court Chamber. No rooms convey the pre–Civil War era, the world of Clay, Calhoun, Webster, and other leaders of that now distant past, as do these three.

Work goes on, even if the results are barely noticeable except to the initiated. In 1988 the central West Front was restored and given a fresh coat of paint. In 1992 the sunken courtyards that once existed between the terrace and the building proper were filled with rooms. There is, in the planning stage, a project to build a three-story public entrance beneath the parking lot of the East Front plaza. It would serve as an elaborate orientation center for the millions who come to the Hill, not just for the Capitol but also for the Jefferson Building of the Library of Congress. (Much of the construction was originally executed in 1961 when there were plans for a 2,200-car underground garage.) The present parking lot will give way to turf and flowerbeds. Visitors, after going up a flight of steps, will find themselves in the Crypt beneath the Great Rotunda. From there they will proceed up the stairways in the House or Senate wings. Better still, if permitted they will proceed to the Great Stairway at the west side of the Great Rotunda. The virtue of this approach is that it repeats the approach to the Great Rotunda that existed prior to the closing of the East Entrance to the public.

We should not slip into the error of thinking of the Capitol solely in terms of architecture. The painter, too, has had his role in recent years. The late Allyn Cox completed the Brumidi Frieze in the Great Rotunda between 1950 and 1953. Two decades later, he was at work decorating the Hall of Capitols and the Great Experimental Hall on the ground floor of the House wing. A conspicuous change over the years, one rarely mentioned, has been the flowerbeds on the approaches to the East Front. Many more flowers, and a greater variety, are now to be seen in summer; in winter, kale, at least, offers some color.

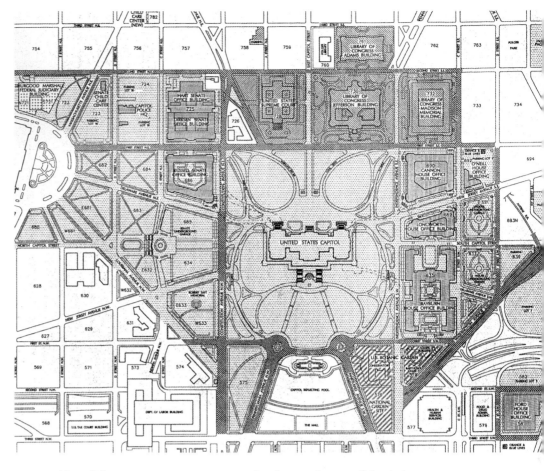

Map of the properties, 273.7 acres, under the jurisdiction of the Architect of the Capitol, 1990. Courtesy Architect of the Capitol.

Listing the several changes in this fashion would seem to make the projects appear numerous until one realizes that they have been strung over the years from 1900 to the present. Furthermore, they have made no difference in the Capitol's silhouette and represent minor differences on the interior, except in the present House and Senate chambers done in the early 1950s. We can wander about the building and exclaim how fortunate we are in its architecture and decoration and in its setting. We may even thank our luck. Yes, there may well have been an element of luck in what we behold. Who could have foretold that a middle-aged Italian, a painter from Rome, would have stopped here only a few years after he landed in New York? Or that he would be the only artist in the country at the time who could execute mural decoration in the grand manner?

While the element of luck is always present, of greater significance is the fact that those responsible, the givers of commissions, were solidly grounded in the heritage of the Western world. What is more, they saw the traditions of this heritage mirrored in the splendid past of Europe, more especially in the world of the Mediterranean. When George Washington turned to Pierre Charles L'Enfant, he did so because this army major had the imagination to see what shape the capital of the new nation should take.

L'Enfant thought in terms of monumental embellishment. The same instinct prompted Washington to choose William Thornton's design in 1793, a building with a rotunda and a dome. In appointing Latrobe architect, Thomas Jefferson acted on the same instinct and the nation was rewarded by two of the finest rooms in the Republic prior to the Civil War: the Old House and Old Senate chambers. Our legislative bodies were to govern in beautiful settings.

The Western heritage inspired the symbols and the details of the abundant ornament. The leaf of the acanthus, a Mediterranean plant, is found here in many forms. Even the baby, so evocative of the classical, made an early entrance in both the Old Chambers. To these were added the pictures that bind us to our history.

The classical tradition continued as seen in the choice of Thomas Ustick Walter as architect and of Montgomery Cunningham Meigs, a mere army captain, yet one with the breadth of culture to know that the Capitol had to be embellished in the grand manner. For this task he chose Thomas Crawford and Constantino Brumidi. Frederick Law Olmsted, in the Capitol terrace, made the last addition to the great composition.

In the end, we come back to the dome. To Walter's and Meigs's genius the nation owes its greatest symbol. Let us rejoice in our good fortune!

The Influence of the United States Capitol

We would be remiss, at this point, if we did not mention and underscore the extraordinary influence of the Capitol on the design of government buildings. We owe it to Thomas Ustick Walter that the high dome—that is, the hemisphere, or cupola, on a columned drum—came to stand for government as well as for religion. From St. Peter's to St. Isaac's, the high dome was limited to being a part of a cathedral or a great church when executed in the classical manner. It is still to be found in churches, but in this country the symbol is also common in structures governmental.

In testimony, we offer views of the best examples, some state capitols built after 1890 and one city hall. Although they have high domes above a rectangular block, each one is different, underscoring the wonderful variety that can be achieved in the great tradition, however similar the basic form may be.

If the high dome indicates major influence, another aspect, no less important, is the presence of sculpture and mural decoration. To walk into one of these state houses is to discover that there was once an abundance of such decoration throughout the country. A good example is the Wisconsin State Capitol (1906–17) in Madison by George B. Post & Sons. Admittedly, the basic plan is not a rectangle but in the shape of a St. Andrew's cross with four distinct wings instead of the customary two. At the center rise the dome on a peristyle colonnade and one attic. Beneath the exterior dome is a second with a large dome, like that of the Capitol, and over the oculus a canopy with a mural. A particular distinction of the building is the quantity of painted ornament, chiefly figurative, by Edwin Howland Blashfield, Albert Herter, Charles Y. Turner, and Hugo Ballin, along with stained glass panels by Kenyon Cox. Nor should the Governor's Room by Elmer Ellsworth Garnsey be passed by. As for the sculpture, it includes the work of Daniel Chester French, Karl Bitter, Attilio Piccirilli, and Adolph A. Weinman. The gilded statue *Wisconsin* on top of the dome is the work of French and stands 15 feet high in comparison to the 19½-foot *Freedom* of the Capitol.

The Missouri State Capitol (1911–18), instead of being between lakes, is on a high bluff overlooking the Missouri River in Jefferson City. It is the tallest building in the town, and its dome can be seen for miles around. The columns at the drum are placed in pairs upholding broken entablatures. Tracy and Swartwout is the architectural firm. The sculptors here were Sherry Fry, who did the statue of Ceres, goddess of agriculture, on the dome; Adolph A. Weinman; Karl Bitter; and Daniel Chester French. Mural decoration in

The Wisconsin State Capitol, 1906–17,
by George Brown Post & Sons. Photo Kenn Jschonek.

The Missouri State Capitol, 1911–18,
by Tracy and Swartwout. Photo Greg Leach.
Courtesy Missouri Department of Natural Resources.

The Washington State Capitol, 1911–21,
by Wilder and White.
Photo Harry J. Halverson.

quantity devolved on Frank Brangwyn; being abundant and ornamental, it is highly effective. Thomas Hart Benton, who is better known, offers figurative panels in the caricatural style that is peculiarly his own.

Another example of a state capitol on a bluff, above Puget Sound, is that of Washington in Olympia, built between 1911 and 1921 on the designs of Wilder and White. With no mural decoration, its interior is largely monochromatic. The colonnade of the drum has advanced and recessed columns in pairs beneath a broken entablature. At the four corners, below the colonnaded drum, are four domed blocks of stone with consoles.

One of the latest of the capitols is that of West Virginia overlooking the Kanawah River in Charleston. Completed in 1932 by Cass Gilbert, architect of New York's Woolworth Building, and Cass Gilbert, Jr., its dome has panels of arms trophies much like those of the dome of the Invalides in Paris.

These capitols were all built with steel frames; even their domes consisted of stone set around frames of steel. Interestingly enough, there were two exceptions: Minnesota's in St. Paul and Rhode Island's in Providence. The former, by Cass Gilbert, was part of the great wave of capitol building that stemmed from the World's Columbian Exposition of 1893 in Chicago. Constructed between 1895 and 1907, at about the time of the Wisconsin capitol, it boasts a similar quantity of mural decoration by, among others, Edwin

Howland Blashfield and Howard Pyle. Even more conspicuous is the sculpture, particularly a gilt quadriga, or four-horse chariot (known to the local youngsters as "the horses"), by Daniel Chester French. An artistic invention of ancient Rome, this one must be one of the less familiar of the several in the country; the best known by far is the one by Frederick MacMonnies on the Soldiers and Sailors Monument in Brooklyn's Grand Army Plaza. As for the dome, its hemisphere has a double row of oeils-de-boeuf. However, the hemisphere has yet another distinction: It is largely of masonry. As shown in the illustration on the next page (top left), it

The West Virginia State Capitol, 1932, by Cass Gilbert.
Courtesy West Virginia Industrial Publicity Commission.

*The Minnesota State Capitol, 1895–1907,
by Cass Gilbert.
Photo John D. Bradford.*

*Drawing of the Minnesota State Capitol dome
partly cut away to show structure. Drawing by
Stephanie Murrill based on one by Alan Ominsky.*

has a cone of steel and brick, invisible to the beholder, which reaches to the columned lantern. This cone serves as support for the cupola sides, which are solid masonry, the stone being marble.

The other dome of masonry is that of the Rhode Island capitol (1894–1903) by the best-known architectural firm of the era, McKim, Mead & White. In fact, it is generally accepted as the third-highest masonry dome in the world after St. Peter's in Rome and the Taj Mahal in Agra, India.

We should perhaps not be quite so astonished by this fact considering the decades in which it was built.

Cast iron was, as we know, so in disrepute at the time that serious thought was given to replacing the Capitol's metal dome with one of marble masonry. Carrère & Hastings, architects of the Russell Senate Office Building and the Cannon House Office Building, did a study of walls required to carry so much masonry only to find that the wide walls would have robbed the building of much of its office space.

One capitol dome, planned some time ago, was finally completed in 2002: the one for the Oklahoma State Capitol in Oklahoma City. The building was under construction during World War I on the designs of S. Wemyss-

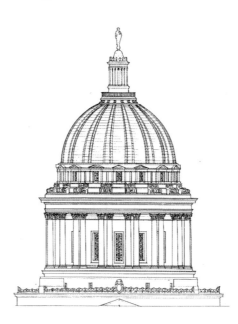

*The design for the dome of the Oklahoma
State Capitol by S. Wemyss-Smith and
S. A. Lalen. Drawing by David Kulick, AIA.*

Smith and S. A. Lalen, but only the main block was finished.

The high, wide dome of the Capitol has rarely served as model beyond state capitols. One notable exception is the City Hall of San Francisco. At the center of the nation's most beautiful civic center, it is clearly in a category by itself. John Bakewell, Jr., and Arthur Brown, Jr., one of the architects of Washington's Federal Triangle, won the competition for its design in 1912 and saw it completed in 1918. Like the Rhode Island State Capitol, it is monochromatic inside, there being no mural decoration. Instead, ornament takes the form of carved stone, modeled stucco, bronze work, and wrought-iron work. While its dome has the triple feature of the Capitol dome—that is, an inner dome with an oculus, a canopy, and an outer hemisphere—it is distinguished on the interior by a Corinthian colonnade rather than piers and pilasters, but what makes for an important difference is its canopy. Instead of having a giant mural like Brumidi's *Apotheosis*, its canopy has a giant relief of the city's seal, symbols of government, and panels of trophies.

Like the Capitol itself, these state capitols and the city hall are part and parcel of the wonders of America's classical heritage.

The Rhode Island State Capitol, 1894–1903, by McKim, Mead & White. Photo Chester Browning. Courtesy Rhode Island Tourist Division.

The City Hall of San Francisco, 1912–18, by Bakewell & Brown.
Photo Moulin Studios.

View of the interior of the dome of the San Francisco City Hall.
Photo Henry Hope Reed.

This also explains the absence of ornament on the 7-foot-high entablature, or horizontal beam, over the peristyle columns. At this point, and elsewhere on the dome, the decoration takes the form of a balustrade above the entablature. What is a balustrade? Simply a substantial railing made of balusters—that is, upright shaped members supporting a rail.[47] The balustrade is present not just as a guard or low wall for the safety of those who are permitted on the peristyle roof, but also to give scale and to serve as ornament.

On the cupola, the ornament takes the form of large toruses, or half rounds, which swell as they descend and, like ribs, divide the curved surface. At the bottom of the half round are antefixae (plural of antefixa) of honeysuckle shape; these are linked by tendrils and globes. In addition, between the lower parts of the half rounds are 9-foot-high windows, sometimes called oeils-de-boeuf, or bull's-eyes, windows set in a curved or flat incline of a roof. At the top of each one is a finial consisting of acorns in cups, and at the bottom is a rosette with pendants of flowers and acorns. The ornament here gives movement to the surface.

In this matter of decoration, we have left to the last one of the more extraordinary parts of the dome, which we have called the secondary attic, the great necklace of giant consoles. Composed of double volutes set on a base and topped by a block, they are 8 feet high and appear to serve as buttresses preventing the spread of the hemisphere. We can grasp something of the scale of this particular ornament if we picture a 6-foot-tall visitor standing between a pair of consoles and reaching the middle of the globes, the size of basketballs, at the sides of the upper volute. More globes are found at the sides of the lower volute, and balls are strung down the center of the console. Acanthus leaves are not absent; the upper volutes are covered with them.

At this point, we pause to consider St. Isaac's Cathedral by Auguste Ricard de Montferrand and its influence on Walter's dome. Certainly the use of cast iron in the former served as precedent for the latter, and there is the fact that there is an unusual sameness of dimensions (*see* Introduction). One can only assume that, having arrived at approximately similar measurements, Walter simply decided to use the same or, at least, close ones. But how important is this similarity in dimensions? What counts, above all, is what we see.

Let us look at the visible elements, you might say, the obvious. St. Isaac's has a dome of gilded copper with no oeils-de-boeuf, the Capitol one of cast iron painted white with oeils-de-boeuf. There is no secondary attic at St. Isaac's and, as a decorative feature, St. Isaac's has winged figures at its lone attic, while the Capitol gives its secondary attic a chaplet of consoles. In addition, this single attic is much lower than the Capitol's main attic. The peristyle at St. Isaac's consists of

Opposite: The dome. (Day)

Lower part of cupola with oeils-de-boeuf. (Day)

Giant consoles between the secondary attic and the cupola. (Day)

The peristyle and drum wall. (Day)

St. Isaac's Cathedral in St. Petersburg by Auguste Ricard de Montferrand. (Photo James Mairs)

twenty-four Corinthian columns with shafts of dark granite monoliths and with bronze bases and capitals, where the Capitol's thirty-six are of white-painted cast iron. Note the difference in the drum windows: St. Isaac's are flat-arched instead of round and shorter.

The differences go well beyond the domes. Where the Capitol is rectangular in plan, St. Isaac's is square. The Capitol's porticoes are at the top of imposing flights of steps between cheekblocks, while at St. Isaac's, the steps are few and are inside the porticoes. The roof of St. Isaac's has small turrets below the dome, and at the corners, splendid giant angels hold torches aloft; even each of the pediments on the four sides have three freestanding figures.

As for the lanterns on the domes, there are differences, with that of the Capitol being larger, and in that respect closer to those of St. Peter's in Rome and St. Paul's in London.[48] Its round temple, or tholos, is 29 feet high with thirteen 15-foot columns and thirteen narrow windows, similar to those below, bearing witness to the fact that repetition is very much a part of classical architecture. Here the number of columns, unlike that of the peristyle, is symbolic in that it reminds us of the number of the original thirteen states of the Union.

The temple-lantern's purpose is not limited to capping the dome; it also serves as a high pedestal for the statue of Freedom and its base, both by the sculptor Thomas Crawford. The latter introduces another curve, concave this time, in the form of a truncated cone. On the cone's surface are rods bound around spears and, at the bottom, wreaths. Jefferson Davis, who, as President Franklin Pierce's Secretary of War, was in charge of the Capitol's construction, explained the symbolism. "The language of art, like all living tongues, is subject to changes," he wrote. "Thus the bundle of rods is no longer employed to suggest the function of the Roman lictor, may lose the symbolic character therefrom and be confined to the single signification [significance] drawn from its other source—the fable teaching the instruction that in union there is strength."[49]

Originally Crawford had her wearing a Phrygian, or liberty, cap, the cap worn by manumitted slaves in ancient Rome—that is, slaves granted freedom by their masters. This did not sit well with Jefferson Davis the slaveholder. "Its history," he said of the liberty cap in 1856, "renders it inappropriate to a people who were born free and would not be enslaved. . . . The liberty cap has an established origin, in this case, as the badge of the free slave; and though it should have another emblematic meaning today, a recurrence to that origin may give to it in the future the same popular acceptation [acceptance] which it had in the past." The Civil War was only five years away.

We may wonder if Davis, soon to be a leader of disunion, ever looked back to the time when he was patiently explaining the symbol to be placed on the Capitol.

The theme of union is again underscored on the statue's base. The cone ends in a globe with a raised band carrying in sunken lettering the Latin motto "E Pluribus Unum" (Out of Many One), which represents our United States of America. In her left hand she holds a wreath and a shield emblazoned with the Stars and Stripes, and in her right a sword.

Thomas Crawford modeled the statue in Rome in 1856 and sent the model (now in the Russell Senate Office Building) to Washington. It was cast in bronze in the northeast quarter, or Bladensburg part, of the District of Columbia. Clark Mills, the sculptor of the equestrian Jackson in Lafayette Park near the White House, did the casting with slaves among his crew.[50] The resulting statue then stood for several years on the Capitol grounds.

They are what the hospital volunteer Walt Whitman saw in October 1863. Calling it the "Genius of America," he described it to the readers of the *New York Times*: "A few days ago, poking about there, eastern side, I found the Genius, all dismembered, scattered on the ground."[51] Of Crawford's answer to Jefferson Davis's request that the Phrygian cap be exchanged for a feathered helmet (a modified version of the war bonnet of the Plains Indians), the poet had this impression: "Of our Genius of America, a sort of compound of some Choctaw squaw with the well-known Liberty of Rome, (and the French revolution), it is to be further described as an extensive female, cast in bronze, with much drapery, especially ruffles, and a face of good natured indolent expression, surmounted with a high cap of more ruffles."

Soon after Whitman had sent in his story, at the end of 1863, Thomas Walter outlined the ceremony of the statue's installation:

It is decided to put the crowning section on the "Statue of Freedom" on Wednesday next, December 2nd at 12 o'clock.

The moment the statue is completed, by the placing [in] position of this section, which will be about 15 minutes past 12 oclock, a large American flag will be hoisted on a globe prepared for the occasion on the scaffolding above the statue. The instant this flag is raised it is desirable that a salute of 35 rounds (one for each state) be fired from a battery of artillery placed in readiness on the grounds east of the Capitol.

It is also desirable that a response be made to this salute from as many of the forts surrounding the city as possible."[52]

The ceremony was to be the simplest, as the War Department requested no demonstrations. Even Walter did not want to be on the dome, "as I do not desire to render myself conspicuous." Instead, "I have ordered Mr. Shoneborn [August Schoenborn, his chief draftsman] to be there in my place, as he has been engaged on the work from the beginning."[53]

So it took place at noon on December 2 with thirty-five salutes, one for each state of the Union, North and South, from the twelve forts that then surrounded Washington.

The cupola, lantern, and statue. (Day)

The tholos, or round temple, of the lantern at the top of the cupola. (Day)

Freedom *by Thomas Crawford.*
The statue now has a black patina. (Day)

Freedom *on the ground, 1993.*
Photo AP, Wide World Photos.

A century ago, cast iron was looked down upon as a base material. This may seem strange in our own time, when we delight in cast-iron buildings. The criteria applied may be found in *The Decoration of Houses* (1897) by Edith Wharton and Ogden Codman, Jr., the best treatise on architectural decoration of all kinds: "If the effect is satisfactory to the eye," observed the well-known novelist and her architect coauthor, "the substance used is a matter of indifference."

In studying the dome one more time, we cannot help noticing vertical lines in the horizontal parts. They are thin joints where the cast-iron plates meet, evidence that the white paint cannot conceal. The most obvious are the cracks in the entablature above the drum colonnade. They are a minor reminder of the metal that, after all, made the dome possible. The key factor was the matter of weight, but there was also the question of the ease of production. The metal, as its name conveys, can be cast repeatedly once the molds

are obtained and can be easily mounted with bolts. For example, the volutes, leaves, and flowers of the peristyle Corinthian capitals were cast separately (in this instance in Baltimore), assembled, and then bolted together.

Could the splendid structure be any better? Some might quarrel with the ornament, considering it coarse, insufficiently refined. However, given the dome's height and sheer size, it could not be otherwise or the detail would appear trivial. There are those who have faulted Michelangelo for the coarse detail at the top of the courtyard facade of Rome's Farnese Palace. Yet Michelangelo, like Walter here, was working on such a scale that refinement had to be sacrificed. Scale is customarily the relation of an object to a module or measurement, the measurement usually being the human figure. At the Capitol dome, the scale is monumental, as can be most dramatically seen in the statue of Freedom and the consoles at the base of the hemisphere.

THE EAST FRONT

I t might seem an anticlimax to turn from the great dome to the East Front below, but this is merely to replace one source of visual pleasure and wonder with another. We have noted the length of the facade: 747 feet and 5 inches. The length of the garden front of the Palace of Versailles is 1,900 feet, that of the Bourbon Palace at Caserta near Naples 810 feet. The length resulted from the north-south expansion, which dictated the need for a high dome. What had been a short facade became a long horizontal block. This horizontal block is distinguished by certain elements. For one, it has three porticoes, or porches, each with a flight of steps and a pediment. Buildings, if they have them, customarily have only one with steps. The United States Capitol has the distinction of boasting three; in this it must be the only building with that many on one facade in the country, and possibly the world.

No less important visually is the presence of a broken facade, which is to say that the East Front is divided into three distinct parts separated by setbacks. As mentioned in the Introduction, Daniel Webster, Secretary of State, suggested that the corridors form the setbacks, and in this he was seconded by President Fillmore. Walter, in his building diary on May 8, 1851, wrote: "Plan wings detached as suggested by Mr. Webster with connecting corridors."[54] The great orator's request was no doubt sentimental, and with good reason. The old center had been the setting of his triumphs. Aesthetically, as it turned out, he was prescient, because the setbacks divide the East Front into three distinct parts. Had Walter done a flat wall without detached wings, the two additional porticoes would have been less effective. What the indentations convey is a visual rhythm to the great front.

We begin our exploration at the center portico, which, as rebuilt, dates from 1960. At that time, the old front at the center, which was of sandstone, was replicated by a new one

The East Front. (Day)

of White Cherokee marble from Tate, Georgia. It advanced the porch along with the wings of the old building and the setbacks of the corridors 32½ feet.

The fact that the extension is a modern duplicate of the original need not deter us from judging it as if it were the old one. What is of particular interest is that the center's design, except for the steps and the flanking colonnades of the portico, goes back to that of William Thornton, the first architect of the Capitol. He was to see at least a portion of it completed before Benjamin Latrobe took charge in 1803. It consisted of the Old Senate wing to the right (north), the Old House wing to the left (south) as far as the foundations, and, in the center, the start of the foundation of the future Great Rotunda. Latrobe followed Thornton's exterior design and, in the rebuilding after the destruction in 1814, continued to abide by it. In fact, the construction of the portico was undertaken by Latrobe's successor, Charles Bulfinch, who simply carried out his predecessor's careful design.

In examining one or the other of the fronts directly on either side of the portico, we see pilasters rising two stories from a rusticated ground floor and dividing the wall into five bays. At the ground level, the bays are divided by rusticated piers, and in the bays are windows in molded frames. Above, the fenestration takes on variety. The two pairs of bays on either side of the central one have, on the second floor, square-headed windows with curved pediments and, above, on the third floor, square windows. In the center bay, the second-floor window has an arch of several profiles—that is, an archivolt which consists of a molding or moldings on the outside of an arch, here an "eyebrow" over a window. Beneath the window's sill is a frieze of rinceaux, an ornament consisting of swirling leaves, mainly acanthus. The third-floor window is round, not square, beneath an archivolt in low relief springing from abutments and rising to the entablature, the horizontal member over columns or pilasters. (For illustrations and explanations, *see* Identifications and Glossary.)

The old center by Thornton, Lastrobe, and Bulfinch with Walter's dome. (Day)

We are now drawn to the portico; our eye automatically turns to the pediment, 61 feet long and 12 feet high.[55] Pediments, like so much of classical architecture, had their origin in antiquity. On ancient Greek temples, they took the form of gables at either end of a sloping pitched roof. The Parthenon in Athens is the great model. Subsequently, the gable was divorced from the roof to become a pediment in its own right with its columns. Pediment and columns were joined to give importance to an entrance, as seen in the public buildings of the ancient Romans. Later, the pediment found its place over windows and doorways in many traditional houses.

The special role of the pediment was as a setting for sculpture. Inside a triangular frame is a recessed wall, called a tympanum, which serves as back to the statuary. Here we see three figures about 9 feet high. In the center is America, having on her right altar with raised lettering, "July 4, 1776." She holds, on the altar, a shield inscribed "USA," along with a spear. Justice, on her right, holds a scroll reading "Constitution, 17 September 1787" in one hand and, in the other, a pair of scales. To America's left, at her feet, is an eagle and, beyond it, Hope with her left arm resting on an anchor and her right arm saluting America. The letters, the spearhead, and the scales are all made of gilt metal.

Out of thirty artists seeking the commission in 1825, Luigi Persico was the sculptor chosen. That there are so few figures in this pediment was due to a request by President John Quincy Adams. According to the architect Charles Bulfinch, Adams wanted none of the "triumphal cars and emblems of victory, and all illusions to heathenish mythology and thought that the duties of the nation or its legislator should be expressed in an obvious intelligent manner." "The whole," he felt, "intended to convey that, while we cultivate Justice, we may hope for success." Such was the "simple didactic message" here expressed.[56]

The President was merely caught up in the architectural fashion of the time, which we today call "Greek Revival." While the style, seen in many buildings, from banks to farmhouses of the Romantic era, sprang from ancient Greek architecture, it had little use for sculpture. This explains why the style produced few statues and little carved ornament, and the result is a spare effect.

When the new East Front was replicated, the sandstone figures were replaced by marble copies carved by Bruno Mankowski in 1959 and 1960. (The sandstone originals are in storage, and the old sandstone columns are now standing in the National Arboretum.)

In his design for the facade, William Thornton provided for a shallow portico with twelve columns and no steps. Latrobe deepened the portico by having a first row of eight columns, a second of twelve, and a third of four. He added the steps, placing them between cheekblocks—that is, facing walls

The House side of the old center wing.
A twin of the Old Senate wing. (Day)

Detail of the House side of the old center wing with rinceaux
panel at second-floor window, a guilloche band below,
and elaborate brackets at first-floor window. (Day)

The center portico by Thornton, Latrobe, and Bulfinch. (Day)

Sculpture of center pediment by Luigi Persico. (Day)

framing a flight of steps. As they proceed upward, the steps are divided horizontally into groups: seven steps and a landing, ten and a landing, and a third set of fifteen. The bottom seven extend partially in front of the cheekblocks. The stone of the steps is not marble but granite, and it comes from Stone Mountain, Georgia.

Inside the porch, the ceiling has coffering—that is, sunken panels—with rosettes.

In designing the columns, Latrobe followed Thornton in choosing the Corinthian order as found in *A Treatise on the Decorative Part of Civil Architecture*, a book by the eighteenth-century English architect Sir William Chambers. First published in 1759, the treatise became a popular pattern book, thanks to its plates, as did other, similar treatises. Latrobe's, and for that matter Thornton's, acceptance of Chambers's capital is a reminder that architects working in the classical style turn to the past. The backward glance does not mean that they copied the model exactly; often they strove for some variation. Chambers based his capital on that of the Temple of Jupiter Stator in Rome and, also, the interior capital of the Pantheon.

The actual carving of the original Aquia Creek sandstone capitals was done on site under the direction of Giovanni Andrei from Carrara, Italy's famous center for marble and marble work. Andrei died in 1824 and was succeeded by another Carrarese, Francis Iardella, who remained in charge until 1827.

We offer a plate from Chambers's *Civil Architecture* for comparison with one of the old sandstone capitals on exhibit in the Crypt. The reader can see the differences, however slight, which are inevitable since Latrobe in his drawing need not have followed Chambers's plate exactly. Nor would Bulfinch have when turning the drawing over to Giovanni Andrei. In producing the finished capital, the sculptor could have made his own contributions in the manner of carving. The differences are seen in the shape of the fleuron and in the presence of rosettes in Chambers's volutes, which are not found in the carved volutes, although they are found on those of the pilasters inside the porch. And there is the V-shaped channeling of the acanthus stalks, not seen in the final product. The old capital in the Crypt does offer a surprise: its size. It is big.

We dwell on the subject of the Corinthian capital because it is central to great classical architecture. Its name is somewhat confusing, for the capital, while it had its origins in ancient Greece, is in truth a product of imperial Rome. Thomas Jefferson, the most knowledgeable American of his day in matters architectural, was very familiar with it, and he counseled Latrobe to turn to Chambers.

The chief ornament of the Corinthian is the acanthus leaf. The viewer, once familiar with it, will be astonished at how often this device of classical architecture is found throughout the building and, for that matter, throughout Washington. With good reason, the late John Barrington Bayley, designer of the new wing of the Frick Collection in New York, always maintained that the acanthus leaf is the morphological symbol of Western art, much as the chrysanthemum is in Japanese art or the lotus in the art of the ancient Egyptians.

Oddly enough, Americans, and not a few foreigners, still see the acanthus design every day—on the nation's paper currency. Even in this age of modernism in the arts, when ornament of all kinds has been banished, our paper currency remains within the classical tradition. Here are examples of the acanthus on both sides of the dollar bill and of the five-dollar bill, currently being phased out of use.

(Only in 1995 did the United States Treasury opt for modern design, beginning with the fifty-dollar bill. Detail such as the acanthus leaf has been eliminated; the design is asymmetrical instead of symmetrical. The result: ugly paper currency.)

The column shafts, it will be noted, are monoliths, meaning that they are made of single blocks of stone. Their surface is plain, without fluting (channeling).

Standing on the steps, we can pause to look back on their role as a continuing stage in our history. The original portico was under construction when John Quincy Adams became President. He took the oath of office and made his inaugural address in the Old House Chamber. Andrew Jackson was the first to have a special platform built on the newly completed steps for the ceremony. On March 4, 1829, he walked along an unpaved Pennsylvania Avenue from his hotel to the Hill. He entered the then small Capitol by another door to avoid the crush of admirers and suddenly appeared on the portico. President Adams was not there to greet him, as he had left Washington the day before and had no intention of being on hand for his successor's swearing-in, there being little love lost between the two. Chief Justice John Marshall administered the oath of office. The inaugural address, which no one could hear, followed. This explains why, at his second inaugural, President Jackson chose the House Chamber for the ceremony. The East Front, as setting for the ceremony, became more or less fixed with the inauguration of President Martin Van Buren in 1837.

Abraham Lincoln took the oath on March 4, 1861—he was sworn in by Chief Justice Roger B. Taney, of the *Dred Scott* decision—and gave his address here. The dome, by then, had reached the attic above the peristyle. At the second inaugural four years later, Crawford's *Freedom* was in place. Once again that master of rhetoric was in command. Time may well have dulled the memory of those of us who first heard it in school,

but these words from Lincoln's second inaugural address, delivered on March 4, 1865, remain familiar:

With malice toward none; with charity for all; with firmness in the right, as God gives us to see the right, let us strive on to finish the work we are in; to bind up the nation's wounds; to care for him who shall have borne the battle, and for his widow, and for his orphan—to do all which may achieve and cherish a just, and lasting peace, among ourselves, and with all nations.

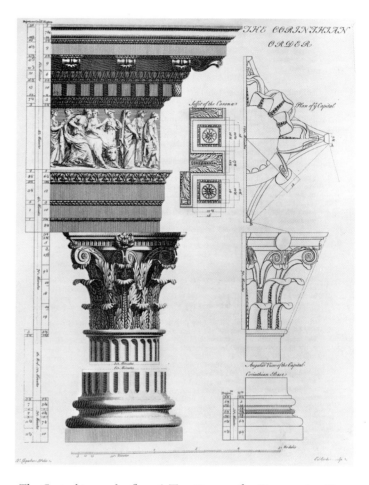

The Corinthian order from A Treatise on the Decorative Part of Civil Architecture *by William Chambers (London, 1759). Courtesy New York Public Library.*

One of the original Corinthian capitals of Aquia Creek sandstone in the Crypt. Note the size. (Day)

Acanthus leaves and laurel leaves on both sides of the old dollar bill.

Acanthus leaves and laurel leaves on both sides of the old five-dollar bill.

were in poor condition, yet no replicas have been made because they depict the American Indian unfavorably. The bare platforms have wrought-iron railings with an anthemion, or honeysuckle, pattern.

The lower levels serve as platforms for bronze lamp standards, ca. 1850.[58] On the bases are the now familiar acanthus and volutes with, in addition, four winged figures. Their presence is a reminder that the human form is very much a part of classical architecture, and not just limited to sculpture and painting.

In addition to serving the long line of visitors on their way to the Capitol's main entrance, these steps are something of a stage. This is also true of those leading to the north and the south porticoes. A band of visiting schoolchildren will assemble on them to be photographed. A congressman will be interviewed by a reporter while a cameraman catches the interview on videotape with, of course, the portico as background. The theater offered is varied and never-ending. Perhaps the most novel are the mute shows of the Passion of Christ at Eastertide. Well, not so "mute," because there is a soundtrack. Helmeted Roman soldiers under a centurion with a white-plumed helmet (the soldiers have red plumes in theirs) stand at attention behind a very lifelike wax figure of Christ on the Cross. Beneath Christ's figure are a live weeping Mary and her live attendants. Music spills out from a neighboring loudspeaker. For some of the year, the wax figure of the risen Christ holding a lamb with two sheep at his feet occupies the landing. Otherwise the spectacle is always changing, in itself a diversion for the visitor.

By custom we should join the stream of pilgrims entering the Capitol, but as

Older visitors will recall that the upper level of the cheekblocks once served as stands for two statuary groups, *The Discovery of America* (1844) by Luigi Persico and *The Rescue* (1853) by Horatio Greenough.[57] Both were removed to storage in 1958 to make way for the new East Front. They our purpose is to study the East Front, we turn right and go north around the cheekblock about ten yards from the steps. Looking up, we obtain a glimpse of the dome overhead much as it appeared prior to the 1960 extension. In doing so today, we are gaining another perspective and a better understanding of how dramatically the dome elements stand out high above the East Front's cornice.

From this spot, at the side of the portico steps, we obtain a clearer view of the ground level underneath the porticoes. A pedestrian passage extends below the center colonnade. Rustication, which is so much a part of the nearby wings, is seen in the piers and top courses of the passage. Under the flight of steps are two additional passages, one for pedestrians and the other, larger one for vehicles. The design is repeated at the other two porticoes.

It should be noted that the base or ground course of the walls here is of granite, not marble. It is the well-known Rock of Ages granite from Barre, Vermont.

(To convey some idea of the amount of masonry work required for a wall without steel frame construction, it is enough to give some measurements. At the base, the wall, or footings, 15 feet belowground is 8 feet 9 inches, then aboveground is 6 feet 7 inches. On the West Front, the footings descend, in some places, as much as 40 feet.)

To go north so as to stand in front of the Senate wing portico, it is best to walk on the east edge of the parking lot. Looking back at the Old Senate wing, one can see a low round turret, or lantern, behind the roof balustrade. It stands over the oculus (the Latin word for eye), a round opening in a dome, of the vestibule to the Senate Chamber; the oculus, as we shall see, has been covered for some time. There is a corresponding lantern over the Old House wing, where it serves to light the Old House Chamber. Flags are flying over both of the Walter wings, evidence that Congress is in session.

We stop in front of the steps of the Senate portico. In designing it, Walter gave it much the same dimensions as that of the Latrobe-Bulfinch central one, but there are differences, as we shall see.

Starting with the pediment, for example, it measures 80 feet long and 12 feet high, thus making it close in size to the central one. The dimensions, by the way, are worth comparing with those of other great buildings. The two pediments of the Parthenon in Athens are 101 feet long and 15 feet high. The one of the Pantheon in Rome is 120 feet and 29 feet; the Panthéon in Paris 101 feet; and the Church of the Madeleine, also in Paris, 150 feet and 30 feet. Among the buildings on the Federal Triangle on Constitution Avenue in Washington, the Departmental Auditorium by Arthur Brown, Jr., of San Francisco has a pediment measuring 87 feet by 19, while the two

Winged figures on the lamp standard on the cheekblock of the center steps by Charles Bulfinch. (Day)

The windowed turret over the Small Senate Rotunda. (Day)

The Senate portico from the southeast. (Day)

The Senate portico from the front. (Day)

pediments of the National Archives by John Russell Pope of New York are 106 feet by 18. The two of the National Gallery of Art across Constitution Avenue from the Federal Triangle are 94 feet long and 10 feet high, but they have no sculpture.

The pediment's chief purpose beyond the decorative is as a stand for sculpture, hardly a surprising virtue. Once again the Parthenon is the supreme example. We have seen that the Greek model was not followed at the center pediment, pursuant to President Adams's request. At the Senate portico, the sculpture is true to tradition in that it has many figures, fourteen all told. They are the work of Thomas Crawford, the same sculptor who did *Freedom*. Like that statue, they were modeled in Rome.

"The Progress of Civilization" is the subject, and the painting shows the triumph of the European settler over the Indian. It reflects a perspective on American history that viewed the vanishing Indian as a casualty of progress. It is part of the story James Fenimore Cooper told in his best-known novel, *The Last of the Mohicans*.

As in such traditional assemblages, the key figure is at the center with the lesser ones to either side. The place of honor is taken by a female figure representing America with an eagle. On her left are a woodsman chopping down a tree, a boy hunter carrying game and accompanied by a dog, a grieving Indian chief, an Indian mother and child, and, last, an Indian grave. On her right, we see a military figure about to draw his sword, a merchant with his wares, two boys, a schoolmaster and a child, a workman resting against a wheel, and, last, an anchor with a sheaf of wheat.

The pediment of the Senate portico with the sculpture by Thomas Crawford. (Day)

Center figures by Crawford in the Senate portico pediment. (Day)

What is interesting about the old figures is that they were carved on the Capitol grounds between 1855 and 1859, most of them by Thomas Gagliardi.[59] It should be explained that sculptors made the plaster models, as, by and large, they still do, leaving the carving to skilled helpers called journeyman sculptors. The common practice in the last century, until journeyman sculptors immigrated to this country, was to ship the plaster models to Carrara, Italy, to be carved; Carrara, famous for its white marble, was and remains a center for the carving of stone. In this instance, Crawford, breaking with custom, shipped the models to Washington, and Gagliardi, trained at Carrara, carved them here.

Crawford was not entirely happy with the height of the pediment, and we can understand why.[60] After he had modeled his statues, he discovered that the central figure, America,

The Corinthian capital by Walter at the Senate wing. (Day)

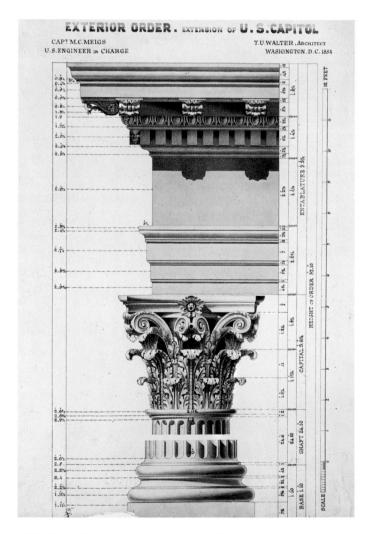

The Corinthian capital and the entablature of the Senate wing. Also seen at the House wing by Walter. Wash rendering signed and dated by Walter and Meigs. Courtesy Architect of the Capitol.

would almost touch the peak of the raking cornices, and he asked Captain Meigs to raise them, which the captain was hardly in a position to order once the portico's design had been done. (The statues were not to be in place until 1864.) One can appreciate the sculptor's dissatisfaction, although the close relation of figure and cornice top is hardly noticeable, nor is it troubling to anyone standing in front of the portico.

The pediment and portico roof rest on twenty-two columns, eight in the front row, fourteen in the back. The observer will discover that there is a slight difference between the marble of the columns and that of the walls. The walls are from Lee (near Stockbridge), Massachusetts, while the columns are from Texas, Maryland, a hamlet fourteen miles north of Baltimore, near Cockeysville. Where the Massachusetts marble has remained unchanged in color, time has given the Maryland marble a soft golden tinge. The plinths, or square blocks, beneath the columns are from Lee. It is worth comparing these columns with the relatively new Georgia marble of the center portico, which is the whitest of all.

The Texas quarry, or quarries, was one source of the marble steps, so conspicuous a part of Baltimore's row houses of the last century. The stone reached Washington via railroad. The marble from Lee was shipped by rail to Bridgeport, Connecticut, and then transported by schooner to the Potomac. (The Washington Monument is built of Maryland marble from one of the quarries near Cockeysville.)

The reason the marble for the columns came from a Maryland quarry is that the one in western Massachusetts could not furnish the faultless blocks in quantity for the shafts. It was not an easy order to fill, the shafts having to be monoliths—that is, single blocks—some 24 feet 1 inch high. What is more, Walter wanted 100 of them for the exteriors of the new wings, in addition to those for the porticoes. Altogether, counting the interior marble columns, all with monolithic shafts, he ordered a total of 174. To these should be added the 36 cast-iron columns of the peristyle and the 12 of the tholos at the top of the dome.

Few buildings in the world have so many, and fewer still were given them at one time. The Missouri State Capitol in Jefferson City has 134, both with monolithic and drum shafts. The famous square in front of St. Peter's in Rome, designed by Bernini, has 284 Tuscan columns, but they form colonnades rather than being part of a building. (Recently there was completed in the Ivory Coast the Cathedral of Our Lady of Peace of Yamoussoukro with 272 Doric columns of *cast* stone, mainly in a colonnaded approach.) Certainly the Capitol qualifies for a line in a book of records simply for having so many columns with monolithic shafts ordered at one time for the new wings. To these can be added the columns of the Old Capitol, 36 on the exterior and 178 on the interior with monolithic and drum shafts.

In adopting the Corinthian order for his portico, Walter, of course, was bound by the precedent of the center portico, but precedent did not prevent him from devising a better one. The result is very successful. The carving is deeper, the serration of the leaves more detailed and more sharply edged. Somehow the leaves have been given the quality of movement; this may simply derive from the depth of the shadows. The volutes, or helices, are in greater relief, with the center curving raised in a corkscrew pattern, much as does the scroll of a violin. For that reason, both in the capital here and in the violin illustrated, the scroll is known as "the spiral of Archimedes." (It takes its name from the famous Greek philosopher and scientist, inventor of the Archimedean screw.)[61] The fleuron of the Walter capital is almost pentagonal, or five-sided, rather than round. The result is that we have here, in Walter's Corinthian, one of the most beautiful capitals in the country. (The visitor can obtain a close view of it from a window on the Senate wing's third floor. *See* "The Senate Chamber," page 129.)

Now Walter, as we know, was not above devising new, or "original," capitals, much as Latrobe had done. But he was careful not to stray too far from the traditional. Furthermore, he produced a telling argument explaining why the architect should abide by tradition. "Columnar architecture, having reached *perfection* [his italics] at the hands of the ancients, any attempt to improve the Orders, or add to their number, would be nothing short of an attempt to improve perfection," he wrote, and he proceeded to quote the familiar lines from Shakespeare's *King John*:

> To guard a title that was rich before,
> To gild refined gold, to paint the lily,
> To throw a perfume on the violet,
> To smooth the ice, or add another hue
> Unto the rainbow, or with taper-light
> To seek the beauteous eye of heaven to garnish,
> Is wasteful and ridiculous excess.

He continued:

These observations are, of course, intended to apply exclusively to the art of building with columns. The architect may produce the most elegant compositions without having any reference whatever to the Orders, but whenever he finds it necessary to introduce an entablature with insulated

The *"scroll of Archimedes" on the head of the Medici viola, Cremona, 1690, carved by Antonio Stradivari. Photo Robert H. Chambers, Portland, Oregon.*

supports, he must turn to the principles developed by the ancients.[62]

(It is of interest that even in our own time, when tradition has virtually disappeared from the arts, there was designed a Corinthian capital in obedience to Walter's injunction. What is more, that capital is in Washington. In 1984 the Philadelphia architect John Blatteau installed Corinthian columns in the grand manner in the Benjamin Franklin State Dining Room in the United States Department of State. This room is the most important classical interior built since the 1930s.)

Another distinction of Walter's columns is that the shafts are fluted, meaning that they have flutes, or vertical channels, separated by fillets, or raised narrow flat band. They should be compared with the center columns, which have no fluting. Such differences may appear niceties, minor variations, but there are very solid reasons why Walter adopted fluting. Let us hear from the architect himself in answer to a query "as to the propriety of leaving the shafts of the Corinthian Order without fluting":

The question is one of no easy solution if we seek to be governed either by ancient examples, or by rule. The practice of the ancients, as you well know, was not at all uniform; sometimes they fluted, and sometimes they left their shafts plain; indeed, we find no two ancient examples of the Corinthian Order exactly alike in any one particular;—they varied the foliage of the capitals, the proportions of the shafts and base, and the details of the cornice on almost every example;—we find that they adapted themselves to circumstances—they fluted their shafts when they were on the outside of their buildings receiving the direct rays of the sun, provided the material was white, or light, so as to define the shadows; but when a dark or variegated stone was used, they always avoided flutes, as did they also in the inside of buildings where no shadows could be obtained. This I think is the true principle, and the only one that has any philosophy about it.— As to rule, we have none, nor have we any uniform examples.

I have followed this principle in the United States Capitol. The outside columns, which are comparatively white and are in the direct light of the sun, I am going to flute, notwithstanding those of the old building [center portico] are plain. There is no reason in this case why the shafts should not be fluted, and there are many reasons why they should be as highly ornamented as possible. If they were of variegated or dark marble I would not flute them. Mr. Latrobe left those of the Old Capitol [designed by Latrobe but executed by Bulfinch] plain because they were a dark variegated stone; they have since been painted white which changes their character—they want flutes.[63]

*The lamp standard by Walter on a cheekblock
of the Senate portico steps. (Day)*

(A footnote to Walter's explanations. As mentioned in describing the center portico, what we see is the 1958–62 front. The old part of the Capitol was of Aquia Creek sandstone, which we shall find, in quantity, inside the building. It is café au lait in color with scattered irregular streaks of brown iron oxide deposits. According to James Fenimore Cooper, it was painted white to conceal the black marks left by the 1814 fire, but in this he was mistaken. The sandstone was painted to protect it from the weather.

It should be added that painting a portion of the old section white continues, as we shall see, on the West Front. There the sandstone still exists, except for places where it has been replaced by Indiana limestone. Both are concealed beneath coats of paint.)

Walter went on to explain:

In the Corinthian columns of the interior of the Capitol, where Tennessee marble is used, I have left the shafts plain (we have 24 of such shafts, with bronze capitals). In one of the grand stairways where the purest Italian marble is used, I have not only left the shafts plain, but had them highly polished;—this I did on account of their receiving their light from above in such a way as to render fluting objectionable. In a long corridor of

Corinthian columns running across the south wing, in the vestibule [Hall of Columns] and in the Senate Retiring Room [Marble Room] I have white marble columns of various modifications of the Corinthian Order, in all of which I have introduced fluting, because the light is received from such points as to make them effective, and because the color of the material is favorable.[64]

Then there follows a paragraph that conveys something of Walter's approach to his art:

So you see that my practice has been various, but always based upon a careful consideration of the circumstances; I have never, in my profession, been afraid to think for myself and I am glad to know that you take the same position. Such I believe to have been the course of the ancients, and I am much more desirous to think as they thought than to do exactly as they did.

This passage might have come from one of today's architects almost as an apology for whatever forms his or her designs might take. For that reason we have to place Walter's thesis in context. First, Walter was a classical architect, which meant that he was bound by the conventions of his artistic heritage. It was, above all, a conservative tradition. No question that he thought for himself, but it must be remembered that he was equally unafraid to abide by precedent, a precedent he gleaned from books of plates and from seeing great buildings.

With so many columns to be carved, as well as window pediments, balusters, and other parts, Walter had at one time 100 marble carvers at work. The crews, in all categories, reached between 200 and 300 men because the monolithic shafts were turned here on the grounds. The extension with the dome was one of the largest nonrailroad construction projects of the decade, costing $13,492,186.02.[65]

To appreciate the Capitol in all its magnificence, we have to understand not just the nature of the classical tradition but also the extent of its presence. The reward of the Capitol is that this tradition, at its most splendid, can be found in abundance.

From this vantage point, if we have a pair of binoculars, we can compare the peristyle columns with those of the portico. The most noticeable difference is the contrast between the refinement of the latter and the coarseness of the former.

The flight of steps at the Senate portico varies from that of the center. Walter makes the climb gentler by having seven steps, a landing, nine steps, a landing, eleven steps, a landing (thus three landings instead of two), and, last, a flight of eighteen steps to the floor of the porch. To be sure, they are also set between cheekblocks, but Walter has the bottom steps going around the block bases, a change that makes the steps more visually pleasing. They "flow," as it were, with a solemn ease.

The cheekblocks are divided into two levels, with the

lower one having an elaborate four-branch lamppost with a center light 13 feet high. It too came from Walter's drawing board; even with this fixture, he did not leave the design to others. On the upper part of the block, there is a balustrade of 3 feet, roughly waist-high. The device, made up of top and bottom rails and balusters, is often adopted just for ornament, to convey a sense of scale, and, on occasion, for security. Both decoration and security would appear to be the reasons for the balustrade's presence on the cheekblocks.

On the roof, on the other hand, it is present for decoration and to give scale. On the roof, the baluster has a different shape. Walter designed one in the form of a truncated cone, without sleeve or belly. It is 2 feet 8½ inches high, set in a balustrade 3 feet 10¼ inches high. Yet a third balustrade is that of Thornton/Latrobe/Bulfinch on the roof of the Old Capitol, which has the same dimensions but has a small belly and a long sleeve (*see* Identifications and Glossary).

The baluster, as the Philadelphia architect Alvin Holm has pointed out, is an exemplar of the classical because it is shaped by the basic profiles (*see* Glossary). For that reason it should be studied along with the column. A historical note: The baluster was unknown to the ancient Greeks and Romans. The first example, dating from the fifteenth century, is supposed to have been made for the Sistine Chapel in the Vatican Palace in Rome. We can be grateful that Walter placed them here, on the cheekblocks, so that we can study them closely.

The same is a virtue of the band of ornament at the top of both levels of the cheekblocks, a guilloche, an enrichment found throughout the building.

Visitors, for reasons of security, are not permitted on the porch. They must examine the columns from the lowest steps. The columns are 30 feet 4½ inches high with a diameter of 3 feet at the base of the shaft; such a proportion, 10 to 1, is the rule of the Corinthian order. The diameter, in this case 3 feet, remains the same for a third of the shaft height; from that point on, the shaft gradually narrows slightly to a diameter of 2 feet 7 inches. This slight curving gives a tapering to the shaft which overcomes the seeming concavity that would result from the eye's distortion were the shaft straight. The term for shaping the silhouette, even to the point of giving the shaft a slight swelling, is *entasis*.

The other notable aspect of these columns—and this is true of the Thornton/Latrobe/Bulfinch ones at the center—is that they stand on square pedestals 3 feet high, simply to give them the effect of greater height without having to increase the column size to achieve the same end.

Complementing the porch columns are Corinthian pilasters that are so much a part of the walls. (If the pilaster capitals, although flat, are the same as those of the column capitals, the shafts are different in having straight sides and

Balusters by Walter for the cheekblocks of the Senate portico steps. (Day)

Balusters by Bulfinch above the cornice of the old center of the Capitol. (Day)

Balusters by Walter for the House and Senate wings. (Day)

Guilloche course on a cheekblock of the Senate steps. (Day)

An ancone, or bracket, at the Senate portico with shucked corncobs. (Day)

not the entasis of column shafts.) The pilasters show the care with which Walter supervised construction. Inevitably he had to face pressure in hiring workers. One instance involved an aged stonecarver who had copied one of the capitals of the center portico to show his skill and who then enlisted the help of a senator to see that he be retained by Walter. Beyond taxing him for proceeding without drawings or models and not carving the capital in marble, Walter said that "the new caps ought to be faultless specimens of the taste and skill of the present age, and not labored copies of one of the earliest specimens of the art in this country." (On the third floor of the Senate wing, on the east side, the explorer can examine the splendid capitals of both columns and pilasters from the corridor linking the Senate and House wings.)

We have already pointed out that the public is not allowed on the porch or on most of the steps. One day, it is to be hoped, security will be less stringent and the public will be permitted once again in both places. At least we can recall the time, several decades ago, when we found ourselves on the porch on a sunny summer afternoon. Standing in the cool shade and surrounded by the pearly glow of the white marble, the setting was Washington at its best.

In a letter to Gridley I. F. Bryant, architect of Boston's Old City Hall, Walter explained why he chose the particular stone for the facade. "As to the question of marble or granite I should go in for marble. Light and shadow are the essence of architecture, and both light and shadow are subdued to gloomy effects in the dark granites of Massachusetts, and the sombre brown stone of Connecticut—these, in some cases, are particularly appropriate and beautiful, but they abnegate all attempts at brilliancy."[66] His thesis is wonderfully illustrated by the portico. (Bryant, it might be added, chose granite for the Boston City Hall.)

The doorway, which can only be studied through binoculars, is suitably enriched. Ancones, or brackets, in the shape of a double volute, support a broken frieze, in turn upholding a cornice. Among the ornaments are the now familiar acanthus leaf; the rosette, which is a frequently adopted device; and a corncob. The last-named is only one of the half dozen or more examples of the fruit of the native plant in the Capitol, a reminder that we are dealing with an American building. At different times, it was simply added to the repertoire of dolphins, eagles, acanthus leaves, oak leaves, ram's heads, and other inherited devices.

Above the door cornice are two reclining female figures by Thomas Crawford. On the left, with a bay-leaf crown, is History; she holds a scroll reading "History, July 1776." Justice, on the right, rests against a globe; in her right hand she holds a pair of scales, and in her left she has a book inscribed "Justice, Law, Order." Crawford made certain that both figures were clearly identified.[67]

The figures of History and Justice by Crawford over the door of the Senate portico. (Day)

The figures are life-size when one would expect them to be heroic—that is, larger than life-size. History is 5 feet 4 inches long and 3 feet 10 inches high; Justice 5 feet 10 and the same height. The total length of the relief is 11 feet 2 inches, while it is 2 feet 2 inches in depth. This last is a key factor in carving substantial relief figures. When almost in the round, the result is supremely effective, depending, of course, on the artist's talent. Measurements, in this instance, are just as important in assessing sculpture as they are in helping the observer to appreciate traditional architecture and painting.

The figures illustrate a major problem with a building like the Capitol: its maintenance. Crawford's original marble, placed here in 1865, was slowly disintegrating when, in 1974, it was replaced by what we see today. The figures were replicated by Francesco Tonelli of the Vermont Marble Company. Tonelli worked from Crawford's plaster models, which are now in the subway connecting the Capitol to the Senate office buildings.

The bronze doors next invite attention. Regrettably, they can only be judged in illustration, or when they are closed, and then only through binoculars. Once again we bow to Crawford. The sculptor designed and modeled them in Rome in 1855, only to leave them unfinished when he died two years later. William H. Rinehart, an apprentice of his who was to gain a name in his own right, completed them

in 1864. The plaster models were cast in the foundry of James T. Ames in Chicopee, Massachusetts, which also cast the splendid equestrian statue of George Washington by Henry Kirke Brown in New York's Union Square. Installed in 1868, the doors portray events in the life of Washington, three battles of the American Revolutionary War, and, in the bottom panels, two allegories. The medallion, depicting Peace and Agriculture, seen at the bottom of the left door shows a father and mother with their three children. They are presumed to be portraits of Thomas Crawford and his family, Rinehart's courteous bow to the dead sculptor.[68]

On leaving the Senate wing, it is worth standing at a distance to compare its columns again with those of the dome's peristyle. The difference in column heights is not as significant as might be expected. Those in the peristyle are actually shorter than the portico columns, 27 feet compared to 30 feet, or 33 feet if we add the square base beneath. Should not the peristyle columns be higher because they are so far away? Evidently not. The columns of the lantern (tholos) are a mere 15 feet. And the statue of Freedom is 19 feet high just to compensate for distance. What Walter did, in the case of the peristyle columns, was to place them on a platform over 10 feet in height. In this he was only doing what the ancient Athenians had done with the Parthenon: setting the columns on a stylobate, a continuous base or platform. In both instances here, peristyle and portico had to be

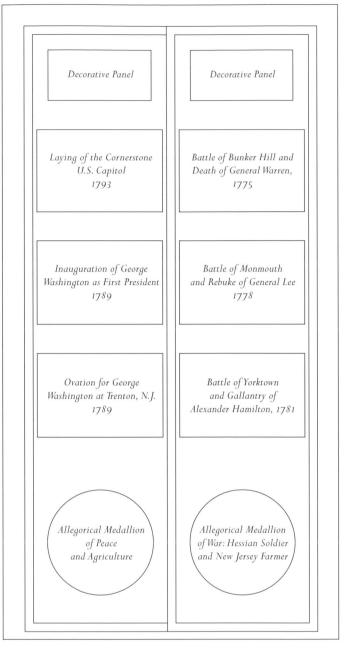

Decorative Panel	Decorative Panel
Laying of the Cornerstone U.S. Capitol 1793	Battle of Bunker Hill and Death of General Warren, 1775
Inauguration of George Washington as First President 1789	Battle of Monmouth and Rebuke of General Lee 1778
Ovation for George Washington at Trenton, N.J. 1789	Battle of Yorktown and Gallantry of Alexander Hamilton, 1781
Allegorical Medallion of Peace and Agriculture	Allegorical Medallion of War: Hessian Soldier and New Jersey Farmer

The bronze door of the Senate portico by Thomas U. Crawford and William H. Rinehart. Courtesy Architect of the Capitol.

Ovation for George Washington at Trenton, *1789*
by Crawford and Rinehart. (Day)

Battle of Yorktown *of the Senate portico door*
by Crawford and Rinehart. (Day)

designed with the proportions of the setting of each in mind, as well as considering the effects of distance.

It might be noted that the peristyle platform, unlike the solid one of the Parthenon, is a hollow "skirt" of cast iron held in place by brackets.

Our tour of the East Front continues south past the center wing to the House wing. We do not know where George Washington laid the first cornerstone on September 18, 1793, but we do know where President Millard Fillmore laid the one of the New Capitol on July 4, 1851. It was at the northeast corner of the House wing. If the President did the honors, it was his Secretary of State, Daniel Webster, who gave the address, his last important speech, for he died later that year:

This is the New World! This is America! This is Washington! And this the Capitol of the United States! And where else, among the nations, can the seat of government be surrounded, on any day of any year, by those who have more reason to rejoice in the blessings which they possess? Nowhere, fellow-citizens! assuredly, nowhere! Let us, then, meet this rising sun with joy and thanksgiving.

There followed a sweeping survey of the nation's blessings. He was not above listing the salient differences in the nation of 1793, the year of the first cornerstone laying, and the nation of 1851. The comparison tells us why Walter had assumed so ambitious an undertaking. The number of states had gone from fifteen to thirty-one, representatives and senators from 35 to 295, the population from 4 million to over 23 million, the country's area from over 800,000 to over 3 million square miles, public libraries from 35 to 694. Whereas there had been no railroads in 1793, there were over 10,000 miles of track in 1851.

We today may smile at the old statesman's boasting, but we must remember that the pride and the sense of accomplishment he expressed were transformed into the marble wonder we see before us.

Admittedly, the steps and portico duplicate those of the Senate wing. Were they not twins, the East Front would not have the balance that is key to so much of its visual power. The authorities Edith Wharton and Ogden Codman, Jr., in *The Decoration of Houses*, have this to say on the matter of symmetry: "If proportion is the good breeding of architecture, symmetry, or the answering of one part to another, may be defined as the sanity of decoration. The desire for symmetry, for balance, for rhythm in form as well as sound, is one of the most inveterate of human instincts." This observation should be kept in mind as we go about studying the Capitol.

If the portico of the House wing is a twin, its pediment sculpture is wholly different. The work of Paul Wayland Bartlett, it is titled *The Apotheosis of Democracy* and was executed in the second decade of this century. At the center stands *Peace Protecting Genius*. Armor-clad and wearing a mantle, Peace rests her left arm on a shield behind which is an olive tree, symbol of peace. Her right arm extends over the winged figure of Genius at her feet. Genius has, in his right hand, the torch of Immortality. The figures beyond Peace's right arm represent Industry. An ironworker leans on his hammer, and behind him a printer holds printed sheets. Next are two metalworkers, one pouring molten metal into a crucible. A spinner measuring cloth and a fisherboy with a boat follow. At Peace's left side, Agriculture is symbolized by a reaper and his son, a husbandman and a bull, a boy with a bunch of grapes, a shepherdess, a child placing a garland on a ram, and, last, a lamb. At either end, in the pediment corners, are waves, those to Peace's far left representing the Atlantic, and those to her far right the Pacific.

Bartlett executed the figures in Paris and Washington from 1911 to 1914. (Since the 1860s, Rome had been replaced by Paris as the training center for the arts of the Western world.) If Bartlett modeled the group, the Piccirilli brothers, as

Allegorical Medallion of Peace and Agriculture, *presumed to be modeled on the Crawford family by Crawford and Rinehart. (Day)*

The House wing portico by Walter with pediment sculpture by Paul Wayland Bartlett. (Day)

The Apotheosis of Democracy *by Paul Wayland Bartlett. (Day)*

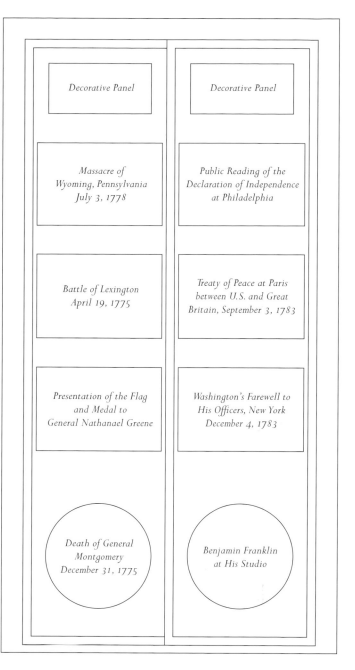

Decorative Panel	Decorative Panel
Massacre of Wyoming, Pennsylvania July 3, 1778	Public Reading of the Declaration of Independence at Philadelphia
Battle of Lexington April 19, 1775	Treaty of Peace at Paris between U.S. and Great Britain, September 3, 1783
Presentation of the Flag and Medal to General Nathanael Greene	Washington's Farewell to His Officers, New York December 4, 1783
Death of General Montgomery December 31, 1775	Benjamin Franklin at His Studio

The bronze door of the House portico by Thomas Crawford and William H. Rinehart. Courtesy Architect of the Capitol.

Presentation of the Flag and Medal to General Nathanael Greene. *Courtesy Architect of the Capitol.*

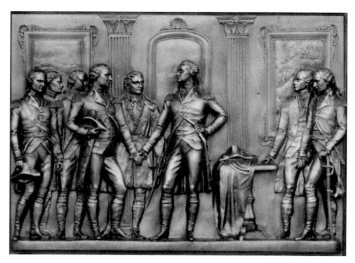

Washington's Farewell to His Officers, New York, December 4, 1783. *Courtesy Architect of the Capitol.*

they did for so many sculptors, carved them in stone, a Georgia marble, at their studio in the Bronx, New York. The figures were set in place in 1916.

It is well worth citing at length Bartlett's comments on the project:

Now, one of the important problems to be solved in this case was the amalgamation of the living forms of today with the classic details of a semi-classic style. In using our brawny types of men and women from factory and field, in modeling their simple working clothes, it was necessary to execute these figures in such a manner that they should not conflict with their distinguished but rather delicate architecture. It was necessary that they should have a distinctive character, in harmony with their immediate surroundings. Too much realism would have been ugly! Too much classicism would have been fatal.

He continues,

Usually pediments are composed for a general front view, and approached by a spacious avenue forming a vista. This happens here only for the central pediment. The fact that this building has such a wide facade and three pediments, that it is generally approached by the sides, and that a person standing on the plaza has a slanting view of at least two pediments, changes entirely the ordinary scheme and has necessitated a new principle of composition. The means employed to meet this contingency are not very visible from the plaza—they were not meant to be visible—but great care has been used in the effort to make the side views equal in interest to the full front view.

(Despite Bartlett's admonition, our instinct is to stand directly east of the portico because we want to obtain the full front view, which is far better than from the side.)

Then, the sculptor explains how he went about composing the whole:

There were other problems, such as the scale and grouping of the figures, the spacing of the groups, and so forth, of which I will not speak. Suffice it to say that with time and study they were solved to my satisfaction. The method of work was as follows: First a small sketch [in clay] was made, then a larger one, and then another. These were changed. Figures were taken away and others put in their places. So on and on in continual effort to improve the scheme until the final models were finished, ready to be carved in marble, erected, doweled, and cemented in place.[69]

It is obvious that Bartlett was very much an offspring of nineteenth-century France in his realism, as were most American sculptors at the time. In this the work offers a sharp contrast to Crawford's to the north. Still, as Bartlett himself observed, realism, in order to rise to the level of the artistic, must have something of the classical. It is the discipline of the tradition, especially in a classical setting, as in the pediment of the House wing, which requires that the figures be linked in a strong composition. In this, as well as in the story conveyed, Bartlett is more compelling than Crawford. One factor that should not be overlooked is his ability to fill the space with so many figures, human and animal, and to give them movement.

On mounting the steps, the visitor finds that here, as at the Senate portico, the public is not permitted inside the porch. Still, we can see that the setting is a duplicate of the one to the north. The bronze door is also the work of Crawford, finished by Rinehart in 1867. The plaster models, done in Rome, were brought to Washington and left untouched in the Capitol Crypt until 1903, when they were cast in Chicopee, Massachusetts, by Melazar H. Mosman. In 1906 the doors were in place, more than a generation after the installation of those in the Senate wing.

Six panels and one medallion depict events of the American Revolution, and a second medallion is of Benjamin Franklin experimenting with electricity.

The visitor goes back to stand before the center portico once again, but, instead of joining the line of visitors, he or she should consider again the success of the East Front. An integral component of that success is the disposition of the center portico and steps in relation to those to the north and the south. The ones before us retreat, some 41 feet behind the pair. In this way, the equivalent of a welcoming forecourt was created, one to which we unconsciously respond. Thus, the Capitol takes us under its protection, a consequence lost were the center portico and steps in line with, or in advance of, its neighbors. Admittedly, the forecourt is not as deep as it was before the center portico was advanced 32½ feet, but despite that change, the sensation of depth has not disappeared. The forecourt remains one more positive attribute of the Capitol.

We now step into the prescribed line of those visiting the Capitol. (What with the many visitors, it is advisable to come here early in the day or during the season of the year when the pilgrimage to the building slackens.) On going up the steps, the visitor passes, on the cheekblocks, the lamp standards, ca. 1850, with a single light, in contrast to those at the Senate and House steps, which have five lights. What are of particular interest are the four winged figures at the standard base, figures that devolve into volutes. They alert us to the importance of the human figure, not just in classical architecture but also in the Capitol. We have its presence in the pediments, on doors, in niches, and atop the dome; here it serves as decoration for a lamp. Remark, too, the varieties of acanthus.

Inside the porch, there is more sculpture. Two freestanding statues occupy niches on either side of the doorway. On the right is the figure of War in the uniform of a Roman soldier, on the left that of Peace holding an olive branch. The originals, installed in 1834, were by Luigi Persico, the sculptor of the center pediment. By the 1950s, erosion had pitted them. When the new East Front was built, they were replaced by the ones we see. Plaster models based on the

Figures of Peace and War, copied from the originals by Luigi Persico, flank the center or Rotunda door by Rudolph Rogers. (Day)

America *on the frame of the center or Rotunda door by Rogers. (Day)*

"Executed in Bronze by F. v. Miller Munich 1860" inscribed on the doorframe amid a band of trophies of arms. (Day)

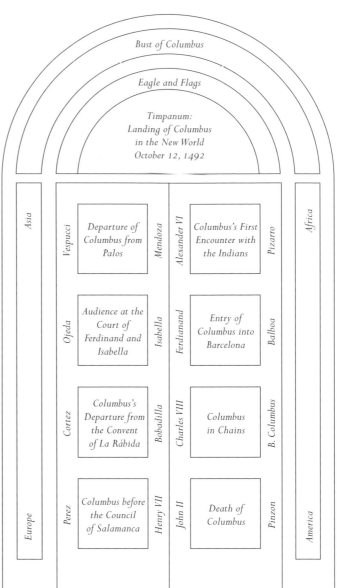

Bust of Columbus

Eagle and Flags

Timpanum:
Landing of Columbus
in the New World
October 12, 1492

Asia	Vespucci	Departure of Columbus from Palos	Mendoza	Alexander VI	Columbus's First Encounter with the Indians	Pizarro	Africa
Ojeda	Audience at the Court of Ferdinand and Isabella	Isabella	Ferdinand	Entry of Columbus into Barcelona	Balboa
Cortez	Columbus's Departure from the Convent of La Rábida	Bobadilla	Charles VIII	Columbus in Chains	B. Columbus
Europe	Perez	Columbus before the Council of Salamanca	Henry VII	John II	Death of Columbus	Pinzon	America

The center or Rotunda door by Rogers relating the exploits of Columbus. Courtesy Architect of the Capitol.

originals were made in 1953 by George Giannetti of Washington and carved in Vermont marble.

Over the niches are panels of a fan of thirteen arrows framed by an oak-leaf wreath, with the wreath in turn bordered by fronds. The original sandstone figures were carved by Thomas McIntosh and Jeremiah Sullivan in 1825, the date of the portico. The ones we see here were made by the Vermont Marble Company based on a model by George Giannetti.

Above the doorway is a third relief, *Fame and Peace Crowning George Washington.* The bust of our first President is in the middle with Peace on the left and Fame on the right, both holding bay-leaf wreaths over his head. Peace is identified by a palm frond, while Fame holds a trumpet of gilt metal. Measuring 18 feet 8 inches long and 5 feet 5¾ inches high, the relief was originally the work of Antonio Capellano and was completed in 1827. What we see, of course, is a marble reproduction executed by George Giannetti and the Vermont Marble Company.

The chief ornaments of the portico, which is to be expected, are its bronze doors, the work of Randolph Rogers. The models were executed at about the same time as those of Crawford. "Designed and modeled by R. Rogers, Rome 1858," reads the inscription in the middle of the left door. Instead of being cast in this country, the doors were cast in Munich by Ferdinand von Miller of the Royal Bavarian Foundry in 1860, as an inscription on the far edge of the right door records.

The panels and the figures portrayed revolve around the story of Columbus and the discovery of America.

The doorframe and the two doors are quite extraordinary for the skill in execution and for the number of figures, found in the leaf frames, the doorframe, and the tympanum at the top, without overlooking those of the panels. The inspiration is Italian, especially the famous bronze doors of the Baptistery in Florence by Lorenzo Ghiberti. The foreshortening of the background and the treatment of the figures are in the style of the great Florentine sculptor.

The Landing of Columbus *in the tympanum of the center or Rotunda door. (Day)*

Columbus's Departure from the Convent of La Rábida
by Rogers. (Day)

Columbus in Chains *by Rogers.*

(Day)

THE GREAT ROTUNDA

A brief historical note. When the door and frame came to Washington, they were installed between the Old House Chamber (Statuary Hall) and the corridor leading to the House wing. That was in 1863. Not until 1871 were they moved here. In order to make space for them, the door, which had been square-headed, was given an arch. (The two doorways of the Senate and House wings are square-headed.)

On a quiet day, it is worth returning here to examine the door. Among the devices to be seen in the nonfigurative parts of the bronze work, along with anchors, globes, and other objects, are several ears of corn, the second example of them met with at the East Front.

Entering from the portico, the visitor is in a square vestibule, created when the East Front was extended in 1960. Overhead is a chandelier of sanded opaque glass resting on bronze arms decorated with acanthus and anthemion. Room and chandelier were designed by Harry Merz under the guidance of the architects Albert H. Swanke and Alfred Easton Poor, who were in charge of the extension.[70] The chandelier was made by Rambusch of New York.

Once past the security gate, the visitor turns right into a narrow hall to examine the wall. It is part of the original facade of Aquia Creek sandstone from the banks of the Potomac in Virginia south of Washington. We see it very much like it was when set in place, even before it came to be painted. This is the sandstone that Thomas U. Walter cited as not needing flutes when adopted for column shafts because of its being "a dark and variegated stone."

Now the visitor abandons the vestibule for the Great

The Great Rotunda. (Day)

Rotunda. It is impossible not to be awestruck. To be sure, we are standing beneath, instead of outside, the familiar dome, but somehow the majestic interior is wholly unexpected. One may even wonder how startling it must have been prior to the construction of the present East Front when one stepped directly from the outside, beneath the portico, into this chamber.

The sheer size of the Rotunda and interior dome with its oculus and the giant canopy over the oculus is breathtaking. We cannot adjust to it at once. Is there anything in the country to be set beside it? The great hall of the San Francisco City Hall, which also rises to a dome with an oculus and canopy (there the hall serves as a stairwell as well as being rectangular in plan)? The great hall of the University of Pittsburgh, Gothic inside and out? A banking room such as that of the Continental Illinois Bank and Trust Company on Chicago's La Salle Street? The Main Reading Room of the New York Public Library? The nave of the Cathedral of St. Peter and St. Paul in Philadelphia? Some state capitols, like those of Missouri and Rhode Island? The Rotunda of the Library of Congress (Jefferson Building) across the way at East Capitol and First streets? Or even the columned hall of the Old Pension Building, now the National Building Museum? No, the Great Rotunda, like the towering dome surmounting it, is one of a kind, unrivaled. No wonder that Frances Trollope, in her *Domestic Manners of the Americans*, declared it: "the magnificent rotunda."

Before studying the triumphant setting, we should begin by looking at the eight pictures set in the surrounding wall, particularly the four on the west half. Historically, these are among the most important in the nation. As an unusual record of our past, it is little wonder that they have become so familiar to us; they have their own special niche in our history books. One fact alone sets them apart: Depicting key events in the American Revolution, they were painted by an artist, John Trumbull, who fought briefly in the Revolutionary War. His father, Jonathan Trumbull, was governor of Connecticut, and he himself was a colonel in the Continental army. It is very rare to find an artist who actually served with the key figures in the events he painted.

These great canvases occupied him at several stages in his long career. Shortly after the Revolution, in 1786, three years after the treaty of peace with England, Trumbull was in Paris, a guest of Thomas Jefferson, our minister to France. They discussed a series of pictures devoted to the history of the Revolution, and Jefferson is generally credited with having suggested that the Declaration of Independence be the subject of one of them.[71] The future President even drew a plan for Trumbull of the room in Independence Hall where the Declaration was signed. The artist then began to paint the portraits for possible use in the series. Even the officers on both sides in the surrender of Yorktown, the subject of the

Another view of the Rotunda. Architect of the Capitol.

third in the series, are based on portraits made by Trumbull when, with introductions from Jefferson, he obtained the likenesses of the French and British officers. Among them was a Swede in the French service, Count Fersen, who went on to become a favorite of Queen Marie Antoinette and who was to be murdered in a riot in his native Stockholm. (He is the eighth in the row of French officers on the left.)

From the moment of his meeting with Jefferson in Paris, Trumbull never relinquished the project. Based on sketches now in the Yale University Art Gallery, the paintings were completed in the following years: *The Declaration of Independence* in 1818, *Surrender of Lord Cornwallis at Yorktown* in 1820, *Surrender of General Bourgoyne* in 1821, *and General Washington Resigning His Commission as Commander in Chief* in 1824.

Inevitably the artist took liberties. Several persons shown in *The Declaration of Independence* were not actually present, such as Robert R. Livingston of New York, second on Benjamin Franklin's right. Trumbull occasionally had to rely on faulty memories. His chief problem, however, was that of drawing the interest of the President and the Congress in the

The Declaration of Independence in Congress, at Independence Hall, Philadelphia, July 4, 1776, *by John Trumbull. Courtesy Architect of the Capitol.*

Surrender of Lord Cornwallis at Yorktown, Virginia, October 19, 1781, *by John Trumbull. Courtesy Architect of the Capitol.*

large—that is, 12 by 18 feet with life-size figures.[74]

There was further delay in their installation in the Great Rotunda, under construction since the summer of 1818. After its completion in 1824, the four pictures were installed.[75]

Trumbull hoped to obtain the commission for the other four canvases destined for the chamber, which he called "the Hall of the Revolution." This was not to be, and the rejection proved to be only one of several disappointments. There was criticism. Perhaps the cruelest came from one of the House of Representatives' more historic eccentrics. John Randolph of Roanoke, Virginia, told the House that "in his opinion, the picture of the Declaration of Independence should be called the 'Shin-piece,' for surely, never was there, before, such a collection of legs submitted to the eyes of man." There was little the artist could do about it. Later he observed rightly to a friend that "the professional reputation of the Artist . . . is a delicate plant easily blighted by a pestilential breath—and—though it may be sport to . . . indulge in ribald witticisms at our expense, yet it is Death to us."[76] In this instance, Randolph's label has survived to this day because of the importance of the four pictures.

The Virginia congressman's caustic assessment need not distract us. How the pictures came to be painted and how they came to be displayed in the United States Capitol is something of a heroic story. We are indeed fortunate in having this almost miraculous record of our country's birth.

ambitious scheme. In 1816 he wrote to Jefferson recalling their discussion in Paris thirty years before.[72] A year later, Congress passed a resolution authorizing President James Monroe "to employ John Trumbull to compose and execute a painting commemorative of the Declaration of Independence."[73]

Trumbull had already reviewed the project in 1816 with President Madison. The latter approved the artist's choice of subjects for the four pictures. More important, where Trumbull had planned to use 6-by-9-foot canvases with half-life-size figures, Madison insisted that the canvases be twice as

Even though the four remaining pictures do not have the historic interest of Trumbull's, they are nevertheless important in recording familiar milestones of our distant past. Facing the main entrance, the visitor has on the left (north) *The Landing of Columbus* by John Vanderlyn, painted in Paris between 1842 and 1846. The great discoverer is shown landing on the island of Guanahani in the West Indies in 1492. Vanderlyn, a New Yorker, was among the first Americans, if not the first, to have studied his art in Paris. He is best known for his picture *Ariadne Asleep on the Isle of Naxos*, now in the Pennsylvania Academy of the Fine Arts in Philadelphia, the first female nude painted by an American.

Next, on the right (south), is *The Embarkation of the Pilgrims at Delft Haven, Holland, July 22, 1620*, the work of Robert Walter Weir done in 1843. The pilgrims are seen aboard the *Mayflower* with Deacon Brewster in their midst holding an open Bible. Weir, who taught drawing and painting for many years at West Point, was the creator of the familiar rotund figure of Santa Claus in red and white which is so much a part of the American Christmas.

To the right of the north doorway is *The Discovery of the Mississippi by De Soto, 1541*, painted in 1853 by William H. Powell. The Spanish explorer is shown on the bank of the river that was to be his watery grave. The scene, it might be added, is highly fictionalized. Far from being handsomely equipped, De Soto and his company were a desperate band by the time they reached the river. The artist was only twenty-three years old when he obtained the commission. His other well-known work, *The Battle of Lake Erie*, is also in the building, in the eastern stairwell of the Senate wing.

The last of the four, on the far right, is *The Baptism of Pocahontas at Jamestown, Virginia, 1613* by John Gabsby Chapman. The Indian princess is shown kneeling with her future husband, John Rolfe, standing behind her. Many viewers are intrigued by the Indian with the six-toed foot who is seen on the right facing the viewer. Chapman, in his time, was famous for his illustrations of the "Harper's Bible," known as such because it was published by the firm now called HarperCollins.

These four pictures are superior to Trumbull's in the handling of the figures and in their composition, especially the paintings of Columbus and De Soto. Today it is fashionable to treat subject matter in a painting as being of no importance. Yet an essential ingredient in most of the world's great pictures is the story. Here the artists had the talent to tell stories and to tell them large, on a scale that warranted their being displayed in the nation's noblest interior.

Surrender of General Bourgoyne at Saratoga, New York, October 17, 1777, *by John Trumbull. Courtesy Architect of the Capitol.*

General Washington Resigning His Commission as Commander in Chief of the Army at Annapolis, Maryland, December 23, 1783, *by John Trumbull. Courtesy Architect of the Capitol.*

The handsome gold frames were designed by Bulfinch. He gave them sides of bound rods, top and bottoms with Greek-key enrichment, and, in the corners, rosettes.

To continue our exploration of this vast interior, we can go to the center, identified by a white marble circle set in the floor of waxed Seneca stone from the Maryland side of the upper Potomac. It is from this central point that the city is divided into four parts: Northeast, Southeast, Northwest, and Southwest, whose initials, NE, SE, NW, and SW, are familiar as part of the postal addresses in the District of Columbia.

At one time the center was occupied by a well-known statue of the seated Washington clad in a toga. The work of Horatio Greenough, it stood on this spot for three years in the 1840s. It was moved to another spot inside the Great Rotunda, then outside across from the East Front, and to several other places, and has finally landed in the National Museum of American History on the Mall.

Except during those few years the center of the Great Rotunda has been bare. In this it differs from the city's other rotundas. Here we have to remind ourselves that Washington is a rarity in having altogether three true rotundas where other major cities have none. There is one in the National Gallery of Art where a ring of green marble columns supports the dome beneath which is a fountain with a modest statue and a large basin. The stone walls have only empty niches for ornament. The diameter between the walls is 103 feet and the dome center is 101 feet 6 inches above the floor.[77]

The other true rotunda is the Jefferson Memorial with an all-white marble interior, 86 feet 3 inches in diameter and 95 feet 8 inches high at the center. Its wall decoration is limited to lengthy inscriptions in dark bronze lettering. Its center, directly beneath the dome, is occupied by the statue of our third President. The general blandness of the two due to the absence of pictures and sculpture in relief, as well as the lack of a high dome, places them in a lesser category. Probably far more important, though this is only a kind of instinctive response, we delight in being able to stand beneath the center of the Capitol dome. One cannot help thinking that the other two rotundas would benefit immeasurably if the fountain and statue were placed elsewhere.

This could also be said of yet another large room with a dome, to be found in the National Museum of Natural History on the Mall to the west of the National Gallery of Art. Not a true rotunda because, like that of the Library of Congress, the space is framed by massive piers rising to a dome, yet its piers are curved, making it seem a walled rotunda. This time the center is occupied by a statue of a giant African elephant, which, as it prevents us from being in the center of the room, makes for an astonishing and successful focus.

It might be added that in the ancient model, Rome's Pantheon, the center was always vacant and still is. (Admittedly, the Pantheon's dome has an oculus open to the sky, which today permits rain to fall into its rotunda. In ancient times, the oculus could be closed in bad weather by means of a giant bronze cover.)

The Great Rotunda of the Capitol is

The Landing of Columbus at the Island of Guanahani, the Bahamas, October 12, 1492, *by John Vanderlyn. Courtesy Architect of the Capitol.*

The Embarkation of the Pilgrims at Delft Haven, Holland, July 22, 1620, *by Robert W. Weir. Courtesy Architect of the Capitol.*

actually smaller in plan than the Pantheon, being 95 feet in diameter as opposed to the other's 142 feet. Here the sense of vastness comes from the high dome. That was true even of Bulfinch's lower dome, and it explains why President Madison asked Trumbull to double the size of his pictures.

Twelve Doric pilasters with fluted shafts divide the circular wall into twelve bays. Eight of the bays are wide, and these contain the pictures; four are narrow, and these have the four doorways. The use of the pilasters is solely for visual purposes. Without them the wall would be repellently bare, and they also serve as apparent supports for the entablature above.

In addition to the pilasters and the pictures, reliefs help set off the empty expanses of wall while evoking our history and our heroes.

Over the four doors are four panels, each with a relief. Above the door (east) by which we entered is an Indian offering an ear of corn to the pilgrims about to land, carved in 1825 by Enrico Causici. William Penn is shown making a treaty with the Indians in 1682 over the north door; the vertical rectangular panel was carved in 1827 by Nicholas Gevelot. At the west door, we see an old favorite, Pocahontas rescuing Captain John Smith in 1606; done in 1825, it is the work of Antonio Capellano. The last of the four, over the south door, is another vertical rectangle carved by Enrico Causici in 1827. Here Daniel Boone is shown fighting the Indians in 1773.

Equally good, and actually more decorative, are the four horizontal panels, over four of the pictures, with portrait profiles in relief attributed to Enrico Causici and Antonio Capellano. They were done between 1824 and 1828. Above *The Landing of Columbus* is the profile of John Cabot, one of the earliest explorers in America. Dispatched by the English, he was, like Columbus, a Genoese sea captain. That of Sir Walter Raleigh, poet-adventurer, the founder of the Lost Colony of Roanoke, Virginia, is over the *Surrender of Cornwallis*. Above the *Surrender of General Bourgoyne* we can see Columbus. The last, over *The Embarkation of the Pilgrims*, is the Cavalier Sieur de La Salle, the French explorer of the Mis-

sissippi Valley. The ornament filling the panels consists of fronds with swirling rinceaux of acanthus ending in rosettes, along with wreaths of wheat stalks and oak leaves.

Four additional panels are above the four other pictures, but they have no portraits. Instead, they consist of an anthemion or honeysuckle ornament at the center, and from this center curve leafy branches of rinceaux ending in rosettes and other floral detail.

We touched on the twelve Doric pilasters dividing the wall. For their detail, the explorer should find the Glossary

The Discovery of the Mississippi by De Soto, 1541, *by William H. Powell. Courtesy Architect of the Capitol.*

The Baptism of Pocahontas at Jamestown, Virginia, 1613, *by John Gabsby Chapman. Courtesy Architect of the Capitol.*

handy in identifying their several parts. Among the rewards of the Capitol is the ease with which we can study the various ornamental devices employed by the classical architect.

This is also true of the modified entablature that crowns the Rotunda. On its frieze, over the pilasters, are oak-leaf and acorn wreaths. On the cornice, a band of pearls and an ovolo, or quarter round, display leaf-and-dart enrichment. The corona has a Greek key, or fret, also seen on the upper and lower sides of the big picture frames below.

We have pointed out that, like Rome's Pantheon, this vast chamber is a true rotunda. There is, however, another distinguishing aspect of the Great Rotunda: namely, that the dome consists of a hemisphere on a drum. The Pantheon in Rome has a low dome. The high domes of such buildings as St. Peter's in Rome, St. Paul's in London, the Panthéon and the Invalides in Paris, and St. Isaac's in St. Petersburg rest on massive piers much as do the domes of the Rotunda of the Library of Congress and of the San Francisco City Hall.

The first entablature, running around the Rotunda, is of stone, 48 feet above the floor. The second is so high that it can be called a wall treated as a modified entablature because there is no architrave. Its frieze is punctuated by a row of seventy-two cast-iron panels with coffers framed by acorns and oak leaves set in plaster. The cornice is of cast iron with a low plain cyma recta, then a cyma reversa with acanthus, a corona, and, last, a cyma reversa molding in leaf-and-dart topped by a fillet.

The cast iron, like the stone and the brick of the building, was made by several firms. In the case of the panels with coffers, the foundry was in Baltimore, while the cornices above and below the third frieze were cast by a New York firm.

William Penn's Treaty with the Indians, 1682, *by Nicholas Gevelot. Photo Architect of the Capitol.*

Between the two iron cornices is a horizontal wall on which there is a frieze, meaning a decorative panel in fresco. (A frieze, as decorative panel, can also be carved in relief, or it can be oil paint on canvas.) Fresco is an ancient method whereby the painting is executed in watercolor on wet plaster. When the plaster dries, this is the most permanent pictorial technique devised. The great example of it is found in the Sistine Chapel in the Vatican: the murals by Michelangelo.

For the artist it presents one difficulty: It hardens rapidly. To make needed changes, the hard plaster has to be removed and the artist must start over again. More often, the artist paints over the unwanted portion of dry plaster with water-based paint in a process known as *fresco a secco*. (*Fresco* is simply the Italian word for "fresh," and *secco* means "dry.")

As we mentioned in the Introduction, there is more true fresco in the Capitol than in all the other buildings in the country taken together. This frieze is one of the Capitol's great adornments, 8 feet 3 inches high and 300 feet long, and some 58 feet above the Rotunda floor. Executed in a form of grisaille, here a gray-brown monochrome (grisaille comes from the French word *gris*, meaning "gray"), it is painted in such a way that it looks like a parade of carved figures.

Actually, sculpture was an option considered by Captain Meigs. Had the captain remained in charge and had Crawford lived, the frieze would have been in carved relief. As it turned out, with an artist at hand skilled in fresco, Constantino Brumidi, the painting medium was chosen.

This is the first example of the muralist's work that we shall examine. Once again we have depictions of great events in our history, beginning over the west door and circling clockwise. From the figures of America and History and *The Landing of Columbus* to the scene of William Penn making his famous treaty with the Indians in 1682 (over the pilaster between the De Soto and the Columbus pictures), the work is by Brumidi. But on October 1, 1879, he fell from the temporary scaffold, saving himself by grabbing the rung of a ladder. He was rescued by several guards. Unfortunately—he was by then seventy-four—he never recovered from the shock and he died on February 19, 1880.[78]

The next episodes, from the settlement of the Plymouth Colony in 1620 (above the painting of Columbus) to the discovery of gold in California in 1848 (over Trumbull's *Declaration of Independence*), were executed by Filippo Costaggini from 1880 to 1888, using Brumidi's cartoons. A 31-foot gap was left to be filled two generations later. In 1953 Allyn Cox, a mural painter like his father, Kenyon Cox, did the episodes from the Civil War (above Trumbull's *Surrender at*

Saratoga) to the birth of aviation—the Wright brothers at Kitty Hawk, North Carolina—to complete the frieze up to the figures of America and History.

The thesis underlying the selection of the historic episodes depicted was explained by Captain Meigs in a letter to Secretary of War Davis. The frieze was intended to show "the gradual progress of a continent from the depths of barbarism to the height of civilization . . . with the illustration of the higher achievements of our present civilization."[79]

Absorbed as we are in studying the Rotunda, we can easily pass over the additional construction required to sustain Walter's great dome. To the existing base, which dated from Bulfinch's time, he added a brick wall, 300 feet long and 26 feet 2 inches high, reinforced with iron. On this would rise the cast-iron dome.

(Interestingly enough, the total amount of iron, both cast and wrought, came to 4,455 tons, with the masonry addition weighing 2,607 tons, for a total of 7,062 tons. This replaced Bulfinch's dome of masonry, wood, and copper, which weighed 5,927 tons. The advantage of iron in the matter of weight alone is obvious.)

The second cast-iron cornice, which is above the Brumidi Frieze, is big. It has to be at that height, being 190 feet from the floor. Its size and the distance from the beholder below

Sir Walter Raleigh, Explorer of Virginia, *by Nicholas Gevelot. Photo Architect of the Capitol.*

La Salle, Explorer of the Mississippi, *by Franceso Iardella. Photo Architect of the Capitol.*

Pilaster capital and wreath on the entablature. (Day)

Relief of anthemion, rosette, and rinceau. (Day)

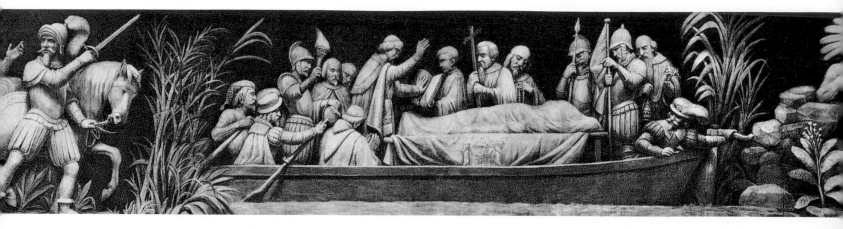

The Brumidi Frieze in the Great Rotunda by Constantino Brumidi, Filippo Costaggini, and Allyn Cox. Photo Architect of the Capitol.

The view of the dome showing the Brumidi Frieze. (Day)

Colonization of New England *part of the frieze. (Day)*

Peace between Governor Oglethorpe and the Indians. *(Day)*

Pilasters and high, round-arched windows of the drum inside the Corinthian peristyle. (Day)

The entablature above the windows.
(Day)

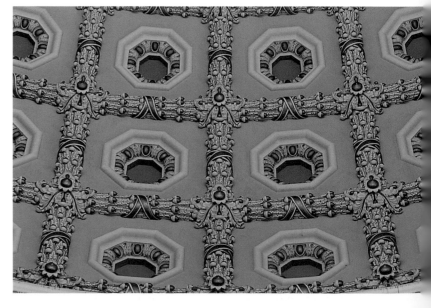

The coffering of the inner dome with its bay-leaf and bayberry toruses in cream and gold. (Day)

meant that Walter had to make changes, not least in the dimensions of the two bead-and-reels, the modified egg-and-dart, and the dentil band. It will be noted that the cymatium, the top profile, is neither a cyma recta nor a cavetto, but a flat surface at an angle.

From this point on, the eye has reached the level of the exterior peristyle. Just as the outside displays thirty-six Corinthian columns, seen through the windows, on the inside are thirty-six Corinthian pilasters dividing the arcade of thirty-six bays. The windows are effective because of their height, and no less impressive because they are set in arch bays whose piers serve as deep reveals (the side of an opening, doorway, or window). The piers have superimposed round-arch openings.

The ornament is as bold as it is on the exterior. The windows have keystones in the form of volutes with short garlands. The Corinthian capitals of the pilasters resemble the special ones of the exterior peristyle, where Walter supplemented the volutes and the acanthus with tobacco leaf, thistle, and cotton flower. As the eye descends along the pilaster shaft, it stops at the plinths, which also serve as posts in the balustrade. The double balusters of the balustrade support a rail that has bead-and-reel and egg-and-dart. Were there no ornament, even at that height, the result would appear heavy and desolate. We must not forget the apothegm of the American philosopher George Santayana: A building without ornament is like heaven without the stars.

The Capitol explorer may be surprised to discover a fleuron missing from a pilaster capital, the one over *The Landing of Columbus*. Its absence shows that, because we miss it, this modest ornamental device is an integral part of the Corinthian capital.

Nearby, two bays to the right, a small black square in the short wall beneath the arch is a modern note: a television camera focused on the floor below.

Set in the reveal-piers of the windows, often overlooked, is the flight of stairs located in a portion of the six bays in the northeast quadrant, high above the pictures of De Soto and Columbus. It is part of the stairway linking the walkway around the foot of the drum with a second flight on the back of the inner dome which ends at the oculus, or dome eye. Once open to the public, access is restricted today.

The window glass of the drum overhead is of French origin, furnished by agents of the Saint-Gobain and associated companies. (The Saint-Gobain Company is one of the largest plate-glass manufacturers in the world.) We know its age thanks to the dates, accompanied by initials, scratched in the glass by visitors years ago. In a letter to Captain Meigs, the agents wrote that they were fixing the price at 56 percent of list price (or 67 percent if duties were remitted), saying that "we can assure you candidly that we will lose money at such a low rate. But as a matter of pride, we are desirous to see our plate glass used in the Capitol of Washington."[80] It is only the old plate glass on the east side of the drum that has lasted; that on the west side has not survived because of prevailing westerly winds.

The drum entablature follows the standard Corinthian model. The architrave has three fascia with a top molding of cyma reversa in leaf-and-dart. The frieze is a plain band. The cornice has egg-and-dart, modillions with acanthus, sunken rosettes and acorns between the modillions, then a corona, bead-and-reel, and, at the top, a cymatium that has the usual cyma recta. This is the last of the entablatures.

This interior dome is divided into panels by large strings of garlands in cream and gold, the garlands being imbricated bay leaves and bayberries bound in ribbons. Where the garlands cross are acorn-shaped rosettes, set on acanthus leaves. At the bottom of the garland grid, above the entablature, are volutes strung together by tendril and acanthus. At the top of the grid is another band of acanthus and tendril, punctuated by nine cones. Over this, in turn, is a band of stars set in a guilloche.

We can now begin to grasp the sophistication of the design of the great dome. On the exterior, we have observed how it was divided into a drum with a peristyle, attic, and hemisphere. On the interior, we find that it is made up of three shells. There is the first one with the giant oculus, 50 feet in diameter, which we have been studying. Then, over the oculus, there is a second, a vast canopy with a fresco. The third is the hemisphere, which is only visible from the exterior.

Once again we see a balustrade, this time to underscore the curve of the oculus as well as serving as a railing for a little-used footway. It is 152 feet 3 inches from the floor to the top of this balustrade.

Now it might well be asked: Why have an inner dome when, presumably, the inner surface of the outer dome that we know so well would serve? Walter had good reason to place the one above us, because the outer dome at this point, which consists of the attic and the cupola, would have been too high. What he required for the interior was a smaller, lower hemisphere that would contain a giant oculus.

Why the oculus? By using such a device, he could have another layer, the canopy with a fresco, a canopy that is 180 feet and 3 inches at its center above the floor. As mentioned in the Introduction, Walter had ample precedents in the Chapel of the Invalides and the Panthéon in Paris, particularly the latter. (We have reproduced, in the Introduction, Walter's drawing of a section of the Panthéon's interior elevation made on his European tour in 1838. *See* illustration on page 16.) Several buildings in the country also have such canopies over inner domes, notably the Wisconsin State Capitol and the San Francisco City Hall.

We cannot help but to rejoice once more that the Great Rotunda is free at its center, much as Rome's Pantheon, and that we, all of us, can stand beneath the glorious dome.

THE APOTHEOSIS OF WASHINGTON

If it was extraordinary that Walter produced a canopy as part of his design, taking his cue from the Panthéon in Paris, it was no less extraordinary that there was, in Washington, an artist who could adorn it. Here Brumidi painted what is one of the nation's great murals: *The Apotheosis* (or *Glorification*) *of Washington*.[81] Like the frieze, it is in fresco, and is a work of art to match Walter's superb dome.

At a height of 180 feet above the floor, it has a diameter of 62 feet and 2 inches, and its concavity, from the canopy's edge to its center, is 20 feet 7 inches in height. In area, the mural is 4,664 square feet. Because of its great distance from the beholder, it is hardly surprising that the figures should, in some instances, measure 15 feet. For that reason they appear life-size to us below; if they were any smaller, they would appear no bigger than children.

We have to remind ourselves that Brumidi introduced fifty-seven figures, not to mention birds and animals, including several horses, a stork, and an eagle. There is even a rainbow.

The beholder should stand in such a way that he or she can see the seated Washington at the center from the front. On one side is the winged figure of the goddess of liberty in her Phrygian cap with an ax and its handle bundled in rods, symbol of government, in her right hand, and a copy of the Constitution in her left. On the other side is the winged figure of Fame, or possibly Victory, with her trumpet. (The visitor comes to recognize symbols and symbolic figures repeated throughout the Capitol.) Completing the circle around our first President are thirteen maidens representing the thirteen states, much as do the stripes in the flag. Two of the maidens hold aloft a banner with the legend "E Pluribus Unum," which also appears at the feet of the statue of Freedom on the dome.

A second, larger circle of figures rings the canopy's edge. Beneath our first President is a group of five representing war. The most conspicuous figure is that of Freedom, with a sword in one hand and, in the other, a shield emblazoned with stripes. She wears a star-studded helmet. With an eagle at her feet, she crushes Tyranny. Going clockwise, the next group, numbering ten, represents the Sciences with Minerva (Pallas Athena) with helmet and spear instructing Benjamin Franklin, Robert Fulton, and Samuel F. B. Morse.

The beholder has to move around the Great Rotunda to see each group in its entirety. Next, holding a trident, is a bearded Neptune in his chariot; with six attendants, he identifies Marine. What appears to be a rope held by the attendants is in fact the first Atlantic cable. Note the cherub riding the dolphin in the lower left; a winged cherub is a favorite subject of decoration throughout the building. The fourth group, entitled *Commerce*, shows seven figures, including Mercury. He is handing a bag of coins to Robert Morris of Philadelphia, financier of the American Revolution. A bale of cotton is at the feet of the god. Brumidi's signature, visible with binoculars, is on the box next to the bale. Between the Mercury and Neptune groups are the twin funnels of an ironclad river steamboat. *Mechanics*, the next group, has Vulcan at the center with five others, including Charles F. Thomas, who, as chief machinist, placed the statue of Freedom on the dome in 1863. Cannons and cannonballs are nearby, and behind the god's right hand is the cabbage stack (later called a "diamond stack") of a wood-burning locomotive.

Last we have *Agriculture*, with seven figures and some horses. The seated goddess is Ceres with a cornucopia, or horn of plenty. America, in a red Phrygian cap, is to her right and is handing her the reins of a pair of horses pulling a McCormick reaper. To her left, with a basket on her head, is Pomona, goddess of the harvest. Flora, goddess of ripening plants or springtime, is at America's knees picking flowers.

At the time, possibly only one large mural existed in the country: that at the center of the auditorium ceiling of the Academy of Music in Philadelphia. Carl Herman Schmolzé, a German immigrant, executed it in oil on plaster in 1854. Actually, the only ones to bear comparison, and that hardly, are two large reredos murals, both by Brumidi, one nearby on North Capitol Street and the other, now gone, in the Cathedral of St. Peter and St. Paul in Philadelphia.

With what great murals of the nineteenth century is the *Apotheosis* to be compared? There is Bouguereau's large mural for the theater in Bordeaux in France. Among the churches in Rome there are the murals of the nave vaults and several chapel walls in San Andrea della Valle. Well known are those of the Paris Opera House by Paul Baudry, which were done in oil on canvas. Baudry's are generally regarded as the century's best. In fact, he executed thirty-three separate compositions, totaling 5,382 square feet compared to the 4,664 square feet of the *Apotheosis*.[82]

Although Brumidi may not be the foremost mural painter of the last century, his work in the Capitol places him among

The Apotheosis of Washington *by Constantino Brumidi. (Day)*

those to be remembered. Yet the artist has not received the honors due him. If he is mentioned at all in the histories of American art, and that surely is rare, it is only to be dismissed. He deserves a line, however short, along with Thomas Ustick Walter, in all our history books.

Fresco, as we have observed, is a difficult medium. Let us see how the artist defined it:

Fresco, derives its name from fresh *mortar and is the immediate and rapid application of mineral colors, diluted in water, to the fresh mortar just put on the wall, thereby the colors are absorbed by the mortar during its freshness, and repeating the process in sections by day, till the entire picture will be completed.*

This superior method is much admired in the celebrated works of the Old Masters, and is proper for historical subjects or Classical ornamentations, like the Loggie of Raphael in the Vatican.[83]

Beyond the difficulty of the medium, there is the sheer size of the *Apotheosis* and the fact that Brumidi had to paint on a curved surface. The plaster of the canopy is three-quarters of an inch thick, held in place by cast-iron lath. It is in two layers, the first of which is called *arriccio*, or "brown coat," on which the artist drew his design in line. It is one-half inch thick. On this is placed the *intonaco*, or finish coat, a quarter of an inch in thickness. The latter has a grainy surface due to the presence of fine sand and mica added to give the plas-

The thirteen maidens attending Washington. (Day)

Armed Freedom crushing Tyranny. Photo Paul Recer.

Ceres, goddess of agriculture, on reaper. Photo Paul Recer.

ter a slight sparkle. The surface varies depending on what Brumidi was depicting. The bright yellow sky of the center is smooth; that of the gray-blue sky below it is rough, with the irregularities giving shape to the clouds.[84]

As is customary, the artist began at the top and worked his way down, thus avoiding having any paint drip on a completed portion below. The face of Washington was where he began, a fact confirmed in the course of a recent conservation. The last portion he painted was part of the Mercury group. Here he gave the face of Brigadier General Meigs to one of the figures, but he was to remove it. Brumidi would do a section technically known as a *giornata* (plural: *giornate*)—that is, a portion completed in a day, from the Italian *giorno*.[85] The section dried quickly, and he moved to another.

A figure usually took two *giornate*, divided at the waist. The upper half with head, torso, hands, and nearby objects as well as some of the sky would be done in one day, while the lower half of clothing, feet, and objects would be done in another. Incredible as it may seem, he also did whole figures, some 15 feet high, in a single *giornata*, as in the Marine group. Altogether, it took him 120 *giornate* to cover the 4,664 square feet.

The great work began in August 1862, a low period for the Union in the Civil War, when Walter invited Brumidi to submit a design. A year later, he had executed the cartoons. With the canopy ready in December 1864, the artist went to work, and by October of the next year he was finished. It had taken about eleven months.

We have dwelled on Brumidi's skill, and with good reason. There is the design with its disposition of the figures in two chaplets and Washington in the center; there is his placing the figures in distinct groups and yet linking them. What is of particular significance is the artist's talent in giving them movement and monumentality, which can only be achieved in the great Renaissance tradition of which Brumidi was one of the last offspring. Nor should we casually accept the extraordinary size of the *Apotheosis* and its setting. Pierce Rice has underscored in his *Man as Hero: The Human Figure in Western Art* that in the present day "we are so geared to books that we tend to disregard size in artistic matters. An analysis of two pictures, one huge and one small, is assessed in matching reproductions and yet the real distinction could be their size."

Rice continues:

In taking art entirely into the area of study and classification, we have let actuality go by the board. Physical presence and conspicuousness, which might very well be thought of as the principal esthetic considerations because they are absolute in determining effectiveness, have simply been lost sight of.[86]

The sheer size of the mural overhead called for someone trained in the outlook and skills of the grand tradition, and Brumidi was among those Romans who were soundly equipped to do so. He had command of the medium, fresco;

he could execute monumental figures; and he was steeped in the artistic tradition of Renaissance Rome. "The task of the artist," to cite Pierce Rice again, "is to indicate nobility and force, while steering clear of histrionics," and this is only possible with a certain "largeness of vision."[87]

We have to remember, for it has long been forgotten, that the highest aim of the artist is the decoration of public buildings. We have, in our time, become so accustomed to associating painting and sculpture with art museums that we find it difficult to accept the fact that great painting has to have a setting and a purpose. (It is an outrage that religious pictures found in museums were torn from their settings and, as a result, lost their purpose, which was to further worship.)

So what we have at the Capitol is a great example of the true role of art. As for Brumidi, few have surpassed him in the art of decoration. One, to offer an example, is Edwin Howland Blashfield, whose work in Washington is to be seen in the Library of Congress and in St. Matthew's Cathedral, but it can also be found from the state capitols of Wisconsin and Minnesota to the Essex County Courthouse in Jersey City.

After the pictures and the *Apotheosis*, the statues in the Great Rotunda are but a minor accent. In fact, they are not part of the fabric of the room as are the reliefs, the fresco decoration, and, to a lesser degree, the great canvases. Several, however, might be singled out. That of George Washington is a bronze copy of the original marble figure in the Virginia State Capitol in Richmond by the Frenchman Jean-Antoine Houdon. Of special interest, it, like the figures in the Trumbull pictures, is a portrait executed when our first President was very much alive. The artist came especially to this country in 1788 to execute it. The statue of Thomas Jefferson nearby, the work of another Frenchman, David d'Angers, is posthumous; it was done in 1833, seven years after the third President's death. The Alexander Hamilton is also posthumous, done in Rome in 1868 by an American artist, Horatio Stone. They are all three heroic in size, being 7 feet 6 inches, 7 feet 6 inches, and 7 feet 9 inches, respectively. It should be explained that there are three figure sizes in sculpture: life-size, heroic, and colossal. Crawford's *Freedom* on the dome is midway between heroic and colossal. The Statue of Liberty is a rare example of the latter.

A recent addition to the Rotunda portraits is the heroic bust of Dr. Martin Luther King, Jr., executed in 1986 by John Wilson. The latest arrival (1997), is the large block of white marble between Trumbull's *The Declaration of Independence* and his *Surrender of Lord Cornwallis at Yorktown*. From the block, carved in 1921 by Adelaide Johnson, rise the busts of the suffragette leaders Elizabeth Cady Stanton, Susan B. Anthony and Lucretia Mott. Working in the style of the French sculptor, Auguste Rodin, Johnson has executed them realistically and shows them only in part surrounded by the white marble. This last is there in quantity to convey a sense of strength and timelessness.

Around the room, next to the wall, are large bronze benches that invite the visitor's attention. Their sides of acanthus and roses are of such solidity that they easily fit into a setting where everything is big. They were actually designed for the present House Chamber, where they were located in the 1870s. A good number found their way to other buildings, but enough were recovered to be installed here.

It is pleasant to sit here and watch the endless stream of visitors from all corners of the nation and, it would seem, from all corners of the world in the spell of the extraordinary room.

Before leaving the Great Rotunda for the Old House Cham-

One of several sketches for The Apotheosis of Washington *given by Brumidi to Thomas U. Walter. Courtesy Athenaeum of Philadelphia.*

Arm and foot of the bronze bench in the Great Rotunda. (Day)

Bust of Martin Luther King, Jr., 1986, by John Wilson.
Courtesy Architect of the Capitol.

Ionic colonnade west of the west doorway. (Day)

ber, it is worth stepping through the west doorway to descend partway down what is known as the Great Stairway, if not restricted. The visitor will be standing between two colonnades of Greek Ionic columns of white Vermont marble. Stairway and colonnades date from about 1900, a date that may puzzle the curious. Why so late? We are in that part of the Capitol where the Library of Congress, the cast-iron one designed by Walter in 1852, once stood before it obtained its own building in 1897.

While the former Library space was converted into offices, halls, and stairs by the Office of the Architect of the Capitol, it is assumed that it did so with the firm of Carrère & Hastings of New York as consultant. (This is the same firm that did the Cannon Office Building of the House of Representatives to the south and the Russell Office Building of the Senate to the north of the Capitol as well as the New York Public Library and the Frick Collection, also in New York.)

The design of the Greek Ionic capitals is modeled on those seen in the Old Senate Chamber and the lobby of the same, first made known to the Western world by *The Antiquities of Athens* by James Stuart and Nicholas Revett in 1762.

When permitted, one can go to the Crypt via the stairway. Instead, I urge the visitor to stop at the sixth step or below and turn to look up through the doorway. Then, proceeding slowly up the stairs, he or she will discover a fresh perspective from which to view the Great Rotunda. The doorway acts as a frame or tunnel, limiting at first what can be seen of the Rotunda, and as one mounts, a whole vision comes into play. It is simply one of several perspectives that make the Capitol so rewarding.

THE OLD HOUSE CHAMBER (STATUARY HALL)

On entering the vast chamber once again, we go south to pass through the doorway between the statues of Washington and Jefferson. The doorway is framed in brown Seneca sandstone from the same quarries on the Maryland side of the Potomac that produced the Great Rotunda floor. We now stand in the Small House Rotunda. While its north and south doorways here have round arches, those to the east and west have lintels and are framed with Greek Corinthian capitals inspired by those of the Tower of Winds in Athens. Like the ancient model, these have a row of palm leaves and a row of acanthus leaves. Two columns guard a west doorway (at one time a window looking into an air shaft), and two guard an east doorway opening on a stairwell.

The low dome has coffers—that is, sunken panels—that are both round- and diamond-shaped. At the top is an oculus with a frame of guilloche and rosettes. The oculus rises to a small glazed lantern. From the lantern hangs a large brass chandelier with many arms, commonly called a Dutch chandelier. (While the general design is of Dutch origin, this particular model is a form of Colonial Revival via restored Williamsburg, Virginia.)

The Small House Rotunda is one of the rare parts of the Capitol designed by Latrobe that survived the 1814 fire. For that reason it has been declared the oldest surviving example of the Greek Revival style of our architecture, according to the architectural historian William C. Allen.[88]

We continue south through an arched vault to the Old House Chamber, which the representatives vacated in 1857. Captain Montgomery Meigs anticipated everyone in proposing that the room be reserved for statues of outstanding citizens, not all elected officials. The choice was left to the states, with each being permitted to select two. Forty statues now fill the hall, with others placed around the building.

The original chamber designed by Latrobe, the one before the 1814 fire, was rectangular in plan with its short east and west ends rounded. With this second one, the architect chose the half-circle plan of the operating room of the College of Surgery in Paris designed ca. 1775 by Jacques Gondouin.[89] (It no longer exists.) This room is the first legislative chamber to have been laid out in the shape of an amphitheater. The congressmen sat in semicircular rows facing the center of the flat south wall. Here there is a colonnade of eight columns, while the curved part of the room has twelve. The shafts are of Potomac marble from the river's banks in Loudoun County, Virginia, northwest of Washington. Called pudding stone, the handsome stone is a conglomerate, or breccia to geologists, meaning a rock made of pebbles and clay and pressed over geological time into marble. The shafts, unlike the monoliths of the East Front porches, consist of three drums (frusta) with no flutes. The Corinthian capitals are of white Italian marble. Giovanni Andrei, who had been working on the Capitol since 1806, was sent to Carrara by Latrobe in 1815 to have the carving done there.[90] The model chosen by the architect was the capital of the Choragic Monument of Lysicrates as found in Stuart and Revett's *Antiquities of Athens.*

The entablature, which is the horizontal member supported by the columns, is divided into the architrave with

The dome of the Small House Rotunda. (Day)

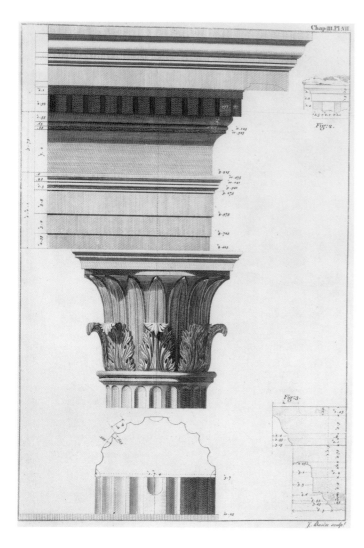

The Corinthian order from the Tower of Winds, Athens.
James Stuart and Nicholas Revett, The Antiquities of Athens
(London, 1762), vol. 1, chap. 3, plate 7.
Courtesy New York Public Library.

The Corinthian order in the Small House Rotunda.
Courtesy Architect of the Capitol.

three fascia and a plain frieze, with a third part, the cornice, enriched with pearls and egg-and-dart, dentil band, block modillions faced with sunken rosettes, and, between the modillions, coffers with rosettes. On the south frieze, there is a piece of sculpture depicting a spread-winged eagle. (Below it was the rostrum of the Speaker of the House.) Above the eagle is a tympanum with a niche filled with a plaster statue of Liberty by Enrico Causici.[91] Her right hand, holding a copy of the Constitution, extends above another eagle, and to her left a serpent, symbol of wisdom, encircles a short truncated shaft. Above *Liberty* is a wide arch that has on its intrados—its underside, which is also known as a soffit—a double row of coffers with rosettes. The extrados, the outside face of the arch, has a band of anthemions and tendrils.

After studying *Freedom* on the dome and discovering that sculpture placed high on buildings can be big, the visitor may not be surprised to find that *Liberty* here is 13 feet 7 inches high.[92] Still, it is a startling fact, as it shows what tricks the eye can play on the inside as well as the outside of buildings.

As for the semidome overhead, much of it is divided vertically by bands of ribbon-bound acanthus. Between them are coffers with white rosettes against a red ground set in a frame of pale blue bordered by acanthus on a cyma reversa. At the top is a band of anthemion, tendril, acanthus, and rosette. The band partly frames an oculus with channeled bands where the fluting is blue and the fillets white. Two bands of acanthus, rosette, and anthemion with volutes of tendrils repeat the ornament found on the arch extrados. Standing beneath the oculus, it is possible to make out its top covered with another band of anthemion and tendril. The detail here, much like that of the column capitals, is from Stuart and Revett's *Antiquities*. The visitor will realize that this is the same lantern south of the dome, which can be seen when examining the East Front.

The brass chandelier is new, a reconstruction based on the one seen in a famous picture by Samuel F. B. Morse, the inventor of the telegraph, showing the House in session. Painted in 1822 and now in the Corcoran Gallery in Washington, it shows what the room was like in those days. The same picture served as the source in reproducing the whale-oil-burning lamps and their brackets mounted on the column shafts as well as for the curtains, red with gold fringe, hanging behind the columns.

The picture, by the way, is a reminder that Morse was a full-fledged artist before he invented the telegraph in 1844.

A piece of sculpture should not be overlooked, *The Car of History*, with Clio, the Muse of history, on the chariot of Time. In relief, on the front of the chariot, are the profile of Washington and the figure of Fame with her trumpet, similar to the one over the door of the main visitors' entrance. The wheel, which holds a clock, rests on a globe with the

The Old House Chamber designed by Benjamin H. Latrobe. (Day)

signs of the zodiac barely visible from the floor. It was executed in 1819 by Carlo Franzoni. (Clio and her chariot appeared on a stamp issued in 1989 on the occasion of the two hundredth anniversary of the first session of the House in New York City, the nation's capital in 1789.)

Easily overlooked are the white marble mantels of the fireplaces on the east and west sides of the chamber's south side.[93] They are copies of a pair found in the Old Senate Chamber that are inaccessible to the public. (The originals are based on drawings done by Giovanni Andrei under the supervision of Latrobe and carved by James Traquair of Philadelphia in about 1812 and installed in 1817 in the Old Senate Chamber.) The side panels have reliefs of a mace adapted from the symbol of the office of the lictors (atten

dants of magistrates in ancient Rome): bound rods here topped by a Phrygian, or liberty, cap instead of the usual axhead. Just above the cap is a splayed sheaf of bearded wheat. At either end of the lintel is a ring of thirteen stars surrounded by a sunburst. More interesting is the horizontal panel, at the center of which are a half dozen cherubs binding rods, symbolic of the thirteen states being united. They are just some of the several hundred babies that are to be found in the Capitol's carved and painted decoration, first seen in *The Apotheosis of Washington*.

Their presence in the building is a reminder of the role of the human figure in Western art; no other civilization has placed the figure at the summit of its hierarchy of decoration. The result is, as the artist Pierce Rice has pointed out

View of the oculus in the Old House Chamber. (Day)

Operating room in the College of Surgery in Paris, designed ca. 1775 by Jacques Gondouin. From Jacques Gondouin, Description des écoles de chirurgie *(Paris, 1780), plate 29. Courtesy New York Academy of Medicine.*

in *Man as Hero: The Human Figure in Western Art*, that the baby is "as much a symbol of the West as the acanthus leaf."[94]

Near the west mantelpiece is the spot where the Capitol guides station their groups of visitors while they go to the opposite spot to the east and whisper; such are the peculiar acoustics that the patient tourists can hear the whispers. It is therefore not surprising to learn that the chamber was never successful acoustically. Curtains were hung behind the columns; carpets were placed at various points to control the sound. Canvas, in one desperate attempt, was stretched beneath the semidome; it put an end to the echoes but absorbed all sounds and cut off light. The floor was raised, all to no avail.

When the House first sat in the chamber, in 1807, it counted 145 members representing seventeen states and three territories. The nation's population in 1810 was 7,239,881. In 1857, when the House moved to new quarters, there were 241 representatives for thirty-one states and seven territories. The population in 1860 was 31,443,321.

In the floor of streaked white and black marble tile are bronze plaques, here and there marking the desks of those of our Presidents who, in the course of their careers, served in the chamber: John Quincy Adams, James K. Polk, Millard Fillmore, James Buchanan, Abraham Lincoln, and Andrew Johnson. Millard Fillmore, who became Vice President in 1849 and succeeded Zachary Taylor a year later, was sworn in as President here; as we know, he was to take more than an ordinary interest in the Capitol's extension. Of them all, John Quincy Adams had the most unusual career as far as the Capitol was concerned. Unlike the others, he had been in the Senate, had become President, and finally settled in the chamber in 1831, two years after leaving the White House. His most famous, and most persistent, effort was fighting a restriction on the people's right to petition. In 1836 the House had voted that all petitions to do with slavery "be laid upon the table" and no further action taken—in other words, a gag rule. Every year Adams called for an end to the gag rule, and every year he was voted down until, in 1844, his motion to abolish it was passed. Not that he was an abolitionist; rather, he saw the right to petition as a privilege guaranteed by the Constitution. In 1846 he was a leader among those who helped establish the Smithsonian Institution, which, today, plays so large a role in the cultural life of the capital city and of the nation. Adams's end came in the chamber. He was seated at his desk on February 21, 1848, at the spot marked by a plaque, when he suffered a stroke. Moved to the Great Rotunda, then to the Speaker's Room nearby, he died two days later at the age of eighty.

Among the more prominent of the nonpresidential members was Henry Clay, Adams's Secretary of State. One of the trio of pre–Civil War statesmen identified with the era that included Daniel Webster and John Calhoun, he was often

Speaker of the House. It was in this chamber that he helped achieve the Missouri Compromise of 1820, the first of several attempts to resolve the slavery issue.

The House was made up of all kinds. Thanks to the movies and to television, we often know more about the lesser figures than about those of the caliber of Clay. Such a one was Davy Crockett of Tennessee, who might be called a professional frontiersman, one who played the part of the rube from Tennessee, boastful and arrogant. After several terms he was voted out of office, and he took off for Texas to die at the siege of the Alamo in 1836. Another was the brilliant John Randolph of Roanoke, Virginia, the most eccentric of all to sit both in the Old House and Old Senate chambers. He thought nothing of bringing his two dogs here.

The House, in those days, was far less formal than it is today. Our nation was much smaller, and while there were crowds, there was nothing like the flood of today's visitors, with the result that they were permitted greater liberties. The public would even find its way to the floor of the House. Vendors collected outside and often inside the room. When some key issue was before the House, the balcony would be packed, notably with women. Chaff and laughter rang out between the floor and the balcony. Frances Trollope, who so admired the Great Rotunda, liked the chamber. She, along with other women, was invited to sit on one of the sofas then between columns, and she enjoyed the spectacle. Charles Dickens, in Washington in 1842, had this praise for the chamber: "The House of Representatives is a beautiful and spacious hall of semi-circular shape, supported by handsome pillars. One part of the gallery is appropriated to the ladies, and there they sit in front rows and come in and go out as at a play or concert. The chair [the Speaker's chair in the middle of the room's south side] is canopied and raised considerably above the floor of the House, and every member has an easy chair and a writing desk to himself, which is denounced by some people out of doors as a most unfortunate and injudicious arrangement, tending to long sittings and prosaic speeches."

Dickens closes, saying that "it is an elegant chamber to look at, but a singularly bad one for all purposes of hearing."

Despite its acoustical weaknesses, the chamber had a strong attraction. We have to remind ourselves that this chamber and the Old Senate Chamber on the other side of the Great Rotunda were the most splendid American interiors prior to 1850 and would not be surpassed until the Capitol extensions were completed in 1860. Along with, we might add, the magnificent interior of the Cathedral of St. Peter and St. Paul in Philadelphia. Also, there is the fact that the only "show" in Washington for decades was the activity on the Hill. There was nothing like today's Smithsonian Institution with its cluster of museums, no National Gallery of Art, no Robert Kennedy Stadium, no Capitol Center, no

The Corinthian capital in the Old House Chamber. (Day)

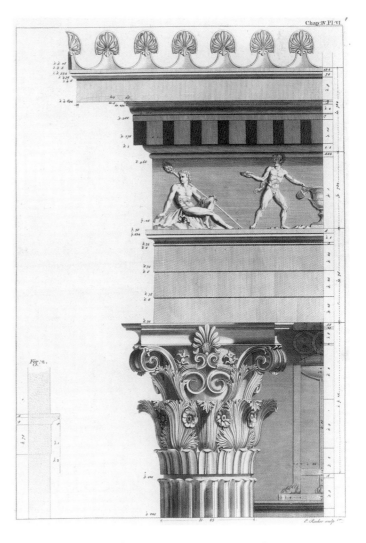

Corinthian capital of the Choragic Monument of Lysicrates. James Stuart and Nicholas Revett, The Antiquities of Athens *(London, 1762), vol. 1, chap. 4, plate 6. Courtesy New York Public Library.*

The Old House Chamber in 1822 *by Samuel F. B. Morse. Courtesy Corcoran Gallery of Art.*

Cherubs on the lintel of the west fireplace in the Old House Chamber. (Day)

Kennedy Center—all those attractions that are now so much a part of capital life.

Of course, in those less crowded days there was a particular virtue to the chamber's size. It was a small public stage that, with easy access, made for an intimate ambience. Its present population of rigid statues is in stark contrast to what must have been all movement and buzz and, on occasion, uproar.

Actually, the chamber, solemnized by the statues, continued as a public resort or meeting place into the 1890s. Vendors of drinks, cakes, and souvenirs, along with lobbyists and visitors, were found here. In a time when there was less need for security, it was a good place to stop a congressman on his way to the House Chamber. Speaker Thomas Brackett "Tsar" Reed cleared out the commercial activity with the approach of the new century.[95]

Not long after, in 1901, the old ceiling of wood was replaced by one of steel, and the decoration, originally painted to suggest decorated relief, became true relief with proper classical detail of coffers and rosettes.

As for the statues, visitors become confused by the abundance of them. Those who are curious seek out the pair that represents their native states. Few of the worthies are well known, so we ask ourselves: Who was he or who was she? At least we can point to one surprise: Among all the lawyers, doctors, businessmen, and others, there is one painter. Representing Montana is the famous portrayer of cowboys and Indians, an artist of the West, Charles Russell. His statue is the fifth to the left as you enter the chamber.

The visitor crosses Statuary Hall, beyond which the Speaker's tribune once stood, to enter the short north-south corridor leading to the House wing. At the corridor's entrances are two arches, the second and smaller of which has views of the Robert E. Lee Mansion, now part of Arlington National Cemetery, and of Mount Vernon, George Washington's home. The decoration was executed in 1902 by Joseph Rakeman. He also painted the pair of arches at the south end, with two views: one of the Washington Monument and the other of Washington's tomb at Mount Vernon. The visitor is not permitted to go beyond this point because the present House chamber is on the other side of the east-west corridor.

We are now outside the old center wing of the Capitol, in that part designed by Thomas Ustick Walter. This narrow hall between the old and the new, it will be recalled, was in accordance with Daniel Webster's suggestion to the architect, seconded by President Fillmore, to have only connecting corridors between the wings. The windows on the west side, facing a colonnade, command a view of the Mall. The columned porch provides a foreground for one of the country's great vistas.

A similar colonnade formerly existed near the windows on the east side. With the construction of the new East Front

The Car of History *by Carlo Franzoni. (Day)*

around 1960 the House Reception Room was placed here, and its wall closed off the other side of the windows.

Of the statues in the short corridor, the one to notice is that of Jonathan Trumbull, governor and chief justice of Connecticut. He was the father of John Trumbull, whose pictures are in the Great Rotunda.

Before turning back, the visitor might glance at the window bays. We know of the role of cast iron on the exterior and the interior of the dome, but we shall discover that it is found throughout the interior of the House and Senate wings built in the 1850s. The window bays, for example, are framed in the metal, and it is also seen in the panels beneath the windows. The acorn and oak-leaf enrichment is part of the detail.

In his first plan for the building, Walter had specified wood for the window bays and the doorway frames because he had been instructed to restrict himself to the materials of the old center of the building. When, in 1853, Captain Meigs was called by Secretary of War Jefferson Davis to take charge of construction, he mandated the shift to cast iron wherever possible. Of course, nothing was easier for Walter, who had worked with the metal, notably in the Library of Congress, completed the year before.

THE OLD SENATE CHAMBER

At this point, the visitor retraces his or her steps, going through the Old House Chamber and crossing the Great Rotunda to its north door. As always in the Capitol, there is a sense of rediscovery on entering the monumental chamber. It is not so much seeing the historic pictures once again as just bathing in the vast space. And, of course, there is the movement, the going and the coming of people of all ages and all kinds, native and foreign.

On going through the north door and a short corridor, we find ourselves in the Small Senate Rotunda. Actually, it is not round but oval, with a round oculus in the floor, and a round dome overhead supported by columns of Aquia Creek sandstone.

We are again in a Latrobe interior executed after the fire of 1814. The architect indulged a fondness for creating a new capital, one of tobacco leaves and flowers carved by Francisco Iardella.[96] The leaves are painted gold, the flowers with smaller leaves red and green, polychromy that actually dates from the 1960s. The tobacco leaf, as a decorative device, was repeated throughout the Capitol; we shall see it in the Senate wing, where Thomas Ustick Walter made use of it.

The small dome above has a glazed oculus. Below it, on the curved surface, are two kinds of coffers: one deep and round with gold rosettes on a red ground and a border of acanthus on a cyma recta; and the other shallow and diamond-shaped with curved sides, its rosettes on a green ground. Lighting for the rotunda comes from a splendid chandelier of Bohemian glass, which came from the Capitol Hill Methodist Church. It was installed here in 1965.[97] The brass sconces, or wall brackets, of the surrounding wall consist of a torch with five arms, the bottom of the torch being held in place by a ring extending from the mouth of a lion mask. Oddly enough, the torch was originally upside down, with the narrow end up holding the arms; the change was made in 1965 by the late Mario Campioli of the Office of the Architect of the Capitol.

The presence of the chandelier and the alteration in the sconces illustrate the subtle improvements that have been made in the building in recent decades.

A short corridor leads north to the vestibule of the Old

Tobacco-leaf and tobacco-flower capital by Latrobe in the Small Senate Rotunda.
(Day)

Senate Chamber. Three sides of the room, square in plan, have walls of Aquia Creek sandstone with doorways; a fourth side, opening on a corridor, has four Greek Ionic columns and two antae (singular: anta), or piers, that are placed on either side of an entrance. The shafts are of the same Potomac marble, or puddingstone, found in the Old House Chamber. The capitals of white Carrara marble were the models for those seen at the Great Stairway, the source being *The Antiquities of Athens* by James Stuart and Nicholas Revett. Between the arches are pendentives on which sit a saucer dome with a glazed oculus. The soffit, or underside, of the dome has wide splayed channels divided by arrises. At the top of the dome, encircling the oculus, is a ring of guilloche enriched with gold rosettes, while at the bottom of the dome is another chaplet consisting of roses bound by a ribbon. The ceiling is, of course, a masonry vault beneath the plaster; it shows one of the many shapes such vaulting takes in the Capitol.

The large brass chandelier hanging from the oculus, installed in 1983, was modeled, as was the one in the Old House Chamber, on the chandelier in the Samuel F. B. Morse picture of the chamber. The sconces, with whale-oil lamps electrified, are the same as those in the Old House Chamber.

Before leaving the vestibule, the visitor might glance at the corners to see the pains a classical architect of Latrobe's stature took in his designs. Instead of using the customary plain right angle, he gave each corner several narrow pilasters and a chamfered narrow vertical panel, with pilasters and panel joining to serve as a pier for the arches and the pendentives. The floor, done in 1901, is made of marble tiles with bands of guilloche and anthemion and, in the corners, a modified United States shield.

We offer such a full description only to underscore the abundance of the decoration and the skill with which it was handled. We might, in addition, try to imagine the Capitol interiors without such decoration. A stark, gloomy building it would be.

From here the visitor steps into the Old Senate Chamber, seat of the United States Senate from 1819 to 1859.[98] The

The dome of the Small Senate Rotunda. (Day)

room's size strikes the beholder at once. We are astonished that so modest a setting was the scene of the great pre–Civil War debates of Daniel Webster, John Calhoun, Henry Clay, and the other orators of the day. We have to remind ourselves that when the chamber was built, the Senate numbered only thirty-four; there were only seventeen states with a total population in 1810 of 7,239,881. By 1859 there were sixty-six senators from thirty-three states with a population of 31,443,321 (1860).

In plan, the room is similar to, if smaller than, that of the Old House Chamber. It too is an amphitheater. Only here the seating has been carefully restored to what it was like in the 1850s. (The restoration was executed by the firm of DeWitt, Poor & Shelton between 1971 and 1975 and the Office of the Architect of the Capitol.) The senators' desks and chairs stand on raised semicircles that face the dais of the president of the Senate. Framing the last tier of chairs is a row of cast-iron columns with modified Corinthian capitals that support a gallery. Paired with the columns are pilasters, Ionic antae, against the wall with shafts of the mottled Potomac pudding stone and capitals of white Carrara marble.

The semidome overhead has coffering with rosettes set in concentric semicircles. At the top, a curved band of anthemion and tendril surround five oculi between which are arabesques of acanthus, rosette, tendril, and anthemion. Within the semicircle is one large half oculus framed by coffers with rosettes and rectangular panels containing anthemion and acanthus. From the frame hangs a very elaborate brass chandelier with abundant ornament where acanthus, rosette, and gadroon are repeated.

Detail of the Small Senate Rotunda dome. (Day)

Lion mask and torch bracket in the Old Senate Rotunda. (Day)

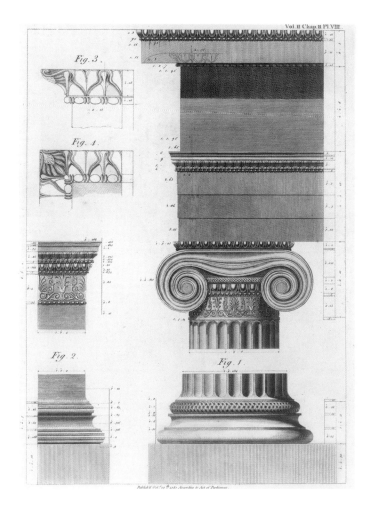

Ionic capital in the Old Senate Rotunda. (Day)

Ionic capital at the Erechtheum on the Temple of Athens. James Stuart and Nicholas Revett, The Antiquities of Athens *(London, 1787), vol. 2, plate 8. Courtesy New York Public Library.*

The Corinthian capital of the cast-iron column designed by Charles Bulfinch in the Old Senate Chamber. (Day)

View of the Old Senate Chamber, designed by Benjamin H. Latrobe. Courtesy Architect of the Capitol.

As for the back of the chamber, it consists of an Ionic colonnade where the Old House Chamber had a Corinthian one. The capitals are the same as those seen in the vestibule outside and at the Great Stairway. Over the colonnade is a massive arch with an intrados of coffers with rosettes, and an extrados, or outside, with clusters of arrows and springs of laurel alternating with stars set on sunbursts in circular frames.

Against the colonnade and rising to the arch is the dais with the chair of the president of the Senate, the Vice President of the United States. Over the dais is a handsome baldachin with a gold-leaf shield bearing the Stars and Stripes, surmounted by a gold eagle holding two gold arrows.

Above the canopy, on the wall beneath the arch, is a well-known posthumous portrait of George Washington painted in 1823 by Rembrandt Peale. Our first President, dressed in black with a white jabot, is seen through a round stone window with a bearded mask on the keystone. It was one of several so-called porthole portraits executed by the artist, this one purchased by the Senate on the Washington centennial of 1832.

Surveying the chamber, we must remind ourselves that,

along with the old House chamber, it was one of the more elaborately decorated interiors, if not the most decorated, prior to the Civil War. This may come as a surprise to those who do not accord the Capitol an important place in the tapestry of American art. What is more, these interiors were not to be surpassed until the 1850s, with the coming of the new wings.

The chamber's great era, when it was "a lofty pulpit with a mighty sounding-board," began almost after the senators filed in 1819. The dominating subject for the next three decades would be slavery. The first attempt to resolve the issue was the Missouri Compromise of 1820, the question before the Senate being the admission of Missouri as a slave state. Henry Clay of Kentucky found the solution in the admission of Maine as a free state, and so began his career as "the Great Compromiser."

A decade later, the subject of debate was the raising of the tariff, which was flatly opposed by South Carolina. The state threatened to nullify it. While the tariff question did not involve slavery, differences over it underscored the growing division between the slave and free states. The two figures that stood out were John Calhoun of South Carolina, the champion of states' rights, and Daniel Webster of Massachusetts, who represented the national or federal position. As Calhoun was Vice President in Andrew Jackson's first administration, and therefore president of the Senate, he left the presentation of his side to Senator Robert Y. Hayne of South Carolina. Thus began the Webster-Hayne Debate in this room in December 1829, which continued into January 1830. The final rebuttal came from the "Godlike Webster" on the twenty-seventh. He closed with a heroic peroration, one that, for generations, has been enshrined in our schoolbooks:

When my eyes shall be turned to behold for the last time the sun in heaven, may I not see him shining on the broken and dishonored fragments of a once glorified Union; on states dissevered, discordant, belligerent; on a land rent with civil feuds, or drenched . . . in fraternal blood! Let their last . . . glance rather behold the gorgeous ensign of the republic . . . not a stripe erased or polluted, nor a single star obscured, bearing for its motto, no such miserable interrogatory as "What is all this worth?" nor those other words of delusion and folly, "Liberty first and Union afterwards"; but everywhere, spread all over in characters of living light, blazing on all its ample folds,

as they float over the sea and over the land, and in every wind under the whole heavens, that other sentiment, dear to every true American ear—Liberty and Union, now and forever, one and inseparable!

The result was decided by President Jackson. A low tariff law was passed, and South Carolina remained in the Union.

The same three statesmen—Calhoun, Clay, and Webster—were on hand again when the Compromise of 1850 was adopted. By then Calhoun was terminally ill; he was to die that year. Two years later, both Clay and Webster would be in their graves. Bitterness was everywhere, and as it turned out, the Compromise would delay but not prevent war. Again Webster, much to the disappointment of a number of his constituents, pleaded for the Union: "I wish to speak today, not as a Massachusetts man, nor as a Northern man, but as an American. . . . I speak today for the preservation of the Union. 'Hear me for my cause.'" It was the last great call before the bloody strife.

In so small a room, before a packed and hushed audience, Webster was awe-inspiring. We today must try to see the chamber solid with humanity, the robust orator all-powerful.

View of the Old Senate Chamber. (Day)

Baldachin with gold eagle over the chair of the president of the Senate. (Day)

The restored Old Senate Chamber, far more than the Old House Chamber converted to Statuary Hall, evokes the milestones of our now distant past. In those days the senators had no offices, nor staffs of clerks and assistants. Except when they could find space in some room in the building, such as the old Library of Congress west of the Great Rotunda, they did all their work at the small desks before us. When the great debates occurred, papers would be stuffed away, the place filled, and the chamber became Washington's center stage.

But the 1850s debates and compromises no longer sufficed. There was fighting in Kansas, "Bleeding Kansas," between proslavery and antislavery men. In the Capitol, language was no longer noble or restrained, former courtesies were vanishing. In May 1856 Senator Charles Sumner, who had taken Webster's place as senator from Massachusetts, denounced the proslavery forces with personal attacks against a South Carolina senator. Two days after his speech, "The Crime Against Kansas," a nephew of the senator's, Representative Preston S. Brooks, assaulted Sumner at his desk.

(Sumner's desk was in the back row, third south of the aisle.) It would only be a matter of time before the nation slipped into civil war.

Although not in the Senate at the time of the incident, one senator would gain fame as President of the Confederate States of America. In 1851 Jefferson Davis of Mississippi was one of the three members of the Senate Committee on Public Buildings that supervised the competition for the enlarged Capitol in which Thomas Ustick Walter participated. It was also Jefferson Davis who, as Secretary of War in Franklin Pierce's cabinet, would be in charge of the construction from 1853 to 1857.

After the senators left in 1859 for their new quarters, the chamber served the United States Supreme Court from 1860 until 1935, when the Court obtained its own building across First Street Northeast. The bench for the nine justices was set against the colonnade; the floor was flat with tables and chairs for counsel and desks for clerks similar to those in the Old Court Chamber below. The luminaries of the pre–Civil War years were never matched, but several stand

Portion of the semidome of the Old Senate Chamber.
Photo John Barrington Bayley.

Arabesque of acanthus, rosette, and anthemion on the ceiling
of the Old Senate Chamber. (Day)

out. One such was William Maxwell Evarts, who was to be Secretary of State under President Rutherford B. Hayes and, later, senator from New York. As early as 1860, he had risen in the bar to the extent of being called to represent New York State in the Lemmon slave case. (It involved the transportation of a slave from one slave state to another via New York.) Another figure was Elihu Root, who was to be Secretary of War under President William McKinley, Secretary of State under Theodore Roosevelt, and senator from New York.

More conspicuous were the justices, especially those of this century who were on the bench. Oliver Wendell Holmes, Jr., son of the author of *The Autocrat at the Breakfast-Table*, was there from 1902 to 1932. Louis Brandeis, a successful Boston lawyer, served from 1916 to 1939. William Howard Taft, the only President to serve on the Supreme Court, was not an associate justice but chief justice from 1921 to 1930. Possibly the most familiar, because of his splendid beard, was Charles Evans Hughes. He was associate justice from 1910 to 1916, abandoning the bench to run for President against Woodrow Wilson. He returned in 1930, oversaw the Court's removal to its present building, and resigned in 1941.

The outstanding cases before the Court chiefly addressed issues involving commerce and the extension of the power of the federal government, such as the application of the Sherman Antitrust Act of 1890, which resulted in the dissolution of the Standard Oil Company in 1911. Still, although a third arm of the government, it remained modest compared to the administrative and legislative arms. When Oliver Wendell Holmes joined the Court in 1902, the justices did not have offices; they did their work at home. Their library, which was housed in the Old Supreme Court Chamber, was inadequate. They had secretaries; their law clerks, recruited from the brightest among law students, were to come later. In fact, in organization it was not far removed from the Court of Chief Justice John Marshall.

By the time the Supreme Court obtained its own building in 1936, the humble days were in the past. Today the Court, like other government agencies, has its own office building, opened in 1991 just east of Union Station.

Before leaving the room, the visitor should not miss the cast-iron Corinthian columns upholding the balcony. They are an early example of the metal's use in the building, having been installed in 1828 by Bulfinch. To either side of the door is a curiosity: a pair of cast-iron stoves. Although they could not have provided much warmth, they are handsome objects. Painted black, they have bronze mounts, one with a ribbon bearing the legend "Novus Ordo Seculorum" (A New Order of the Ages [Is Born]), which appears on the great seal of the United States and on the reverse of every dollar bill. Each one is surmounted by an obelisk with a gold spread-winged eagle standing on a gold ball. The feet at the base are in the shape of lion paws.

On leaving the Old Senate Chamber, the tour goes back to the Small Senate Rotunda and descends the Old East Senate Stairway. Like the chamber, it is the work of Latrobe, a good example of giving monumentality to a small space: the north part with the upper landing square, the south curved to encompass the flight of steps. A nice touch is the architect's inclusion of a semidome over the curved portion.

At the foot of the stairs, the visitor is in the vestibule made famous by the columns with the "corncob capitals" and shafts of clustered cornstalks. We have seen ears of corn in the doorframes of the porticoes of the East Front, and we shall come upon more elsewhere in the building. These are, by far, the best known. Although called "corncob," they are really bunches of partially shucked ears. Designed by Latrobe as an "American Order," fully approved by Jefferson, carved in 1809 by Giuseppe Franzoni, they reflect somewhat more than a passing fancy of the architect's.[99] He was working in a style not wholly familiar to most of his countrymen; the acanthus, so abundantly present in the Capitol, is a Mediterranean plant. With corn, Latrobe was reaching out to the public with a plant familiar to all. Jefferson, beguiled by it, delighted in having a copy at Monticello, his famous residence near Charlottesville, Virginia.

Latrobe's famous corncob capital. (Day)

We can cite the comments of Thomas Ustick Walter, who, in his Capitol extension, was to have several special capitals of his own. "Many examples exist in our own country of columns and entablatures, which differ widely in their decorations from anything the ancients ever did," he wrote in 1841 when at work on Girard College.

Mr. Latrobe, for example, made an Order in the entrance of the Supreme Court Room in the Capitol in Washington which is often denominated the American Order, and if any modification of either the three grand divisions [Doric, Ionic, and Corinthian] of columnar architecture is entitled to the distinctive appellation as an Order, that undoubtedly is; the shaft of the column is ornamented with the representation of twenty-four stalks of Indian corn, instead of the ordinary flutes and fillets; and the capital has the form of an inverted bell surrounded with eight ears of corn, a portion of the grains of each ear being gracefully displayed between the open-

ing husks; the astragal between the shaft and the capital is made to represent a rope. But this Order, novel and ingenious as it is, can only be considered a modification of the Corinthian, having the same proportions, a bell-shaped capital, and foliated embellishments.[100]

Latrobe's capital has rarely been imitated, with examples being found only at the Litchfield Villa in Brooklyn's Prospect Park and in the Playmates Theater of the University of North Carolina at Chapel Hill, both by Alexander Jackson Davis. It may well be asked why there are so few like it. The simple reason would appear to be that their novelty and the association they called up were not enough. They are not as beautiful as the capitals of the traditional orders—the Doric, Ionic, and Corinthian—which are found throughout the building. For that reason the corncob, as ornament, was not adopted again, even in the 1900s when columned buildings were rising up on all sides in the decades that saw the United States become the great classical country of the world, at least in the realm of architecture.

From the vestibule the tour passes through a doorway to the north into the Old Supreme Court Chamber, restored in 1975 by the United States Senate Commission on Art and Antiquities. As might be expected, reflecting ancient Greece, it is by Latrobe.[101] We see a space, in plan a hemicycle, which has been carefully restored to what it was between 1810 and 1860, when it served our highest court. At the straight side, on the east side, there is the justices' bench. Behind it, supporting three wide arches, is a colonnade of six short Doric columns. The hemicycle ceiling is an "umbrella" vault—that is, cone-shaped with the wide ends locked in nine round arches and the narrow ends abutting the half circle of a semidome. The straight side of the semidome is attached to a wall pierced by the large arches springing from six Doric columns. These columns with fluted shafts were inspired by those of the Temple of Neptune (or Hera) at Paestum, which is south of Naples. Latrobe's source was probably plate 14 in chapter 6 of William Weaver's *Antiquities of Magna Graecia*, published in 1803.

Latrobe's skill is revealed in the unusual vaulting, vaulting made possible thanks to the assistance he received from skilled masons. We have the name of the master of them, George Blagden, an Englishman who began to work on the Capitol in 1794 and who was to die there in 1826 as the result of an accident.[102] We shall meet with him again when we come to the Crypt, where he worked for Charles Bulfinch.

At the back is a lunette—white relief on a blue ground—of Justice with scales and sword; an eagle guarding the law symbolized by books; and a winged male figure, topped by a sunburst, who is holding the Constitution in one hand and pointing to it with the other. Executed in plaster in 1817, it is by Carlo Franzoni. The relief obviously came after the fire that left the room so damaged that the vault had to be rebuilt. With its mahogany desks and brass lamps, plain ceiling and walls, we can imagine the black-robed justices seated here, properly sober-faced.

Just before entering the chamber, we passed the bust of Chief Justice Roger B. Taney, on the bench from 1836 to 1864. On March 6, 1857, Taney delivered the Court's decision on the *Dred Scott* case, one of the last of the key episodes leading to the Civil War. Augustus Saint-Gaudens, famous for

his equestrian statue of General William Tecumseh Sherman on New York's Fifth Avenue, did the bust around 1877. In the chamber are the busts of four other chief justices. They are John Jay, 1789–95, by John Frazee, America's first native-born sculptor; John Rutledge, 1795, by Alexander Galt; Oliver Ellsworth, 1796–1800, by Hezekiah Augur; and the best known of them, John Marshall, 1801–35, by Hiram Powers, the sculptor who did the handsome Benjamin Franklin to be seen on the second floor of the east staircase of the Senate wing. The Marshall bust, by the way, was done from life.

What strikes the visitor most is the room's small size. If there were acoustical problems with the Old House Chamber, the problems here were poor ventilation, dampness, and inadequate light. In fact, the bad ventilation and the dampness are believed to have shortened the lives of more than one justice. (Today no daylight enters the chamber because the present East Front is some 32 feet beyond the old one, as we became aware when examining the exterior.)

There is a display case with documents and other items on the famous cases that were heard here: *McCulloch v. Maryland,*

The bench side of the Old Supreme Court. (Day)

The semicircular part of the Old Supreme Court Chamber with its unusual vault. (Day)

Gibbon v. Ogden, Cohen v. Virginia, Brown v. Maryland, and *Ogden v. Saunders.*

We are reminded again of the Capitol's activities in those days; like the House and the Senate, the Supreme Court was part of what might be called the theater of Washington. Many senators and representatives were, like Daniel Webster, lawyers. It was nothing for them to appear before the Court and then dash upstairs to their respective chambers, that of the Senate, of course, being directly overhead. Webster was retained in no fewer than 170 cases tried here; in 1827, for example, he argued as many as 16 cases. No one matched him in his day, nor have any since.

Like the Old Senate and Old House chambers, the Old Supreme Court Chamber was a magnet, particularly when important cases were being argued. Here is a description of what the packed crowd saw when Webster was before the Court: "It is something to see him moved with anxiety and the toil of intellectual conflict; to see his lips tremble, his nostrils expand, the perspiration start upon his brow; to hear his voice vary with emotion, to watch the expression of laborious thought while he pauses, for minutes together, to consider his notes, and decide on the arrangement of his argument."[103] Such was the observation of one woman present. Among the great man's admirers, the ladies were in the

van. The courtroom would be packed for the famous lawyer, but once he stated his case, the crowd would leave.

Again, as with the Old Senate Chamber, the smallness of the room must have added to the drama. We have the same reward today if we have the good fortune to see a well-acted play in a small theater. In both instances, we are a long way away from the ubiquitous microphone and public-address system.

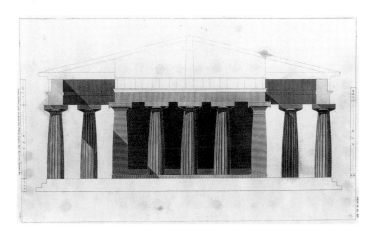

Latrobe's inspiration for the columns: those of the Temple of Neptune (or Hera) at Paestum. William Weaver, Antiquities of Magna Graecia *(London, 1803), chap. 6, plate 14. Courtesy New York Public Library. (Day)*

THE CRYPT

Perhaps with a final glance at the display cases on the Court's history, we follow the prescribed route for visitors by leaving through a second doorway to step onto the ground floor of the Small Senate Rotunda. A plaque on the wall tells us that it was from the old Supreme Court chamber that Samuel F. B. Morse in 1844 sent the famous message "What Hath God Wrought" to Baltimore, thus announcing the invention of the telegraph. Actually, the artist-inventor sent it from a nearby room.

Morse was one of the leading painters of the day, but, no different from artists of any era, he had a very hard time obtaining commissions. He was particularly bitter about not having been asked to execute a picture for the Great Rotunda. It was one of the reasons he abandoned his art to devote himself solely to inventing and to politics.

Here we stand in the circular arcade that supports the colonnade of the second floor. Through the oculus that we saw from above, we can make out the polychrome capitals and dome from another angle. With other visitors staring back at us, we can enjoy another diversion offered by the play of space in the Capitol. The ceiling ringing the arcade is a barrel vault of brick masonry with a plaster surface.

The Crypt. (Day)

The tour goes south to the Crypt, a room directly beneath the Great Rotunda. A crypt is defined as a chamber beneath the floor of a church to receive tombs; this one is actually above a small room built to house Washington's tomb. His body, as it happened, was not to come to the Capitol because his descendants, abiding by his wishes, kept it at Mount Vernon, where it remains. Above the small room was to be a statue of our first President at the Crypt's center, and overhead, an oculus was made to allow those in the Great Rotunda to look down at it. The oculus was subsequently filled because John Trumbull, in the 1820s, pointed out that the damp air rising from the Crypt was damaging his historic canvases.

The small room below contains the simple black catafalque on which Lincoln's body rested in the Great Rotunda in April 1865. The catafalque still serves to receive the bodies of those lying in state in the Rotunda. (On occasion the room can be seen on guided tours.)

This solemn round chamber in which we stand, where ornament is at a minimum, is divided by two rows of Greek Doric columns: an inner circle of eight single ones and an outer of sixteen, all made of Aquia Creek sandstone. The capitals consist only of an abacus, a flattened echinus, and a necking of acanthus leaves, the only enrichment in the room. The columns are similar to those in the Supreme Court Chamber, but the shafts have no fluting. Like those columns, these were inspired by the ones of the Temple of Hera in Paestum.

The Crypt was designed by Charles Bulfinch, Latrobe's successor, and its construction fell to George Blagden, the master craftsman who had worked with Latrobe in the Supreme Court Chamber. What is extraordinary about the room is not the columns or its shape, although that is unusual, but the ceiling. What gives this ceiling a special place in American architecture, and not just in the Capitol, is that it offers a most elaborate example of vaulting, even more striking than that of the Supreme Court Chamber. It is a reminder of the importance of masonry vaulting prior to the coming of the cast-iron and, later, the steel beam. Masonry vaulting, despite the cost, had distinct advantages over a wood-beam ceiling: It was fireproof and it was permanent.

The vaults rest on what are called entablature blocks on top of the columns. At the center, the visitor stands beneath a vault in the shape of a stilted dome—that is, a dome raised vertically at the edges as if on stilts. Girdling it, between the ring of single and double columns, is a series of groined vaults—a series repeated between the double columns and the circular wall. The vaulting plan shows how intricate it is and what obvious skill was required of the mason. Not only is there elaborate intersecting of the groining but also the vaults change shape. For example, on the inner portion, at right angles to the columns, the vault is elliptical. But with the outer ring, the part next to the wall becomes round. Admittedly, it is so skillfully done that the visitor hardly notices the form.

The innermost abacus with its curved side. (Day)

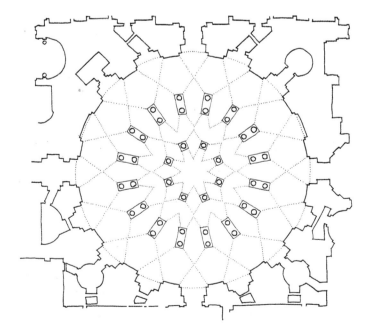

Outline of the vaulting of the Crypt showing the pattern of the groins. Drawing by Stephen Piersanti.

Octagonal room directly south of the Crypt. (Day)

Yet, on examination, the abstract pattern of the ceiling is pleasing in its intricacy. This is true although there is no recourse to ornament. When we stand near the wall and look to the center, we discover perspectives between columns, particularly those starting at one of the four main doors. We are intrigued by the changing shapes of the arching and the presence of groining.

Another touch, and an indication of Bulfinch's attention to detail, is found at the abacus of an inner entablature block. The curious can see that the inner side of the abacus is concave, conforming to the inner circle beneath the stilted dome, while the outer side of the abacus is convex, aligning with the outer side of the inner colonnade.

As we shall see, vaulting so effectively achieved here by Latrobe and Bulfinch was undertaken with equal skill by Walter. In his case, we shall encounter the plain and the enriched, just part of the range of treatment to be found in the Capitol.

The most spectacular object in the room is of a kind not often seen at close hand. It is one of the original capitals of Aquia Creek sandstone that were part of the original center portico. From the layers of paint and the fact that one volute has to be held in place by wire, we can understand why a new porch was needed, and of marble far more durable than sandstone. It should be compared to the reproduction of the plate from Sir William Chambers's *Treatise on the Decorative Part of Civil Architecture* reproduced in Chapter 3, "The East Front." Beneath it is a base of the column. Studying both, we can now understand why Walter was determined to design a new capital for his two porticoes. His displays a deeper serration, a crisper outline of the leaves, thus achieving a stronger contrast of light and shadow. Also, he gave his a bolder volute by using a screw of Archimedes.

The Crypt offers a changing exhibition devoted to the Capitol. It is most compelling, but it should be reserved for study after an exploration of the building. Not every display is to be found in the cases; the drawings and designs to be seen on the walls should not be overlooked.

Besides the Corinthian capital, there are several other permanent objects installed. One is a small Ionic temple of wood dedicated to the Medal of Honor, the nation's highest military decoration for bravery. Near it, in a wall niche, is a large clock that was, at one time, in the chamber of the House. With a case whose design is credited to Walter and Meigs, it is topped by a bronze eagle by Guido Bottin, and to either side are bronze figures of an Indian and a pioneer by William Henry Rinehart, who executed the bronze doors of the House and Senate wings designed by Crawford.

To leave the Crypt, the tour goes out by the south door to an octagonal room that is beneath the Small House Rotunda. The ceiling has an octapartite (eight-part) vault with ribs covering the groining. Directly east is the Old House stairwall, which is wholly different from that of the Old Senate wing. In plan it has three straight sides with the fourth curved to hold the stairs. In the square part are pairs of columns in shallow niches on two sides and forming part of an opening on the third. We have seen these last on the way to the Old House Chamber; they were the ones with the simple capital of palm leaf, pod, and acanthus. Overhead, the dome consists of panels radiating from an oculus, while over the stairs is a semidome with vaulting in the shape of a scallop shell.

Opposite the foot of the stairs are the leaves of the Amateis bronze door, executed in 1910 by Louis Amateis. On the theme of "the intellectual and physical progress of the country, or the Apotheosis of America," they were intended for a doorway in a new West Front, never built. After a peripatetic journey, they were placed here in 1972. In execution they are a total contrast to the bronze doors of the East Front. The style is realist, and it can be easily made out that the bronze replicates the rough clay in which the sculptor modeled the figures and ground.

The route goes east to a small room with a groined vault overhead and a semidome at one end. At the north end is a bust of Lincoln, 1908, by Gutzon Borglum, famous for his huge presidential portraits at Mount Rushmore, South Dakota.

Of particular interest is a nearby plaque listing the Northern regiments from Massachusetts, New York, and Pennsylvania, which were briefly quartered, in the building during the Civil War.

We can gather what the Capitol was like in the spring of 1861 when it was converted into barracks. Here is Thomas Walter describing the setting to his wife in May 1861:

There are 4,000 [troops] in the Capitol, with all their provision, ammunition and baggage, and the smell is awful—The building is like a grand water closet—every hole and corner is defiled—one of the Capitol police says there are cart loads of —— in the dark corners; Mr. Denham says in one of the water closet rooms where he made an attempt to step in, some 200 must have used the floor. The stench is so terrible I have refused to take my office into the building. It is sad to see the defacement of the building everywhere.[104]

The stairwell of the Old House with the scallop-edged semidome. (Day)

THE BRUMIDI CORRIDORS

Up to this point, the tour of exploration has been through the old building. We should come away with a clear understanding of what the Capitol was like up until the 1850s. Now the route proceeds north from the Crypt to the new Senate wing, part of the Capitol extension. It is the floor that signals the change from the old to the new. Where we were walking on Seneca sandstone in the old part, we step on polychrome tile as we enter the Senate Connecting Corridor, which, with Daniel Webster's encouragement, Thomas Ustick Walter designed to serve as a link between the old and the new.

The flooring, known as Minton encaustic tile, is very much a product of the nineteenth century. It came into fashion in the 1840s, and this particular variety was made by Minton, Hollins and Company of Stoke-on-Trent, England. It is the flooring in the houses of Parliament in London, restored in the 1840s after a bad fire. Once common in this country, it is even found in the Terrace overlooking the Lake in New York's Central Park and is still to be seen in the New York State Capitol in Albany. Between 1856 and 1860 Captain Meigs, in charge of the Capitol extension, ordered it in quantity through a New York firm. "Encaustic" defines the tile because it consists of several colored clays inlaid on a base of brick clay and then baked. It should be added that the New York importer Miller & Coats executed the design. It consists of a variety of classical ornament, such as the guilloche with rosette, Greek key, rosette in a hexagon, a textile-like pattern, and others. In some places, there is an arabesque of acanthus. On the whole, the tile has stood up well under the tramping of millions. The inevitable wear and tear, however, shows; but the worn tiles have been replaced by new ones made by H. & R. Johnson Tiles Ltd., heir to the old Minton company.

The windows on the corridor's west side look beyond a small court to the terrace and the Mall. The conspicuous accents on the Mall's north side are the domes of the National Gallery of Art and the Natural History Museum, with the Washington Monument in the distance. We can appreciate, as we could on the second floor of the House Connecting

A favorite subject of Brumidi's, this time in bronze, on the railing of the Brumidi Stairway. (Day)

Corridor, how narrow are the "hyphens" linking the old and the new at the Capitol. Prior to the 1960 extension of the East Front, the visitor could look out with equal ease to the east. Now the windows are blocked by the Senate Dining Room.

Being familiar by now with vaulting in the building, we can easily recognize it overhead. It consists of groined vaults set in rectangular spaces between arches. The wide sides of the vault fit into round arches over the corridor, while the narrow ends over the windows fit into elliptical arches. It is a pattern frequently repeated. As at the Crypt, this is brick masonry vault covered with plaster.

On leaving the connecting corridor, we enter several small square halls with groined vaults with this difference: They have painted decoration. The decorative aspect of the vault is now underscored. Much of the variety of ornament found in the Minton tile is repeated on the ceiling, such as the rinceaux, guilloches, and stars. Four lunettes beneath one set of four sets of panels have a version of the famous eagle and wreath from the Forum of the Emperor Trajan in Rome. (It is now on the porch wall of the Church of the Apostles in Rome.) Known as Trajan's eagle, it can be seen on many American buildings of the first decades of the twentieth century. It served as model for the "Ruptured Duck," the discharge button of those who served in World War II. As with the original, the head is thrust through a bay-leaf wreath; however, unlike its model, this one holds arrows in its claws. Beneath the vaulting on the east and west sides are lunettes with trophies of arms and flags to either side of a shield. They were executed in fresco a secco—that is, tempera on dry plaster, tempera consisting of pigments mixed with a glutinous substance and water.

Off a second small hall, with another groined vault, is the Refectory of the Senate, an oasis for the hungry or thirsty visitor.

One more small hall, with little decoration, is bisected by an east-west corridor. At this point, we turn left (west) into another spare setting. Simply painted, the hall's decoration is confined to four round panels, one of which depicts lynxes

*Trajan's eagle on a vault in the corridor leading
to the main Brumidi Corridor. (Day)*

*A pair of lynxes about to devour a rabbit.
(Day)*

*Pomona and Vulcan in the panel of the west wall of the
west north-south corridor next to Room s-129. (Day)*

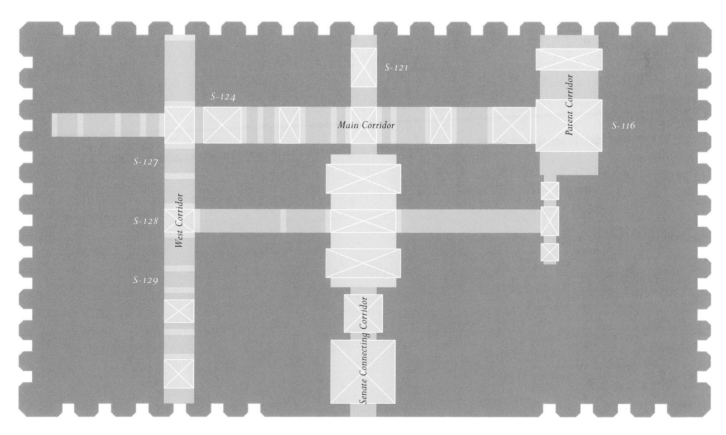

*Pattern of the groins (blue) and the arches (beige) in the Brumidi Corridors.
Based on the drawing by Cunningham-Adams. Courtesy Architect of the Capitol.*

Arch in the main Brumidi Corridor near the north entrance to the Senate wing. (Day)

about to devour a rabbit. We must assume that we are in a corridor featuring the plain colors Thomas Walter deemed best for spaces without daylight.

At the West Corridor (north-south), we are not permitted in the south section. At least we can see the white Carrara marble of the West Senate Staircase and the lunettes executed by Constantino Brumidi toward the end of his life: *Authority Consults the Written Law*, *Columbus and the Indian Maiden*, *Bartolomeo de La Casas, the Apostle of the Indians*, and *Bellona, the Roman Goddess of War*. We are now in the corridors for which Brumidi, if he did not execute the decoration, made the required sketches and certainly supervised the project. His work here, as with *The Apotheosis of Washington* and the frieze in the Great Rotunda, conveys the extent of his labors in the Capitol.

(South of Room s-129 in the west wall, we can make out two panels, an upper one with two figures standing on a tripod: Pomona, goddess of the harvest, with a cornucopia of flowers; and Vulcan, god of fire and metalworking, with a hammer. These figures were seen in the panel *Agriculture*, in *The Apotheosis of Washington*.)

On turning north (right), we stop at the door to Room s-127, the main room of the Senate Appropriations Committee. On occasion the door is open, allowing the room to be seen through a second glass door. (For a description, turn to the section of the book entitled "Closed to the Public.") To the left of the door is the first of the vertical panels that we shall examine in detail. Like all the Brumidi Corridors, it was designed by the artist and executed, under his supervision, by assistants. (Bear in mind that not all the animals and flowers depicted on these and other panels to be discussed are identifiable.)

LEFT OF S-127 [105]

T o p

(left)		(right)
	ruby-throated hummingbird	
Anna's hummingbird		*yellowthroat*
scarlet tanager		*lazuli bunting*
	butterfly	
eastern bluebird		*yellow-rumped warbler*
bird		*prothonotary warbler*
angel wings (butterfly)		*ruby-crowned kinglets*
	snail	
eastern bluebird		*black-headed grosbeak*
	cicada	
sulphur butterfly		*painted bunting*
ruby-throated hummingbird		*bird*
cabbage butterfly	*snake*	*swift*
	bird	

(20 birds altogether)

B o t t o m

OPPOSITE PANEL ON EAST WALL

T o p

(left)		(right)
bird		*bird*
yellow warbler		*horned lark*
bird		*vermilion flycatcher*
cardinal		*Anna's hummingbird*
bird		*bird*
ruby-throated hummingbird		*yellowthroat*
female blue grosbeak		*male blue grosbeak*
cicada		*buckeye butterfly*
	painted bunting	
purple finch		*painted bunting*
		dark-eyed junco

B o t t o m

At this point, what is quite overwhelming is the abundance of the decoration, the sheer opulence of it. The mural work is hardly confined to the walls; it is overhead. At Room

Barrel vault at Room s-127. (Day)

Barrel vault in the north arm of the West Corridor. (Day)

s-127, for example, there is an elaborate barrel vault, with rinceaux of acanthus, fans, bunches of flowers, more acanthus in a variety of shapes, and winged figures. These last are not so much cherubs as boys sprouting from acanthus leaves.

We cross the main Brumidi Corridor to enter the north arm of the West Corridor. Above the walls with the portraits of Robert Morris of Pennsylvania (west) and Charles Carroll of Maryland (east) is another barrel vault with two landscapes in ovals. Here, in addition to sixteen winged cherubs, are signs of the zodiac (painted by Brumidi in 1860), birds, and two heads of Indians. On the walls, the birds have not been overlooked; hummingbirds are on one panel to the west. (The murals here were restored by Cliff Young, ca. 1980.)

At the entrance to the main Brumidi Corridor, we have panels, again to the right and to the left, with more birds. These, like many of the long vertical panels, have designs that stem from those of Raphael in the Loggie di Raffaello in the Vatican. Brumidi, who had worked in the Papal Palace, was familiar with them. To see how closely he followed the sixteenth-century master, we offer an eighteenth-century engraving of several of his panels. Raphael included a few birds and ani-

mals, whereas Brumidi had them in quantity, finding them in native species. Interestingly enough, Brumidi left the fauna to be painted by James Leslie, his English-trained associate, much as Raphael had the fauna executed by Giovanni da Udine. Leslie found his models among the stuffed specimens in the Smithsonian Institution. The birdwatcher and ornithologist may be disappointed in Leslie's lack of absolute accuracy, but we must not forget that he was decorating walls, not executing scientific illustrations.

What sets these panels apart is the basic pattern of acanthus, tendril, ribbon, urn with flowers, and other objects, with the fauna being an added touch. The depiction of animals, as well, was suggested by ancient Roman examples in both Raphael's and da Udine's cases by the decoration of the Golden House of Nero, which had been discovered in the early sixteenth century. (A good example of an ancient Roman relief with rinceaux and animals is one embedded in the garden front of the Villa Medici, seat of the French Academy in Rome. In the Metropolitan Museum of Art in New York those interested will find a pilaster of ancient Roman origin where, in addition to floral rinceaux are birds and cherubs.)

Ruby-crowned kinglets, black-headed grosbeaks, an angel-wing butterfly, and a cicada on panel to the left of Room s-127, the west wall of the North-South corridor. (Day)

Drawing of an ancient Roman panel set in the garden facade of the Villa Medici, seat of the French Academy in Rome. Drawing by Pierce Rice.

Wall panel from one of the Raphael loggias in the Vatican. Engraved by Volpato. Courtesy Bibliothèque Nationale.

Pairs of great blue herons at southeast corner of the West North-South Brumidi Corridor and the main Brumidi Corridor. (Day)

A pair of motmots with racket tails beneath portrait of General Joseph Warren. (Day)

Panel on the south wall of the main Brumidi Corridor. Above a cluster of acanthus leaves, the viewer can make out a tortoiseshell butterfly, a field mouse, a lizard, and a weasel. (Day)

The bronze appliqué of a cherub framed by acanthus leaves. Here the symbols of Western art are joined by Brumidi. On occasion exhibited in the Crypt. (Day)

Pair of cherubs at the top of panel on the north side of the main Brumidi Corridor where it joins the West Brumidi Corridor. (Day)

A pair of little blue herons on the underside of the same arch. (Day)

A side panel of the door of Room s-116. (Day)

A canephore, a maiden who, carrying a basket of flowers on her head, was an attendant at ancient ceremonies. Here on the underside of the arch. (Day)

Beyond the long panel are several short ones, directly to the left of the door to Room s-124. The lower panel has a whippoorwill and, above it, a song sparrow.

Next, on the right, is the West Brumidi Stairway, one of four in the building (two in the Senate wing and two in the House wing). With the approval of Walter, Brumidi executed the design, which was modeled in Philadelphia by Edmond Baudin, French-born and French-trained, and cast in bronze by Archer, Warner, Miskey & Company in Philadelphia in 1858. The design consists of a continuous rinceau of acanthus, flower, tendril, and vine leaf placed between upper and lower guilloches with stars. Mixed with the traditional detail, as in the corridor panels, are animals, those here being eagles, stags, squirrels, pigeons feeding their young, snakes and lizards, along with hydrangea, hibiscus, magnolia, cattails, and bunches of grapes. And, of course, there are the cherubs that are always so much a part of Brumidi's designs.

The cherub here is a reminder that we first met with it in *The Apotheosis of Washington* and the horizontal panel of the fireplace in the Old House Chamber. We see cherubs again, painted, in the nearby panels, and here they are in bronze, along with acanthus. Such babies, in whatever form, "are the purest artistic devices, in the absence of any narrative role, as much a symbol of the West as the acanthus leaf," stipulates the artist Pierce Rice in his *Man as Hero: The Human Figure in Western Art*. "More, in the absence of any such phenomenon in actuality [where do babies float on clouds? where do they have wings? where do they grow out of acanthus leaves?], the depiction of the winged infant requires of the artist creative rather than transcriptive abilities," Rice continues. "Unlike their human counterparts, barely able to support themselves on the railing of their playpens, the babies of Western decoration are in full command of their activity, yet not in the least earthbound. The model is in art itself, and the conditions dictated epitomize the essential nature of pictorial invention."[106] (A sample of Brumidi's work is a nearby picture of a cherub between acanthus leaves, illustrating perfectly the symbols of Western art.)

At either side of the foot of the stairway are more panels with birds and animals mixed with ancient masks. On the left are a vermilion flycatcher, yellow warbler, gray squirrel, horned lark, and weasel, and on the right a chipmunk, weasel, and cardinal can be identified.

View east in the main Brumidi Corridor. (Day)

OPEN TO THE PUBLIC

It is obvious why Brumidi is so honored here. He was the designer not just of the stair railing but also of the wall and ceiling decoration. Of course, he was not alone. We have mentioned James Leslie, who did both designing and painting. There was also a separate crew of decorators under Emerich A. Carstens. Names of some of the staff of painters are known to us: Joseph Rakemann, Albert Peruchi, Ludwig Odense, George Strieby, Jr., and B. B. Bergman. (Bergman was to assist Brumidi at the Church of St. Aloysius Gonzaga on North Capitol Street.) What is of particular interest is that, like the draftsmen in Walter's office, many were of German origin, "forty-eighters," refugees from the political suppression after the revolution of 1848.

As we go east, we pass panels with portraits in profile of Revolutionary War heroes painted to resemble carving, a form of cameo. Beneath the portrait of General Joseph Warren is a pair of motmots with racket tails. The bird is native to Central America, although it is sometimes found as far north as the Mexican border of the United States.

Between the security gate and the north entrance is a short barrel vault painted in tempera by Emerich A. Carstens. As it was cleaned recently, it gives us a good idea of what some of the mural work looked like when new.

Nearby, at the crossing of the two corridors, there is an arch over the east arm of the main Brumidi Corridor. On it are two female figures bearing baskets on their heads; they are

In the Patent Corridor looking south and west along the main Brumidi Corridor. (Day)

supports each volute, and the roset [*sic;* by which he means the fleuron] is a magnolia, modelled on nature."[108] Washingtonians and Southerners will easily recognize the flower. The corn leaf and the tobacco leaf are also to be seen.

The visitor may wonder why Walter devised this variation on the Corinthian. Only a few feet away, just outside the entrance, is the Senate portico with a traditional Corinthian order for which he offered so cogent a justification (*see* "The East Front," page 51). Of course, with the portico order he had to follow the precedent set by the Thornton / Latrobe / Bulfinch capital at the center porch. A markedly different design would have been out of place.

Much as we admire, in our time, originality, we tend to forget that the primary aim of the artist is to create beauty, as Walter made clear, not to be different for the sake of being different. A great designer, in working close to tradition, hardly considers his talent restricted as opposed to "free" when producing variations, no matter how elaborate. In the example of the capital before us with its tobacco leaf, corn leaf, and magnolia flower, he was only thinking in terms of producing a pleasing object, to be sure an unusual one.

A question of appropriateness enters architecture with the importance of place. The portico is far more important than this short corridor in scale, position, and purpose. To repeat the portico order here would be, in its way, demeaning; Walter felt a new one was needed for the corridor as a minor, rather than a major, accent.

This interpretation is underscored by the Corinthian capital of the Senate Retiring Room, also known as the Marble Room (*see* "Other Rooms Closed to the Public," page 165). The Retiring Room order resembles that of the portico because it reflects the importance of the Senate and, therefore, in matters of decoration, is placed in the higher echelon of the hierarchy.

We shall see another of Walter's special capitals in the Hall of Columns in the House wing.

For all the presence of the native plants, the capital here is rarely noticed, even in the surveys where Latrobe's "corn-cob" capitals are discussed. But, then, the Corinthian of the Senate portico goes unobserved, although it is one of the most beautiful in the country.

Despite Walter's stricture that interior columns should be nonfluted shafts, these shafts are fluted. The explanation is that there is plenty of light in the hall, making for pleasing shadows.

The marble ceiling consists of deep sunken panels of Lee, Massachusetts, marble with egg-and-dart enrichment in the coffers. Three of the coffers have, instead of marble, stained glass.

At one end of the elevator lobby is a high doorway of cast iron

Opposite: The Senate Reception Room looking south. Every surface is decorated. Courtesy Architect of the Capitol.

The saucer-dome ceiling in the Senate Reception Room designed by Brumidi. (Day)

Seven cherubs floating in the center of the saucer dome. Painted by Brumidi. (Day)

with a door whose leaves are of satinwood. It opens onto a tiny vestibule off the floor of the Senate Chamber. The vestibule ceiling is a curiosity. White balls of varying size are set in V-shaped patterns with the V-point meeting at the center. The style? Authorities have suggested a variety of Gothic, the only example of its kind in the building. A chandelier is suspended from a cluster of acanthus. (It is visible only when the door is open.) The wall to either side is in scagliola, a mixture of gypsum, glue, and color and, then, polished to resemble marble.

At the other end of the lobby is the door to the Senate portico that we examined from the exterior.

Another bust nearby is that of Richard Milhous Nixon by Gualberto Rocchi. Vice President from 1953 to 1961 in both Eisenhower administrations, Nixon became President in his

Power, a pendentive by Brumidi in the Senate Reception Room.
(Day)

*Photograph of Michelangelo's Sybil in the Sistine Chapel.
Courtesy New York Public Library.*

America, Patron of the Arts and Sciences, *east panel
in rectangular vault. (Day)*

own right from 1969 until he resigned from office in 1974.

Continuing north, the visitor steps into the Senate Reception Room (S-213), one of the most elaborate of the Capitol's public rooms. What is fascinating about its design are the pains taken by both Walter and Meigs to achieve the sheer abundance of ornament, with most of the credit going to the captain. Moreover, it is disposed symmetrically by Walter, not easy given the presence of so many doors. We are once again reminded of Edith Wharton and Ogden Codman, Jr.'s apotheosis that symmetry is the "sanity of decoration."

Let us examine how Walter went about achieving the symmetry. He began by dividing the room's rectangular plan into two parts, the larger one to the south being a square and the smaller to the north being an east-west triangle at right angles to the room plan. The first is identified by a saucer dome adorned with octagonal coffers, set in three narrowing circles, with tobacco-leaf rosettes alternating with those of acanthus. At the top, in the middle, is a round fresco of seven babies romping with cloth swags on clouds.

Beneath the saucer dome, at the four corners, are four pendentives, also in fresco, filled with symbolic figures. In the southeast triangle, we see Jurisprudence holding a book in her left hand and the rod of authority in her right. She is accompanied by one winged cherub with a pair of scales and another with a bay-leaf wreath. In the southwest triangle, Prudence accepts reins and a bridle from a winged cherub, while to her right is a cherubic pair, one pouring water from a ewer into a jug held by the other. Prudence has a frond in her right hand. Power, a maiden with a lion-skin headdress and a club (both the trappings of Hercules) is in the northwest pendentive. She is shown with two cherubs, one holding a wreath and the other carrying an ax bound in rods on his shoulder. The fourth and last, to the northeast, Wisdom holds a mirror in her left hand with the help of a cherub. Two other cherubs are on her right, one with a snake, wisdom's symbol.

In the game of counting cherubs, there are ten, nonwinged, in the ceiling with two in two of the pendentives and three in the other two, all winged.

The monumental treatment of the symbolic figures is solidly in the grand tradition. Michelangelo's Sibyls in the Sistine Chapel ceiling were probably the most important of the influences reflected in the positions of the figures. As for the cherubs and the handling of cloth, Brumidi learned his lessons well at the Accademia di San Luca, which offered special instruction in both subjects.

Between the pendentives are three lunettes where the decorative panels are in a different key. Maidens with cherubs playing with garlands are depicted in grisaille in imitation of sculpture against red drapery. The lunettes remain unfinished, as we can tell from the empty spaces, such as the rounds that were evidently reserved for busts or portrait reliefs, as seen in the Brumidi Corridor. The decorative portions were done

Washington, Jefferson, and Hamilton in a panel surrounded by decoration. (Day)

Female figures and cherubs frame empty panels. (Day)

in the late 1850s, while the one figure panel, in the south lunette, was done in 1870–73. George Washington and Thomas Jefferson are shown seated with Alexander Hamilton standing.

The number of cherubs is fourteen, which, added to the seventeen in the dome and the pendentives, makes for a total of thirty-one.

Beneath the lunettes are five wall panels enriched with gilt relief. They are the work of Ernest Thomas, a Frenchman from New York, who, on being commissioned, was commanded by Captain Meigs to do his best. Thomas, as a result of his work here, was in charge of modeling most of the plaster ornament in the extensions. At the center of each panel is a portrait of a Senate worthy, done in 1959: John C. Calhoun by Arthur Conrad, Henry Clay by Allyn Cox, Daniel Webster by Adrian Lamb, Robert M. La Follette by Charles La Follette, and Robert A. Taft by Deane Keller.

The second, rectangular part of the room has a groined vault for ceiling. Each of its four parts has a panel with symbolic female figures and one to three babies. In the western one is a fierce "America at War" with a star-crowned helmet wielding a sword in her right hand and carrying a shield on her left arm. A cherub with a rod-bound ax sits astride an eagle. In the lower right corner, hard to make out, are soldiers.

"America at Peace" is the subject of the north panel. A seated America with a Phrygian cap cradles a rod-bound ax in her left hand, and from her right unfolds the Constitution. One cherub points to the document while a second grasps sprigs of laurel and olive. To her left, a third cherub with a United States shield has a ribbon inscribed "E Pluribus Unum," which an eagle holds in its beak.

The east panel presents a standing flower-crowned "America, Patron of the Arts and the Sciences," shown with paintbrushes and a triangle in one hand and a laurel branch in the other, while a nearby cherub holds a horn and another is about to throw a shield down on a pile of arms.

Industrial Arts, or *Industry and Agriculture*, has a seated veiled America in the south panel. She is holding, in her right hand, a cornucopia filled with a pineapple, wheat stalks, an ear of corn, and plums, while her left hand rests on a plow. Over the plow floats a cherub with a flowering tobacco plant. A second cherub has a left hand on the cornucopia, and in his right he holds a caduceus, symbol of commerce. Beside him is a woodburning locomotive with a cabbage stack.

Beneath *War* and the *Arts and Sciences* are two more lunettes similar to those beneath the saucer dome—that is, they are in grisaille with the same two female figures and the four cherubs. Altogether, there are sixteen cherubs in this part of the room.

The frames of the vault panels here have a greater variety of gilt relief. Ernest Thomas, foreman of plasterers, showed off his skill not just with floral swags, fruit-filled vases, eagles, and acanthus but also with stags. Similar enrichment is found in the thin vertical panels of the arch abutments.

Here, along with the fruit-filled vases and arabesques, are ears of corn and beards of wheat.

As we look at Brumidi's work in the Senate Reception Room, we can see that it was centered on the depiction of the traditional figure, not the realistic or naturalistic figure of the nineteenth century or, for that matter, of the twentieth century. The artist gives the body a generalized form that ennobles the human figure. Here is the explanation of the artist Pierce Rice in his *Man as Hero: The Human Figure in Western Art*:

> The quirks and accidents that animate actual appearance are nowhere to be found. We are offered, instead, a kind of synthesized view of nature. The continuity of the arm is emphasized, not its interruption by elbow and wrist. . . . The knuckles and the joints of the hand are subdued toward the same end. With the human head it is the rotundity that registers on us before individuality. But the limbs and heads themselves are subordinated to the unity of the body itself.
>
> The body, in short, has been so conceived as to bring it as close as possible to being a single form without sacrificing its human character. The result is a degree of grandeur of aspect far beyond anything we are provided by mere unassisted sight. The graphic loftiness, conveyed by means of the generalized contour, is the hallmark of the art of the West.
>
> Breadth of execution, then, is the indispensable ingredient, but the ennoblement of the human figure, of which this breadth of execution is the instrument, would be so much grandiloquence in the absence of appropriately heroic nominal themes.[109]

Here in these figurative panels of babies and adults we see the emphasis on the round and the elimination of the quirks. A glance at the profiles in two of the pendentives shows that Brumidi abided by the tradition that began with the female profile of the ancient Greeks and that, in the pendentive of *Power*, came to the artist by way of Michelangelo.

We come back to that symbol of Western art that Pierce Rice has called the baby. We have not counted all of them here, there being more of them in the hexagons between the arch abutments of the room, numbering twelve. Altogether, that makes fifty-nine cherubs in the Senate Reception Room. We smile at their abundant presence and delight in Brumidi's extraordinary talent in making them so much a part of the Capitol's decoration.

In concentrating on the decoration, we have forgotten that here, as elsewhere in the building, we are in a room with masonry vaulting covered with plaster. The alternative could be a vault solely of plaster and lathe suspended from beams by trusses, as on the second floor of the Jefferson Building of the Library of Congress—that is to say, a shell vault within a structural frame. Were we to go behind the plaster in this room, we would find bricks and mortar.

As for the plaster ornament, much of the work, being duplicated, can be obtained by the use of molds. For example, the rosettes in the dome coffers, like the coffers themselves, come in three basic sizes easily cast in molds.

A stag in stucco by Ernest Thomas. (Day)

Corn in relief on the wall. (Day)

Cherub with cornucopia on wall. (Day)

Female mask on the Minton tile on the floor. (Day)

The floor in Minton tile reflects, in part, the ceiling. Bead-and-reel, leaf-and-dart, ribbon, guilloche, diamond shape with leaf, basket weave, and rinceaux, along with female masks and dolphins, are part of the elaborate pattern.

The marble fireplace is by Walter, as are most of them in the extensions. Here oak leaves and acorns, acanthus-bound rods, and a cartouche of volutes and acanthus make up the detail. The mirror above is set in an elaborate gilt frame from which extends valances over the two windows.

The window embrasures, along with the doorframes, are of cast iron.

Other than the mural decoration and floor tiling, the elaborate ceiling and the mirror with valances, what sets the room apart from run-of-the-mill American architecture is the use of false doors to achieve symmetry and balance, which Wharton and Codman insisted were so important. For example, the door on the west side of the room's rectangular section is false; it is there simply to balance the door to Room s-128. At the east half of the south wall, the door and doorway also are false, serving to balance the doorway by which we entered the room.

One final accent is the two crystal chandeliers. They are the final contribution to the sustained opulence of the room, the most elaborate of those open to the public.

THE SENATE CHAMBER

Leaving the Senate Reception Room, we retrace our steps to the elevators or the East Grand Stairway. At the stairway, the visitor will notice that the balusters of dark Tennessee marble have the same conical design as those of Walter's roof balusters. Over the staircase, in the cast-iron ceiling, is a panel of stained glass (or daylight glass, meaning a ceiling window) backed by artificial light. The design with its varieties of acanthus leaves is by Brumidi and was executed by J. and G. H. Gibson and Company of Philadelphia.

At the third-floor landing is the *Recall of Columbus* by Augustus G. Heaton and two busts, one easily recognizable: that of Lincoln (1868) by Sarah Fisher Ames and the other of Senator Charles Sumner (1894) by Martin Milmore, both obviously posthumous.

In the elevator corridor nearby, the visitor should step to the nearby window, if that section is not closed to the public. Peering up through the windows to the capitals of the East Senate portico, it is possible to make out the following incised inscription on the side of a coffer:

THOMAS U. WALTER
ARCH^T F^t U.S. CAPITOL
(Ft = Fecit; trans. designed)

(Captain Meigs's name was on the cast-iron beams of the Senate and House roofs, but they were removed in the 1950s.

On this particular matter concerning recognition, the architect won out over the engineer.)

Actually, of greater interest is the Walter capital, which we can study here at close hand. (If this section of the hall is off limits to the public, the capitals of nearby columns can be seen from the corridor that links the Senate and the House wings, along the east side of this floor.) We are familiar with the attention given Latrobe's corncob and tobacco-leaf capitals in contrast to the neglect of Walter's magnolia and tobacco-leaf capitals on the second floor. But the triumph of his skill are these wonderful examples of the Corinthian in the traditional mode. In examining them from the outside, we learned of the architect's care in their design and his concern that they be carved by skilled craftsmen because he wanted them to be better than the Thornton/Latrobe/Bulfinch ones of the center portico.

The route goes back to the stairway landing and into the corridor that runs along the south flank of the wing. There is no mural decoration on the third floor. Here the ceiling consists of two saucer domes separated by three groined vaults. The presence of the saucer domes is a reminder that Walter had ample practice in designing them for the interior of Girard College. Polychromy is, as we might expect, in the Minton tile of the floor. There is one surprise, however, in this floor: winged cherubs, which we are accustomed to finding on walls and ceilings.

Compared to the Old Senate Chamber, this "new" one, opened in 1859, is much bigger. It is also much simpler in its decoration. This last is to be explained by the fact that it was rebuilt and redecorated in 1949–51 based on the designs of John Harbeson of Harbeson, Lough, Livingston & Larson of Philadelphia and Francis P. Sullivan of Washington.

From the south corridor we go to the south gallery, which faces the tribune of the president of the Senate, who, we must remind ourselves, is also Vice President of the United States. The one hundred mahogany desks for the one hundred senators, two to each state of the Union, are set in semicircles in descending levels and focused

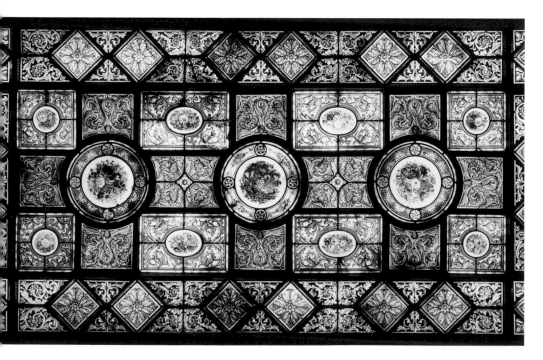

Stained glass ceiling of the Senate stairwell. Courtesy Architect of the Capitol.

"Thomas U. Walter" carved in a lintel of the Senate portico. (Day)

on the tribune. The walls of the lower part of the chamber are set off with Doric pilasters with shafts of red Levanto marble from Italy and capitals of cream Hauteville from France. At the doors in the center of three sides and at the two doors on the tribune are pairs of Greek Ionic columns of the same marble. The same columns are found behind the desk of the Senate president. Over three of the entries to the chamber are figurative panels of cream Hauteville, representing Courage (west), Patriotism (east), and Wisdom (south), by Lee Laurie and carved, respectively, by Bruno Mankowski, Louis Milione, and Edward H. Patti. Beneath the panels are the following inscriptions: "Novus Ordo Seculorum" (A New Order of the Ages [Is Born]) on the west; "Annuit Coeptis" (God Has Favored Our Undertakings) on the east; and on the south "In God We Trust." On the tribune or north side, the two entries have panels of clustered flags and other ornament, also in Hauteville marble.

The same marble, it should be added, can be seen at the entrance to the gallery and in the wainscot of the gallery wall. Above the wainscot, the walls are covered with golden damask. The parapet wall of the gallery is of Hauteville marble on the Senate side and of Alabama marble on the gallery seating side.

The sconces are worth a glance. They consist of an upright in the form of a cornucopia, or horn of plenty, with a light bowl at the top and a curved tail at the end from which spread wings.

Clearly visible from the visitors' gallery are the white marble busts of the Senate presidents set in bowl niches. Some are easily recognized, such as those of John Adams (1890) by Daniel Chester French and Thomas Jefferson (1889) by Sir Moses Ezekiel, both above the presidential tribune. Among the unfamiliar is the bust of Millard Fillmore (1895) by Robert Cushing on the east wall, second in from the south. As the visitor is well aware, Fillmore remains one of the least known of those Vice-Presidents who became President. Yet in the history of the Capitol, he looms large because he appointed Walter architect of the Capitol extension.

No likeness of Fillmore's successor, Franklin Pierce, exists in the Capitol, the reason being that he was never Vice President. However, he should be represented in the building because he was the one who transferred responsibility for the Capitol's expansion from the Interior to the War Department, where Jefferson Davis, as Secretary of War, placed Captain Montgomery Cunningham Meigs in charge of the Capitol construction.

Another bust tends to be overlooked. Its subject is in our history books because of one of the more singular incidents that occurred in this chamber: the attempt to impeach a President. Andrew Johnson of Tennessee has a bust here because he was Vice President in Lincoln's second term. On becoming President in 1865, he found himself opposing the so-called Radicals, the group of Republicans demanding strict reconstruction of the defeated South. At no point in its history, before or since, was the Congress as powerful as in this

Close-up of the Corinthian capital designed by Walter. (Day)

post–Civil War decade, and the Radical leader was a representative from Pennsylvania, Thaddeus Stevens.

It may be asked, if a member of the House was so important, why did the event occur in this chamber? Under the Constitution, a President facing impeachment has to be tried by a committee of the Senate with the chief justice of the Supreme Court (in this case, Salmon P. Chase) presiding. Thaddeus Stevens dominated the Senate Chamber as he did that of the House. We turn, not to an American, but to a French correspondent for a description of the representative from Lancaster, Pennsylvania, Georges Clemenceau. The future Prime Minister of the French Republic was in this country for several years, and he devoted part of his sojourn to filing stories for *Le Temps*, a leading Paris newspaper.[110]

Here is Clemenceau's description of Stevens, who was then very close to death in the spring of 1868 (he was to die that fall):

Mr. Stevens is carried in, his illness progressing rapidly, but his energies mounting still faster. Once in a while, a sardonic smile, like a grimace, flickers over his livid face. If it were not for the fire smoldering in the depth of his piercing eyes, one might imagine life had already fled from that inert body, but it still nurses all the wrath of Robespierre [the leader of the Jacobins in the Terror during the French Revolution].

What riveted the young Frenchman was Stevens's single-mindedness:

Devoted heart and soul to the service of one ideal, the immediate abolition of slavery, he threw his whole self with no reserve and no personal afterthoughts into the cause he had chosen. It must be admitted that Mr. Stevens stands out a man of only one idea, but that does not matter a whit, since he had the glory of defending that idea when it was trodden in the dust, and the joy of contributing largely to its triumph. That should be enough accomplishment for one man, when the cause to which he has devoted his life and soul is that of justice.[111]

It is hardly to be wondered at that Stevens continues to excite controversy. Again, his single-mindedness is exactly what appealed to Clemenceau. We can only speculate about whether memories of his visits to the chamber came to him in the Great War and after, when "the Tiger," as he was known, pursued his ends in the same way as the representative from Pennsylvania.

The move of the upper house to its new chamber and its expansion over the years to its present number of senators, one hundred, made for considerable change. Gone were the orators of the pre–Civil War years; the postwar senators stand out more as figures of power: Henry Cabot Lodge of Massachusetts, Elihu Root of New York, Robert M. La Follette of Wisconsin, Arthur H. Vandenburg of Michigan, and Robert Taft of Ohio. As for the more recent senators, we think of John F. Kennedy and Lyndon Baines Johnson.

The visitor will probably be disappointed to find only a partially filled or even nearly empty chamber when Congress is in session. Television has only underscored the fact that much of the work of legislative bodies has long been done in committee or by staff. Still, we are startled to be in the visitors' gallery and discover a single senator present reading a speech to an empty chamber. The senator does have an audience of his colleagues, but it is via television in nearby offices and, at times, on a nationwide channel. The drama has long since gone, except for an occasional close vote or an incident where a senator ordered by the Senate president to attend is carried bodily into the chamber by the staff of the sergeant-at-arms, and the nation laughs.

On leaving the Senate Chamber, security permitting, it is worth going west on the south corridor to windows overlooking a corner of the center building and the West Terrace. The visitor can see the pilasters of Thornton/Latrobe/Bulfinch and, turning sharply left, see the columns of Walter. It is simply another opportunity to compare different capitals at close range.

The Senate Chamber. Courtesy Architect of the Capitol.

THE HOUSE CHAMBER

The route doubles back to a long, narrow corridor, part of the 1960 extension, which goes south to the House Chamber.

The corridor windows that face east look out on the Walter colonnade, part of the link between the old center and the Senate wing. With plenty of light, it is the best place to study the architect's Corinthian capital. After a short turn in the corridor, the visitor finds, on the right, two windows giving on the Old Senate Chamber. The windows are repeated farther on, again on the right; only here they face Statuary Hall. After yet another bend in the corridor, windows on the left permit views of another of Walter's colonnades.

We are now in the corridor off the House Gallery. From the windows nearby, on the north, we can see both Walter's capitals and those of the Thornton/Latrobe/Bulfinch pilasters across the way. In the volutes of the latter are rosettes, absent from Walter's, and the relief of the acanthus leaves is flatter and the serration more repetitive than those of Walter, who varied them nicely. Also, the onlooker can see that the stone is Georgia marble of the type used in the 1960 extension.

At the west end of the corridor are more windows; here we have one of the great views of the Capitol. Looming above the beholder is the magnificent dome with its templed lantern and statue. Like the Great Rotunda beneath it, there is nothing in this country quite like this hemisphere. A special touch (a human note?) is the ladder climbing up the curving slope. In the chapter devoted to the dome, we pointed out the importance of size in the ornament here, especially the consoles. Seeing them at close range, we can grasp how important they are in Walter's design.

We can also examine the pilaster capital on Bulfinch's center of the West Front. As with those at the center of the East Front, their volutes have rosettes instead of scrolls, and here too the acanthus leaves are flat compared to those of Walter's capitals nearby. At the East Front, we noticed the different shape of the roof balusters. The ones here reflect the same differences: Bulfinch's have the customary bellies and sleeves, and Walter's, to the right, are cone-shaped.

The corridor is not too different from the one outside the Senate Gallery. Minton tile, as there, introduces a variety of color. On some tiles there are symbols. One, for example, is a Corinthian capital representing architecture, a harp representing music, a palette and brushes and a scroll representing painting and poetry, and, last, an anchor and a wheel rep-

View of Walter's Corinthian capital of the Senate wing portico from the corridor going to the House Chamber. (Day)

The best close view of the cupola, lantern (tholos), and the statue of Freedom. Here the visitor gains a notion of the size of the ornament around the oeils-de-boeuf, having the ladder to give scale. (Day)

THE HALL OF COLUMNS, THE HALL OF CAPITOLS,
THE GREAT EXPERIMENT HALL,
AND THE WESTWARD EXPANSION MURAL

It seems puzzling that the West Grand Stairway of the House wing shrinks to one narrow flight of steps to reach the first floor. It is a reminder, as with the stairs elsewhere at this level, that the Capitol's first floor is a ground floor, the second being the main one, the *piano nobile* of the Italian palace or the *bel étage* of the French town mansion.

At the foot of the stairs, the visitor stands in the short west corridor running north-south. On the barrel vault is the last of three mural decorations executed in recent decades in the House wing. Based on a general scheme by the late Allyn Cox and Cliff Young, it was executed in 1993 by Jeffrey Greene and the Evergreen Painting Studios. Known as "the Westward Expansion Mural," it consists of generously labeled maps showing the nation's growth from the Atlantic coast to Hawaii.[112]

At the north end, in a lunette beneath the vault, is a surprise: a portrait of Montgomery Cunningham Meigs, the army captain to whom, along with Thomas Ustick Walter, we Americans owe so much. (It may well be asked why this squeezed portrait of General Meigs is here pushed up against the vault. By rights he should be among those portraits of the artists and architects in the Hall of Capitols at the east end of the west-east hall known as the Great Experiment Hall. One comes away from this unfortunate portrait with the feeling that today's architects and architectural historians have avenged Meigs for the difficulties he made for Walter.)

At this point, the visitor should go directly to the center north-south corridor of the House wing, the Hall of Columns, the most monumental of the public halls in the Capitol. Fourteen pairs of columns with monolithic shafts of Massachusetts marble line the corridor. The shaft treatment consists of channels, or fluting, with the fluting stopped, which means that the channels are filled to a third of the shaft height. Much as he did on the second floor of the Senate wing, Walter attempted an original capital with thistle and tobacco leaves and included thistles on the molding of the nearby pilaster capital.[113]

Yet Walter, ever the traditionalist, did not diverge sharply from an ancient model: the capital of the Tower of Winds in Athens. He only substituted tobacco leaves for palm leaves and added the thistle. Note the absence of volutes.

The walls are not of marble but of scagliola, this time a café au lait and orange color given a breccia pattern. In identifying the material, the curious can see that it is warmer to the touch than marble and that, unlike marble, it has hair-thin irregular cracks, mostly vertical, scattered throughout. Scagli-

The Corinthian capital of the Hall of Columns. Walter modeled it on that of the Tower of Winds in Athens. See the plate from Stuart and Revett on page 92 (top).

ola was adopted on the orders of Captain Meigs, much to the annoyance of Walter, who protested. Walter maintained that marble would have cost less and would have been less fragile.

This is, in part, a technical question, but as the wall itself testifies, scagliola ("scag") stands up very well. What is more, even in Rome, a city blessed with all varieties of marble, scagliola is found on all sides. The disagreement over material is only one example of the conflicts that divided the army engineer and the architect.

There is no Minton tile on the floor here. Between 1920 and 1924 it was replaced by squares of Alabama white and black marble from Glens Falls, New York.

Overhead, the lintels and coffers are of cast iron, the metal Walter had made much use of in the colonnades of Girard

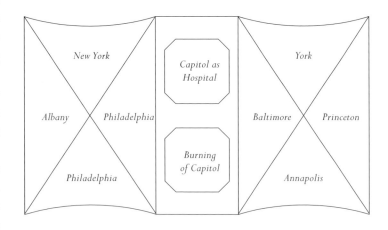

Plan of murals in the Hall of Capitols by Allyn Cox.

The Hall of Columns. (Day)

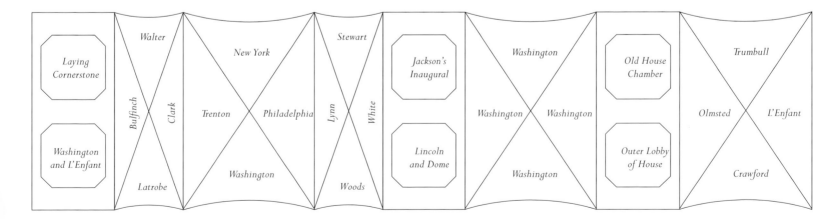

(Plan of murals continued)

Independence Hall, *a panel by Allyn Cox for the Hall of Capitols.*
Courtesy Architect of the Capitol.

College. The coffer enrichment consists of bands of acanthus, bead-and-reel, and egg-and-dart. Cast iron, now so familiar to us, frames the doorways.

Because Statuary Hall could hardly accommodate all the statues presented by the states, many were placed here. Standing between the columns, they do not jar as they do in Statuary Hall, where they crowd the beholder's vision. Here each has his or her bay, and as a result, they add to the quality of the hall without being overwhelming.

In a way, the Hall of Columns may be said to represent assertiveness on the part of the architect. Walter left no wall and ceiling space for the artist. As it turned out, Brumidi was to do no mural painting in the House wing corridors. In fact, he had only one commission, his first, in the

House wing, which is to be seen in H-144: that of the Subcommittee of the House Appropriations Committee.

It was left to a later generation to fill the nearby corridors with decoration. The United States Capitol Historical Society and the Daughters of the American Revolution conceived the project of a series of murals surveying the nation's history. To execute them they turned to Allyn Cox, the artist who completed the Brumidi Frieze in the Great Rotunda, and he was at work on them from 1969 to 1982.

They are in two corridors: the Hall of Capitols and the Great Experiment Hall. To reach the first, begun in 1973, the visitor goes via the main east-west corridor, the Great Experiment Hall. Once at the Hall of Capitols, the tour should start at the north end, where there is a portrait of Brumidi, in a lunette above a window, executed in grisaille. This is the same style of execution, an imitation of carved relief, which is found in the Brumidi Frieze. Cox's grisaille is very successful here because it resembles stone. The medium is not fresco—that is, water-based paint mixed with plaster—but oil paint on canvas.

What he depicted in this corridor were former capitols where Congress and its predecessors had met, alternating with portraits of the architects of the Capitol and others associated with the building.

Most of us will be surprised to see identified as the first

Rotunda During Civil War, 1862,
a panel by Allyn Cox in the Hall of Capitols.
Courtesy Architect of the Capitol.

View by Allyn Cox of the cast-iron Library of Congress formerly on the west side of the Capitol, designed by Thomas Ustick Walter.
Courtesy Architect of the Capitol.

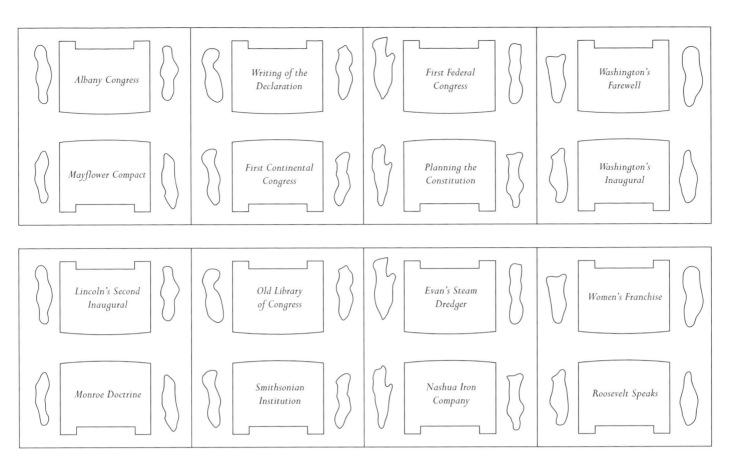

| Albany Congress | Writing of the Declaration | First Federal Congress | Washington's Farewell |
| Mayflower Compact | First Continental Congress | Planning the Constitution | Washington's Inaugural |

| Lincoln's Second Inaugural | Old Library of Congress | Evan's Steam Dredger | Women's Franchise |
| Monroe Doctrine | Smithsonian Institution | Nashua Iron Company | Roosevelt Speaks |

Diagram of the ceiling of the Great Experiment Hall. Courtesy Architect of the Capitol.

capitol the long-gone Stadt Huys of Albany, New York. Yet it was there, in 1754, that representatives from several colonies met to initiate a possible federation. At least we can recognize the building with the label "Philadelphia, 1775" as Independence Hall. Not until we come to the picture labeled "Washington, 1800" do we see the beginnings of the present Capitol.

Of the scenes showing the present Capitol, the most startling is *Rotunda During Civil War, 1862*. We have discussed elsewhere (*see* "The Crypt," page 108) what the building was like when the first Northern regiments briefly settled there in the spring of 1861. At that time, the Virginia front was still not far south of the Potomac, but a year later all had changed: the building was cleaned and hospital beds were everywhere, even around the scaffolding of the dome in the Great Rotunda. Here is Walter's description of the scene depicted in one of Cox's panels, dated 1862:

The excitement here is very great, and the presence of so many wounded greatly affects the sensibility of all who have any feeling—poor fellows, what they must suffer! They have taken the Capitol as a hospital, and the beds are now up in the rotunda, the old Hall of Rep's. and the passages—one thousand beds have been put up. It does not interfere with our work in the least, and I think the move is a good one."[114]

(Unfortunately, the comforting scene in Cox's picture was not to last. A month later, the architect reported in a different vein: "I have been compelled to move by the filth and stench and livestock in the Capitol—there are more than 1000 sick and wounded in the building and it has become intolerable especially in the upper rooms.")

At the south end are four portraits of those (other than architects) who had a part in the building's history. They are Major L'Enfant, who, in his plan for the Federal City, picked Jenkins Hill to be the Capitol site; John Trumbull, who painted the revolutionary war scenes in the Great Rotunda; Thomas Crawford, who modeled the statue of Freedom on the dome, and the bronze doors of the Senate and House wings; and, last, Frederick Law Olmsted, who laid out the Capitol grounds and devised the terrace that is such a prominent feature of the West Front. (The missing portrait is, of course, that of Montgomery Cunningham Meigs, which ended up in the corridor with the Westward Expansion Mural, noted above.

The Great Experiment Hall, running east-west, is along the route to be followed to get to the Hall of Capitols. Retracing his or her steps, the visitor can pause to see the different murals. One panel is of special interest, at the west half of the corridor; it depicts the former Library of Congress built by Walter after the 1851 fire. It was this work that broadcast the name and talent of the architect, confirming President Fillmore's wisdom in his choice of Walter.

We meet the Hall of Columns once again. The exploration of the public portions of the Capitol is over. We proceed to the south entrance to take a walk around the building.

We have underscored elsewhere the fact that the United States Capitol is a working building and not a museum. Visitors, however disappointed they may be, must accept this reality. They must take pride in the fact that the nation's greatest building is still consecrated to the purpose for which it was built: the business of government. They should also be proud to know that their representatives work in beautiful surroundings. The purpose of art, above all else, the French painter Dominique Ingres maintained, was the decoration of public buildings, and our own George De Forest Brush insisted that the artist's highest aim was the painting of "a noble subject on a wall."

If one were to seek a historic building where elected officials, admittedly of an oligarchy, once met in splendor, the supreme example would be the Doge's Palace in Venice, but it is a museum today. Two decorated legislative buildings remain, besides the United States Capitol, the Palace of Westminster in London and the Parliament Building of Hungary in Budapest. Captain Meigs never saw the Palace of Westminster before the Civil War, but he was familiar with its reconstruction after the fire of 1834. If there was any influence stemming from the rebuilding of the palace, it was its abundance of decoration. The Capitol would have decoration, too, but it would be in the building's style from the beginning, in the classical tradition. For this reason Meigs turned to the Italian Renaissance. He desired that the affairs of state be conducted in a setting that was the visual equivalent of the powers and responsibilities of the legislators. We as citizens can only rejoice that there was on hand an architect, Thomas Ustick Walter, and an artist, Constantino Brumidi, who were able to design and execute the required settings—with, of course, the captain as patron.

Nor let us overlook the fact that in the important decorated rooms and corridors—that is, those by Brumidi—there is little difference between the public and the nonpublic parts of the Capitol. Those desiring to study Brumidi's work, for example, have the Senate Reception Room and the Brumidi Corridors. As for Walter's special orders, the columns, like those of Latrobe, are in the public spaces. What we offer here, in discussing the rooms closed to the public, is simply an additional slice of the spectrum of the Capitol's decoration.

Center of Brumidi's ceiling in the President's Room with the four figures, counterclockwise from right: Liberty, Legislation, Authority, Religion. (Day)

THE SENATE COMMITTEE ON APPROPRIATIONS

Room S-127

Having said that there is little difference in the Brumidi decoration between the parts opened to the public and those closed to it, there is one important exception, namely, several of the rooms of the Senate Appropriation Committee, notably Room s-127. (At least when Congress is not in session, it can be seen through a partially glazed door from the West North-South Brumidi Corridor.) Designed in 1856 for the Committee on Naval Affairs, it was decorated in a classical manner wholly different from that of the neighboring corridors. Here Brumidi chose as model the mural work of Pompeii, the ancient resort near Naples that was buried in 79 A.D. by the eruption of Mount Vesuvius. Only a century before Brumidi was at work in the Capitol, it was discovered, and has been the object of continuing excavation and, we might add, of pilgrimage ever since.

Part of the buried city's fascination has been its abundance of fresco that, inevitably, came to inspire artist and architect. The influence was confined to the "Pompeiian rooms," and of these only a few were executed in this country, as in one New York mansion of a Vanderbilt. (Today "Pompeiian" walls are occasionally found in bathrooms of private residences.) Actually, Room s-127 is rare, the only example of such public work being seen at the Roman Villa of the J. Paul Getty Museum at Malibu, California. (The villa is a reproduction of a villa in Herculaneum near Pompeii. It was executed for Mr. Getty under the authority on Roman architecture, the late Dr. Norman Neuerburg.)

The room, rectangular in plan, is divided by an arch with a two-part ceiling made of groin vaults. Each quarter of a vault has nereids, or sea nymphs, riding sea goat, sea horse, dolphin, swan, triton, and turtle. Also in the vaults, in elaborate frames, are the figures of America and sea gods conveniently labeled Iolus, Amphitrite, Neptune, Nereus, Thetis,

Pisces, part of the zodiac that is depicted in Room s-127. (Day)

Oceanus, and Venus. Around the frames are eagles, United States shields, cornucopias, and winged cherubs wrapped in acanthus leaves. Of these last there are sixteen.

Four doors, one of them false, have figured overdoors, each with two winged cherubs rising from acanthus leaves. They bring the total baby count to twenty-four.

Decoration hardly stops with the ceiling. On the walls are floating female figures on a dark ground. They hold symbols of the sea, such as the sextant. One panel on the east wall has, in addition to the female figure, two cherubs, which brings the total of them in the room to twenty-six.

One particular distinction of the Pompeiian style of mural work is the use of architectural elements, such as columns. Unrestricted by structural conditions, the artist devised his own. They were usually with thin and fancifully enriched shafts. We see them on the ceiling to either side of the frame of the figurative panels. In the lunettes, they took the form of aedicules. In the only lunette completed—it is not by Brumidi and the rest were only partially done or left empty—there is a temple-like structure, like an open pavilion at the end of a garden. This fanciful architecture, like the floating figures on the walls, is the closest link to the interiors found in the buried city.

At the west end of the room, between the windows, is a fireplace with a high mirror in a handsome gold frame, consisting of half-engaged Ionic columns upholding an anthemion frieze. The fireplace, if not the mirror frame, was designed by Walter.

The ceiling, by the way, is in distemper and fresco, as are the walls. (Brumidi's beautiful sketch for the room is occasionally on exhibit in the Crypt.) As for the handsome chandeliers, they, like most of the crystal chandeliers in the Capitol, were installed in this century. The center one here comes from the White House and was probably made by the well-known firm of E. F. Caldwell & Company of New York.

The Naval Appropriations Committee was not here for long; other committees used the room. The Senate Committee on Appropriations has occupied it since 1912.

Opposite: Room s-127, one of the rooms of the Senate Committee on Appropriations. The best example of the wall decoration of ancient Rome and Pompeii in the country. (Day)

Ceiling detail in Room s-127. A special quality is the liveliness of the figures. (Day)

Some refined detail: two birds and a spray of stalks. (Day)

Volutes and a vase of flowers. (Day)

An overdoor with winged cherubs. (Day)

Portion of the completed lunette showing fanciful architectural detail of the ancient Romans. (Day)

A mask of an Indian on the center arch. (Day)

A swan and the top of a column framing a wall panel. (Day)

The Boston Massacre, 1770. *Courtesy Architect of the Capitol.*

Decorative panel in the vault groin. (Day)

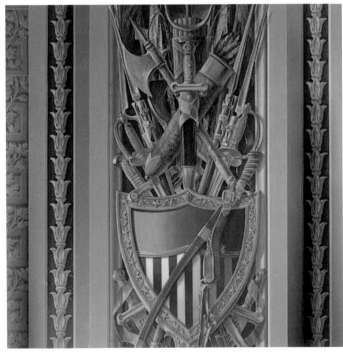

Portion of a wall panel of arms painted by James Leslie based on the design of Brumidi. Courtesy Architect of the Capitol.

Room s-128 is also part of the domain of the Senate Appropriations Committee. Where Room s-127 had been designed for Naval Affairs, this one was for the Military and Militia Committee, and was not given to Appropriations until 1906. Episodes of the American Revolution by Brumidi are the chief ornament, to be found in the lunettes: *The Battle of Lexington, 1775* and *Washington at Valley Forge, 1778* are on the south wall, the *Boston Massacre, 1770* and the *Death of General Wooster* are on the north wall, and *Storming Stony Point, 1779* is on the east wall. If the first three are familiar, the last two are not. David Wooster, Connecticut-born and a Yale graduate, was in the British navy and he fought in the French-and-Indian War. He met his death in a raid on the enemy-held Danbury, Connecticut. Stony Point was a fort on the west side of the Hudson River commanding a main road between New England and Pennsylvania. Its successful capture was a major step in the career of General Anthony Wayne.

What is typical of Brumidi is that, in painting the title-panels of each lunette, he framed them with flower garlands, scrolls, acanthus and, of course, a pair of cherubs for each.

As with s-127 the ceiling has two groin vaults separated by an arch. Each vault has, at the top, a series of half circles and wreaths, along with trophies of arms and small figurative panels in a gray-green monochrome. The rest of the vault detail is in rinceaux and arabesque on a ground of gold and gray squares painted in imitation of mosaic.

Equally unusual and effective are six vertical panels, more than 7 feet high, of trophies of arms, flags, musical instruments, and American shields. There must be six or more flags and more than a dozen arms in each. Topping the clusters is either a shako or a plumed Roman helmet. They are by James Leslie, the English artist who assisted Brumidi in the corridors and, for that matter, in Room s-127.

The fireplace, as in s-127, is the work of Walter. Here the frame, by an unknown hand, extends arms from the top to form valances over the windows. The cornice at the center, with its United States shield, is set against a cluster of arms, banners, and acanthus.

For those who work in these quarters, one of the rewards is the view west. The windows, in their cast-iron reveals, open on the bars of the arcade of the West Front to command a framed perspective of the Mall.

S-129 has much less decoration than the first two rooms. Not painted until 1870, and then only in part, the room served the Committee on the Library. Brumidi's work is confined to the ceiling, as one might guess from the presence of six cherubs. In the quadripartite vault, the east panel has a figure, Architecture, holding a view of the center of the Capitol with the help of a cherub while, on her right, a second cherub unfolds a plan of the Capitol. In the north panel, a flower-crowned maiden is seen with brushes and palette; a cherub helps her hold a portrait, presumably of Samuel F. B. Morse. This would be most fitting for one representing painting. A winged figure, Science, with a bay-leaf crown, sits in the west panel. Her right hand is on a star-studded globe with a telescope nearby. A printing press is to her left. Two cherubs serve her. In the last one, to the south, another maiden, Sculpture, with a winged cherub sits holding a mallet and chisel. Facing her is a marble bust where a second cherub is inscribing the name of Washington Irving. The arts would seem to boast of three representatives, the sciences one. Brumidi's usual interest in detail is present in the arabesques of acanthus around the panels with rinceaux, scallop shells and volutes, and, instead of cherubs, four female masks.

A ceiling panel with the figure of Painting by Brumidi (Day)

THE PRESIDENT'S ROOM (S-216)

Where one of the rooms of the Senate Appropriations Committee evokes ancient Pompeii and another one simply has elaborate decoration, the President's Room, with the Brumidi Corridor, can be placed in the School of Raphael. Befitting its purpose as the Capitol sanctuary of the President of the United States, it has as much embellishment as the corridor, only it has more figurative panels.

Completed in 1860, at about the time of the Senate's move to the then new north wing, it reveals the artist in full command of his art. Here is a most unusual interior; there is nothing quite like it in this country.

The President's Room is small, 20 by 20 feet with an 18-foot ceiling. The windows with deep reveals face north and thus command a view of Union Station as well as the massive red brick Government Printing Office on North Capitol Street. At first glance, our eye is caught by the three mirrors where we see our own reflections. There are pier glasses on the east and west walls and a mirror over the mantelpiece of the fireplace between the windows. All three have elaborate gilt frames, installed in 1860, whose most conspicuous elements are the columns at the sides. They are of no particular order; the thin shafts, rising from richly treated pedestals, are encircled by ribbons and rose garlands. At the top are broken entablatures between which is a segmental arch with a crown of flowers, leaves, scrolls, and volutes. Even the centers at the bottom of the pier glasses have a curious device: a pedestal of elaborate detail with a white marble top.

For all the distinction of the mirrors and mirror frames, what counts are the walls. They are divided into five wide vertical panels consisting of diamonds and hexagons with the latter containing portraits of Washington's first cabinet, and of the Postmaster General. They were Thomas Jefferson, Secretary of State; Alexander Hamilton, Secretary of the Treasury; Henry Knox, Secretary of War; Edmund Randolph, Attorney General; Samuel Osgood, Postmaster General. The frames are placed in beds of palmettes and acanthus, with the acanthus linked to the frames by scrolls. The diamonds are filled with vases of flowers. The vertical frame that binds diamond and hexagon in the vertical panel has an ivy-leaf band and a border of a leaf-and-dart cyma reversa.

Opposite: The President's Room looking northeast. The clock with its bronze of a man taming a horse is no longer there. Also, crystal pendants have been removed from the chandeliers. (Day)

Looking southeast in the President's Room. (Day)

Of equal interest is the ornament of the narrow vertical panels next to four of the portraits. Here are seen four intricate polychrome arabesques consisting of leaves in scrolls and a cherub rising from a cluster of acanthus leaves, the whole painted on gold leaf. One cherub holds a caduceus, symbol of communication and commerce, a second an anchor that represents shipping, a third a sword for war, and a fourth a sheaf of wheat, the symbol of agriculture.

As in the Brumidi Corridors, Raphael's influence here stems from the vertical panels of the loggias in the Vatican.

If the portraits of the members of Washington's first cabinet are here, where is our first President? He is found in the lunette of the south wall. To either side of the frame are winged figures, along with cherubs. Pairs of cherubs are also seen in the lunettes to either side of the tops of the pier glasses. One of them on the west, beneath the label "Legislation," has a winged cherub tying up bundles of state papers, laws, and congressional debates. At its feet is the signature "C. Brumidi," and the date, 1860. Another cherub, on the east

Top of a pier-glass frame in the President's Room. (Day)

Cherub, "Shipping," with anchor on a wall panel. (Day)

*Portrait of Thomas Jefferson as part of wall decoration.
(Day)*

*Acanthus and arabesques of leaf, tendril, and rosette
at base of wall panel. (Day)*

Portrait of Columbus with globe seen on the ceiling. (Day)

side near the label "Executive," holds a sword in his left hand and a pair of scales in his right with a law book at his feet. There are eight cherubs in three lunettes that, with four in the vertical panels, add up to twelve for the walls.

The walls are only an introduction, as it were, to the groined vault overhead. Called a quadripartite vault, it is divided into four panels, each of which has a portrait of a seated historic figure. They are Deacon Brewster of the Plymouth Colony (*Religion*), Christopher Columbus (*Discovery*), Benjamin Franklin (*History*), and Amerigo Vespucci (Latin name: Americus Vespucius), the explorer whose first name is the eponym of America (*Exploration*).

Every figure is identified with a label placed in a triangle of a pendentive along with cupids. Brewster's label has three babies (actually not painted by Brumidi), Columbus's two, Franklin's one with an eagle, and Vespucci's two.

If there are cherubs at the bottom of the portraits, there are cherubs seated on pairs of volutes in frames above the portraits. Brewster's pair is winged, with one of them holding a bow and carrying a quiver of arrows and the other reaching for an arrow. In the case of the two over Columbus, one of them, winged, holds a globe and the other reads a map. One of Franklin's holds a ribbon with the legend "E Pluribus Unum," the other the bound rods of the lictor symbolizing the state. Vespucci's two babies, without wings, are playing with branches of laurel, symbol of fame and victory. Along with the cherubic pairs are a United States shield and a spread-winged eagle.

Where these famous men are portrayed in rectangular frames, there is, between and above them, another row of symbolic female figures in round frames, these frames (like

Two cherubs above Columbus. (Day)

Two cherubs beneath Columbus. (Day)

Raphael's ceiling in the Stanza della Segnatura, Vatican Palace, Rome. Photo Studio Canali.

the others) having been painted to resemble true frames. The one representing liberty is seen to the south, above George Washington. On the west side is Legislation with a sword in her right hand. With her left hand she points to the Constitution held by a cherub. On the north or window side is Religion with a veil. The fourth and last, to the east, is Executive (Authority) with a scepter; she has, to either side, a cherub, one of whom holds a torch. As to the cherub count, the portraits have respectively five, four, three (one with an eagle), and four outside the frames, for a total of sixteen. Two cherubs each were allotted by Brumidi to the symbolic figures, making a total of eight.

(In the illustration of the vault's center, an octagonal panel depicts four cherubs. This panel is no longer there. Several decades ago, the chandelier fell, taking with it Brumidi's original four cherubs. It was replaced by another, the one shown here. In a recent cleaning of the decoration, the decision was made to remove the replacement since it was deemed to be the work of another artist. Today's version has no cherubs,

only a gray-blue surface. The ceiling, which originally had twenty-eight cherubs, now has twenty-four, and the room presently has some thirty-six babies.)

We have mentioned Raphael's influence on Brumidi. Clearly, with the ceiling here, Brumidi looked to the great artist's Stanza della Segnatura (Room of the Signing), one of the suite known in the Vatican Palace as the Stanze di Raffaello, or Rooms of Raphael. (It should be added that the Vatican ceiling is not entirely the work of Raphael, there being parts by Bramante and Sodoma.)

All the figurative ceiling panels are set in what seems a common border, so carefully are the outer parts of their frames linked. This common border, a continuous band, consists of leaves, mostly acanthus and anthemion, executed with such skill that the arabesques formed are models of their kind. Punctuating the band are small United States shields—that is, shields consisting of red and white vertical stripes and a small field of blue, the same as the ones found above the portraits. In addition, the portraits have special frames consist-

The continuous framing band of the ceiling. (Day)

Seals of states and territories in the framing band of the ceiling. Beneath Religion *is the seal of Ohio. (Day)*

A female mask repeated in the Minton tile of the floor with the elaborate frame of rinceaux and other detail. (Day)

Bronze figures and other ornament on the chandelier. (Day)

are fixed on shafts of intricate arabesques rising from pairs of dolphins with intertwined tails.

Even more astonishing than the quantity of cherubs is the beauty of their treatment. They are far from being presented as immobile statues, especially those in the lunettes and on the ceiling. They are all in movement, at work or at play. Brumidi's skill in making them so lively is the artist's chief attribute, placing him among the outstanding mural decorators of the last century. On this score, no other painter in our history has rivaled him, except the sculptor Philip Martiny, who did the babies on the grand staircase of the Jefferson Building of the Library of Congress across from the Capitol.

The ornament of the Minton floor tiles is as detailed as any in the Capitol. At the center is a gold and white rosette on a red ground placed in a star. Then come circles of bead-and-reel, leaf-and-dart, and a wide band of circling ribbon, a band of acanthus arabesques on a red and blue ground, and, last, a large double guilloche. All have a square border with a cloth pattern. The triangular spaces between the double-guilloche circle and the square border form triangles with rinceaux and a female mask. In its own way, the floor is as spectacular as the ceiling overhead.

And there is the chandelier with its many bronze arms and bronze figures in a dark patina. The top row of figures consists of four men in armor. The next row has eight cherubs. A third row has eight more male figures, labeled Washington, Franklin, et al. With all the room's ornament, such a chandelier would appear unnecessary. However, the question may be posed: How else to light such a room?

Two busts are in the room: a marble one of President James A. Garfield by Charles H. Niehaus and a bronze one of President William McKinley, Jr., by Emma Cadwalader-Guild.

One example of the care with which the room was decorated can be found in the small rectangular panels beneath the windows. Each is adorned with a red star-shaped arabesque set against a gold ground framed in bands of oak leaf and acorn. The other curiosity is the presence of a false door, much like those in the Senate Reception Room. It is not really a false door because it does open on a shallow closet, which is rarely used. Still, the reason it is there is that Walter desired symmetry in the south wall to balance the two windows to the north. He had to have one door for an entrance. He found the answer by including a second that serves virtually no other purpose than that of decoration.

Although in recent years the room has chiefly served as a venue for Senate press conferences, Presidents have found it useful for ceremonies. Abraham Lincoln was the first to do some signing here; that was on March 4, 1861, the day of his inauguration. Most subsequent Presidents have only used it for signing at the end of their terms of office. President Grant was one of the more frequent users throughout his presidency. Recent presidents have customarily retired to it after inaugurations.

ing, at the sides, of Corinthian pilasters painted to resemble stone and with shafts of very elaborate arabesques that descend to pairs of dolphins with intertwined tails.

One more item of ornament is the round shields set in the common border. They depict the state seals of the period, light red on a dark red ground. In the border beneath *Religion* on the north side of the ceiling is the seal of Ohio. With difficulty the viewer can make out a top half with six rays coming from a tiny globe—that is, the sun—and beneath it, a sheaf of wheat and a cluster of arrows. One seal, with a beehive, represents a territory, Utah; it is in the southwest corner beneath the cherub with an eagle, just below Franklin's portrait.

With such an abundance of ornament, it would not be surprising if we overlooked the decoration on the sides of the portrait frames. It is as elaborate in its way as that of the continuous band. Here are Corinthian pilasters whose capitals

THE LYNDON BAINES JOHNSON ROOM (S-211)
AND THE OFFICE OF THE VICE PRESIDENT (S-212)

On the second floor of the Senate wing, there is a hallway leading to the east portico where we encountered the "magnolia columns," if they may be so termed, of Thomas Walter. Standing near the entrance and facing the portico, we have, on the right, the bust of Calvin Coolidge by Moses A. W. Dykaar nearby and, beyond it, the door to the John Fitzgerald Kennedy Room, s-210. It is part of the office of the secretary of the Senate. The rooms are handsome with their high-vaulted ceilings and high windows in deep reveals, but there is little mural decoration. For that we have to turn to the Lyndon Baines Johnson Room, s-211, on the left (north).

(In a niche near the door is the bust of Thomas R. Marshall, Vice President in the Wilson administration. He is remembered best for telling the nation: "What this country needs is a good five-cent cigar.")

When Walter designed the room, it was originally assigned to the Senate Library. However, when completed, it became the Senate Post Office, which accounts for the subjects of the Brumidi frescoes. Later, it was the room of the Committee on the District of Columbia, a reminder that the District was governed until recently by committees of the Senate and House. President Johnson made it his in 1959, when he was Democratic majority leader, and kept it as president of the Senate when he was elected Vice President, only to give it up on the fateful day of November 22, 1963.

That he made it his was, to be sure, evidence of his somewhat autocratic nature, but it must be remembered that no Vice President of the United States had spent so many years in the Capitol. In 1931, at the age of twenty-three, he came to the Hill as a congressman's secretary. After an absence of a few years, he settled in the House upon winning a by-election in 1937. Service in the navy took him away for several years. In 1948 he moved to the Senate, eventually becoming Democratic majority leader. In 1961 he was, as Vice President of the United States, president

The Lyndon Baines Johnson Room with ceiling and lunettes by Brumidi. (Day)

of the Senate, and he only left the Capitol to move to the White House.

In the Johnson Room, we behold another triumph of Brumidi's. The ceiling vault, divided into four parts by groining, has four figurative panels. Designed in 1857, only one of them was executed by 1861. The rest were done in 1867. In all probability, the first to be painted was *Telegraph* on the west side of the vault. A seated America with a Phrygian cap rests a left arm on an anchor and cradles a caduceus, Mercury's staff, symbol of commerce and communication. Beside her are an eagle, a cornucopia, a cannon, two ramrods, and a flag. Behind the eagle is a telegraph pole. Cannon and ramrods remind us that the Civil War had begun when the artist set to work. Extending her right arm, America is welcoming Europa, who is riding a bull festooned with flowers—an allusion to the Greek legend where Zeus, the king of the gods, took the body of a bull and carried away the beautiful Europa. Here she obviously represents Europe. Between her and America is a cable held by a cherub; the panel celebrates the laying of the first Atlantic cable between England and this country in 1858.

Brumidi, by the way, received $500 for this panel and the decorative scheme on the groin next to it. In 1866 he was called in to complete the ceiling with the assistance of a journeyman painter and a laborer. *Physics*, the north panel, has as

its chief figure a bay-leaf–crowned woman reading a railroad map held by a youth. Beyond his right is a steamboat. To her left, Vulcan is seen with a pair of railroad wheels, and behind him is a woodburning locomotive with a cabbage stack. The east panel has the figure of Geography, her left hand resting on a globe and her right hand holding a pair of calipers. To her left, a winged figure unfolds a map of the Western hemisphere, and to her right, another winged figure holds the model of a woodburning locomotive with its cabbage stack, and a protractor, an instrument for measuring angles. *History* is the title of the south panel. History is shown with a quill in her right hand writing in a book. To her right is a table with a manuscript, inkpot, and quill, along with a printing press. In the distance is a battle scene.

The invention, the design, the handling of the figures show the master in command. The decorative portions are no less skillfully executed. On three of the groins, he placed three maidens, the center one bearing a basket of fruit on her head in the manner of a canephora, a maiden in ancient Greece who carried a basket of sacred objects on her head when participating in religious ceremonies. We have met with the figure before in the underside of an arch in the main Brumidi Corridor. The fourth groin, on the southeast side, consists of two maidens, and a youth, with a flower basket on his head, is the canephorus. Each group stands on a splendid base—a leafy pedestal set in an arabesque of acanthus and volutes and rosettes—and to either side are fruit garlands and swirling acanthus. At the center of the ceiling, an elaborate rosette consists of acanthus, anthemion, and rinceau. No less elaborate is the large crystal chandelier.

The lunettes beneath the vaulting are simple. A United States shield is shown in a scroll frame bordered by scallop shells and sprigs of bay leaf. To either side is a decoration of tendril, acanthus, and rosette.

It is easy to recognize Walter's hand in the marble chimneypiece. The mirror frame, among the simpler ones in the Capitol, has sides in the shape of modified Corinthian columns with beribboned shafts and, at the top, a flat pediment enriched with a cabochon. The cabochon is placed in an oval frame held up by acanthus volutes between which is a frieze of rinceaux.

The Minton tile of the floor is concealed by a protective carpet, leaving only a border visible. Winged boys spring from acanthus on either side of lamp standards with rams' heads and lions' paws; boys and standards hold up a ribbon-bound laurel garland.

We met with two false doors in the Senate Reception Room on the other side of the west wall, and now we discover a third one here on this side of the same wall. It is the left one of the pair in the west wall. Some use has been made of it in recent decades as a shallow closet for china and glassware. Both doors, arched, are set in cast-iron frames that in

Decorative figures between the panels with symbolic figures. A youth at the center with a flower basket on his head between two maidens and two eagles. To the left is a part of Geography, *and to the right,* History. *(Day)*

Geography, *a ceiling panel in the Lyndon Baines Johnson Room. (Day)*

turn have been placed inside a third cast-iron frame, also arched. What, it may be asked, was Walter trying to do? He was simply balancing the two windows opposite with a single large doorway frame containing two doors. Had there been just the single door, the one opening to the Senate Reception Room, it would have been off-center, and therefore off-balance in relation to the two windows. The result is a large double-door frame, not the door itself, in the center of the wall, with the active door centered on the wall of the Senate Reception Room.

In the southwest corner, in what looks like a large cupboard, or armoire, is actually a small bathroom with sink and toilet. It replaced a large bathroom installed here by Vice President Johnson. The bathroom wall did not reach the ceiling, thus leaving the Brumidi vaulting untouched. The room then was a

working office lit by bullet-head lights hung from the ceiling, and there was, in addition, a kitchenette. Today the restored Lyndon Baines Johnson Room is reserved for meetings.

Next to the Lyndon Baines Johnson Room is Room s-212, a staff office of the Vice President, formerly the office of the sergeant at arms. Here, on a segmental vault, Brumidi painted *Columbia Welcoming the South Back into the Union.* We know the date as the artist signed it "Brumidi 1876." On the coves of the ceiling and on lunettes, as was his custom, Brumidi painted panels, this time in grisaille. Cherubs frolic in rinceaux of acanthus and rosettes. Several small panels show America destroying arms with one hand while with the other she holds an olive branch.

Again we can marvel at the artist's skill in handling decoration, so brilliantly shown in the corridors that bear his name.

THE DEFENSE SUBCOMMITTEE OF THE HOUSE
APPROPRIATIONS COMMITTEE (ROOM H-144)

I n one of the most extraordinary episodes in the history of American art, a middle-aged immigrant called on Captain Montgomery C. Meigs in 1854 with the proposal that he be employed to decorate the Capitol. What was singular about the occasion was not just that Constantino Brumidi, an artist from Rome, was a skilled mural decorator, but that the patron, in this instance a captain of engineers in the United States Army in charge of the Capitol construction, knew exactly what had to be done. We have already cited the captain's discussion of the matter with his friend Gouverneur Kemble, the cannon maker on the banks of the Hudson (*see* page 23). Meigs had a clear idea of what had to be done; the walls were not to be left undecorated plaster. The question was: Who was to be the artist? A few days after Christmas 1854 Constantino Brumidi was in the captain's temporary office, actually Room H-144. In labored French on both sides it was agreed that the artist would do a careful sketch for the east lunette, the subject to be the calling of Cincinnatus from the Plow.[119]

From January to March 1855 the artist worked away. The result was a picture with nine figures, a pair of oxen, and other elements. Lucius Quinctius Cincinnatus, a Roman hero, is seen with a delegation from the Roman Senate. Having led the Romans to one victory and gone back to his farm, he was being asked to lead them to another. As Meigs pointed out, the story appealed to Americans, most often in connection with George Washington. In the right-hand corner is a youngster, modeled by one of Meigs's children, who is holding a rake with a crossbar inscribed "1855 C. Brumidi," concealed by cove lighting.

Cincinnatus Called from the Plow, *Brumidi's first mural in the Capitol. Courtesy Architect of the Capitol.*

The artist found a parallel to the legend, other than our first President, for the opposite lunette on the west wall. In the *Calling of Putnam from the Plow to the Revolution*, he told the story of Israel Putnam, the Connecticut farmer. In June 1775, hearing that the English troops then occupying Boston were about to march out of the city, he gathered volunteers and joined the American forces at the Battle of Bunker Hill.

The two other walls have more elaborate decoration. On the south one is the profile of Washington, executed as if in carved relief, set in a bowl with an octagonal frame. On one side stands America with the flag, on the other an Indian with a bow and a quiver of arrows. Five cherubs, winged and non-winged, play with a fruit garland around the frame. The background, with tendrils, is painted to resemble carved stone. Beneath it is a rectangular panel showing reapers with sickles at work in a wheat field.

Opposite, on the north side, is a similar portrait of Jefferson accompanied by Fame (left) with a bay-leaf crown and holding a sprig of bay and by the Republic (right) wearing a Phrygian cap and holding a tablet. Cherubs play with a fruit garland while one of them helps the Republic hold the tablet.

Beneath it is another panel depicting the harvesting of wheat, only this time with a mechanical reaper. The McCormick reaper had recently been invented in the Shenandoah Valley, and Captain Meigs wanted it depicted here. A doorway, with a cast-iron frame, is beneath each of the panels. The rest of both walls have only large painted frames. At the top of each frame is a cherub head between cornucopias.

It is, however, on the ceiling, not on the walls, where Brumidi triumphed. In this small room, only 20 feet by 18, Walter built a groined vault that not only made possible the lunettes for the walls but also provided curved surfaces on the ceiling, ideal for the artist. Like the vault at the north end of the Senate Reception Room, it is divided into four parts by four groins radiating from a central oval. Each part is given over to a figurative panel devoted to one of the four seasons. Starting with Spring on the east they depict, clockwise, Summer on the south, Autumn on the west, and Winter on the north. Each is symbolized by a graceful figure seated on clouds and surrounded by cherubs, most of them winged. In composition they are very fine, wonderfully in balance and all in motion. As we can see, it was not enough for the artist to give the figure form and grace; he must give it movement, especially movement in defiance of gravity, as the gods and goddesses rest on clouds attended by the gamboling babies.

If we study Spring, we see a maiden with a white rose in her left hand while, with her right, she motions upward. The cherubs are busy, one bringing her a flower crown, another holding aloft a swirling mantle, a third releasing a dove. Three others are equally active, two with a basket of flowers and one with a bunch of roses. Summer, reclining on a cloud,

Portrait of Thomas Jefferson between the figures of Fame and Liberty. Beneath it a picture of the newly invented reaper. Courtesy Architect of the Capitol.

Ceiling. Courtesy Architect of the Capitol.

has a sickle in her right hand and a scythe at her left side. Here a cherub has a bow and arrow, another binds a sheaf of wheat, a third is emptying a cornucopia, and three more are holding drapery caught in a breeze. Autumn is a youth receiving a bunch of grapes from a flying cherub overhead; in his right hand he holds a thyrsus, a rod with a beribboned pinecone at one end, which was the attribute of Bacchus, god of the harvest and of wine. Five cherubs celebrate the harvest, one with a jar of wine, a second with a basket of fruit, while three others are cheerfully playing the flute, the tam-

Framing detail on the ceiling in grisaille. (Day)

Cherub with bow and arrow in the ceiling panel Winter. *(Day)*

bourine, and castanets. Winter, strangely enough, is represented by a middle-aged man with black hair and beard instead of, as is customary, by an old man with white hair. On the left, three of his cherubic helpers are at work creating a snowstorm, two with a wineskin of wind and another pouring snow from a jug. On the right, two more are doing the same while two others huddle in a blue sheet and a third cherub, his back to us, blows on a conch shell. The play of drapery, as in the other panels, is very much a part of the composition. Obviously, Brumidi's training in drawing cloth as well as babies had not been in vain.

Separating the four panels are four grisaille bands springing from the corners of the ceiling and running along the groins to the grisaille oval at the center of the ceiling. The virtue of grisaille is that the artist is simulating carved relief to set off the polychromatic figurative panels. What is unusual about the bands here is that although they are in the category of decorative painting, they too have plenty of animation. In the oval at the top, for example, a rosette of acanthus and anthemion is placed in a bowl bordered by a scroll frame with scallop shells on four sides. Revolving around the frame and shells is a riot of tendril and acanthus growing from flowers. The whole oval is then encircled with ribbon-bound garlands. The liveliness, gray as it is, is astonishing.

The center of the composition is the oval at the top of the ceiling. From it radiate the four bands of grisaille along the groins. Each band has a cherub who, while holding a beribboned garland of the oval, stands on a vase whose support descends to a fruit-filled bowl. The bowl rests on a pedestal, bordered by anthemion, and rises from yet another bowl of fruit on yet another pedestal with an elaborate base. Two

cherubs are seated on the bowl to either side of the second pedestal. At the foot of the groin, where there is a shield of splayed acanthus, are two more cherubs. The ornament finally stops at the springing of the groins. The play of leaf, tendril, bowl, and cherub is entrancing.

As if three cherubs were insufficient, Brumidi has yet two more below the base of the lowest bowl holding the ribbon-bound fruit garlands strung along the bottom of the figurative panels. Moreover, these same garlands are upheld at the middle by volutes in the panel frames. Beneath the gold volutes are gray eagles gripping arrows and laurel in their claws.

The gilt frames of the ceiling panels, like the arches on the ceiling's four sides, are false; treated with gold leaf, the enrichment consists of a Scotia in leaf-and-dart and bead-and-reel. That these gold frames are flat and not in relief is betrayed by the fact that Brumidi placed one hand of each topmost cherub against a frame. He also has fruit garlands spilling over on two of the frames.

As in the Senate Reception Room, the cherub is omnipresent. Their presence here was only a foretaste of what Brumidi would include in his Capitol work. There are twenty-five babies in the ceiling panels and another twenty in the grisaille bands. The wall portraits have five each, for a total of ten. Last, there are four cherub heads between the cornucopias on top of the wall panels. The grand sum of babies is fifty-nine.

The decoration of the entire room was executed in fresco. In assisting him, Brumidi had a painter, one L. Franze, for 156 days and Michael Lang, a laborer, for 240 days. He himself worked 329 days, for which he was paid $2,632 ($8 a day, the pay of a congressman, was his wage.)[120]

OTHER ROOMS CLOSED TO THE PUBLIC

Three Architects' Rooms: The Senate Retiring Room, the House Retiring Room, and the Sam Rayburn or House Reception Room

Among the rooms in the Capitol was one that was Thomas Walter's sole responsibility: the Senate Retiring Room. No painter, no sculptor, not even a stucco craftsman participated in the decorating.

The Senate Retiring Room is directly north of the Senate Chamber. Known as the Marble Room, it is, as might be expected from its informal name, all marble. The walls are of dark Tennessee, while the ceiling and four columns are of Carrara. Indeed, the four columns, of a splendid Corinthian order designed by Walter, are the room's chief adornment. In what is a sober interior, a crystal chandelier and mirrors provide a cheerful note, while leather chairs and couches convey a relaxing touch.

In the old days, the public was admitted, but lobbyists became such a nuisance that in 1921 it was closed to all except the senators.

Its equivalent in the south wing, the House Retiring Room, occupies a similar spot in relation to the House Chamber. It has a big advantage over the other in that it faces south, which makes for a more cheerful ambience. The elaborate ceiling of the central bays is of cast iron; Walter executed the design. Each bay has an elaborate ceiling made of sunken panels that hold an elaborate rosette of acanthus and acorns with a boss or pendant in the shape of a pinecone at the center. The detail is picked out in gold.

Walter made up for the absence of ornament on the walls by having elaborate sconces for lighting. In each the main element is a cherub springing from acanthus. With upraised hands, the baby holds a globe from which extend five arms bearing lights. The still-present petcocks are evidence that they were originally piped for gas.

The single additions at either end are different in their decoration, dating from the turn of the century. The ceilings are groined vaults embellished with rinceaux of vines and flowers, bound rods set on bay-leaf wreaths, and eagles and flags. Beneath the vaults are lunettes with symbolic figures, masks, and a variation of the United States seal. A chandelier is in each of the additions, totaling three for the room.

Between the House Chamber and the House Retiring Room is a narrow corridor called the Speaker's Lobby. No doubt heavily frequented in the old days, it is now a portrait gallery. Here are pictures of the Speakers of the House of Representatives, some of whose names and even faces will be familiar: Henry Clay (Speaker 1811–14, 1815–20, 1823–25), James G. Blaine (1869–75), Joseph G. Cannon (1903–

11), and Sam Rayburn (1940-46, 1949-52, 1955-61). Length of service makes obvious their importance. The more curious should note the portrait of Thomas Brackett Reed (1889-91, 1895-99) of Maine (no relation to the author), whom authorities consider the most brilliant of them all. Of his picture executed in 1891 by John Singer Sargent, Speaker Reed remarked: "His worst enemy wouldn't say that the portrait in any way resembled him."[121] So much for this particular work by one of America's best-known artists, who was very much of the realist school.

In the lobby's center are a desk and chair of oak designed by Walter for the House Chamber. In their elaborate detail,

The Senate Retiring, or Marble Room, by Thomas U. Walter.
Courtesy Architect of the Capitol.

The House Retiring Room, designed by Thomas U. Walter.
Courtesy Architect of the Capitol.

Speaker Thomas Brackett Reed, *1891,*
by John Singer Sargent. Courtesy Architect of the Capitol.

Cherub sconce in the House Retiring Room.
Courtesy Architect of the Capitol.

they are very much a part of the Civil War era. Again, the ceiling overhead is of cast iron.

Another "architect's room" is the Rayburn Room, or House Reception Room. Its significance lies in the fact that it is a rare classical setting recently executed, designed, and constructed in our time, actually in 1963. As such, it will stand out for future generations when so-called modern art will have disappeared and the nation in its art will once again be solidly in the classical tradition. The room was designed by the architect Harry Merz, under the direction of Messrs. DeWitt, Poor, and Shelton.[122] What is most impressive is the walnut paneling, pilasters, and Corinthian columns made by Knipp & Company of Baltimore. Unusual in such rooms where the entablatures are customarily of stucco given a wood stain, here even the entablature is of walnut. With marble fireplaces at two ends and a wall on the west side, the fourth side on the east is demarked by four Corinthian columns setting off a passageway. The two large brass chandeliers were made by Rambusch of New York. The most important ornament of the room is a portrait of George Washington by Gilbert Stuart.

Certainly the House Reception Room is a complete contrast to its Senate equivalent (open to the public), where the sumptuous note is Brumidi the artist's decoration. Here the sumptuous touch is the walnut woodwork by Knipp & Company following the architect's design.

Rayburn or House Reception Room by Harry Merz under the direction of Messrs. DeWitt, Poor, and Shelton. (Day)

A Corinthian capitol in the House Reception Room carved in 1963 by S. Knipp & Company. (Day)

The Speaker's Room

Ceiling decoration in the Speaker's Room. Courtesy Architect of the Capitol.

As might be expected, the Speaker's Room is strictly reserved for the Speaker of the House. Originally it was set aside for the Committee on Territories, a fact that explains much of the decoration. James Leslie, Brumidi's talented assistant, was given the following orders for the room in 1856 by Captain Meigs: "Its decoration should be suitable for the objects of the labors of this committee. Objects relating to the settlement of our new states, to the chase, the life of the Indian and the trapper. The ordinary implements of this life may be advantageously introduced." Animals, arms, and Indian objects in the decoration answer the captain's request. In addition, there are the seven shields of the seven territories that would soon be admitted as states: New Mexico, Washington, Minnesota, Kansas, Oregon, Utah, and Nebraska. All are accompanied by frames and bands of ornament, such as guilloche and rinceaux. In 1940 the Lone Star of the Texas seal was added, as was the seal of the House, by Sam Rayburn, the Speaker who hailed from Texas.

It was during Rayburn's speakership that the most dramatic incident in the room's history took place. One afternoon—it was on April 12, 1945—Rayburn was in what was known as the "Board of Education"; actually, the Speaker disliked the label and referred to his room as "downstairs." At the end of a working day, he would invite several colleagues to gather for a drink. On this particular day, Vice President Truman arrived around five to be told that the White House had called and that he must return the call. He promptly did so and got a request to hurry over. "Jesus Christ and General Jackson!" was his astonished comment as he put down the receiver and, turning to the others, ordered: "Boys, this is in the room. Something must have happened." He left and ran through the Hall of Columns, through the silent Crypt—it was after visiting hours—to the Brumidi Corridor and then up the East Brumidi Stairway to retrieve his hat in the Vice President's Room, down the stairway again, and out beneath the portico to his waiting car. Not knowing the cause of the urgent summons, he arrived at the White House to be received by Mrs. Roosevelt and several members of the family and staff and was told that the President was dead. He was now President.

Mural decoration in the Capitol continued, as we know, after Brumidi suffered his accident in 1880 while working on his frieze in the Great Rotunda. Admittedly spasmodic, it was spurred, especially after 1900, by the World's Columbian Exposition of 1893 in Chicago and the splendid decoration of a few years later in the Library of Congress (Jefferson Building). The work is to be found in the corridors and rooms that replaced the old Library of Congress west of the Great Rotunda. Among those who worked in these spaces as well as in the new Library of Congress was George Willoughby Maynard, who executed floating female figures much like those he did in the new Library, now the Jefferson Building. Another was Elmer Ellsworth Garnsey, supervisor of the new Library decoration under Edward Pearce Casey. Garnsey painted lunettes in Room H-132, first occupied by the Committee on the Louisiana Purchase Centennial and, later, by the Committee on Industrial Arts and Expositions. (Today it is one of the rooms used by the House Republican leader.) Garnsey devoted three lunettes to the main buildings of three world's fairs: the 1876 Centennial Exposition in Philadelphia, Chicago's 1893 Columbian Exposition, and the 1901 Pan-American Exposition in Buffalo. As the Louisiana Exposition in St. Louis had yet to be built, the artist just had an uppercase "L" in the fourth lunette, covered by Napoleon's symbol, a bee, because he had sold the territory in 1803 to this country. The decorative detail is restrained, nothing on the order of Brumidi.

A second room of the period is H-231. Originally that of the House Committee on Public Buildings and Grounds and now allotted to the House Republican Leader, it looks to the arts in its decoration. The ceiling has symbols of painting, sculpture, and architecture. In the four lunettes are portraits in green grisaille of great Italian architects and sculptors, along with one American. They are:

North	*G. Barozzi da Vignola (1507–1573)*
	William Thornton (1759–1828)
	Antonio da Sangallo the Younger (1483–1546)
South	*Arnolfo di Cambio (1240–1302)*
	Jacopo Sansovino (1486–1570)
East	*Benedetto da Maiano (1442–1497)*
West	*Domenico Fontana (1543–1607)*
	Andrea Palladio (1508–1580)

Thornton is certainly in excellent company.

Most ambitious of all is probably the work in Room H-143 of the House Appropriations Committee done in 1903. At the time, it was home to the Committee on Insular Affairs. Henry Lyman Saÿen was commissioned to do four lunettes: *Primitive Agriculture*, *Good Government*, the *Rule of Tyranny*, and the *Rule of Justice*. In style they are wholly different from the figurative panels of Brumidi. Where his figures are traditional (as we can see in the Senate Reception Room), Saÿen's are wholly realistic, reminding us that realism, or naturalism, as it was once called, replaced the older style beginning around 1880 in this country.

The colonnade and the statue of the Republic at the World's Columbian Exposition of 1893 by Elmer Ellsworth Garnsey. Courtesy Architect of the Capitol.

Stucco Enrichment: Its Role

We have dwelled on the Capitol's painted decoration for obvious reasons. In so doing, we could easily slip into neglecting another kind of decoration that is splendidly represented in the building, namely, stucco ornament. Stucco, an Italian term, is customarily reserved for fine plasterwork, the kind presumably found in enriched detail. We have met with it in the Senate Reception Room, especially in the framing of ceiling panels. We know who was responsible for the work, the craftsman Ernest Thomas, and we know he was encouraged by Captain Meigs. In all probability he was in charge of the stuccowork throughout the extension of the 1850s.

Nearly all of it is to be found in the corridors closed to the public. We can only catch a glimpse of it as we go up and down the main stairs. Elaborate arabesques in gold are placed against the vertical panels of red or brown of the walls and the soffits, or undersides, of the arches. Mixed in with tendrils, vine leaves, and varieties of acanthus are snakes, ears of corn, and a female mask. In the arch panels, there is greater variety, what with dolphin heads, stylized scallop shells, goats' heads, and storks' heads.

Wherever there is a sunken panel, which is everywhere, including the saucer domes and their pendentives, along with the arches, enrichment can be found. Even wall vents have their ornament, thus making them models of their kind.

In assigning credit for the ingenious treatment of these corridors, which, like the Brumidi Corridors, are broken up by arches, barrel vaults, and even saucer domes, we give the first palm to Walter. For the enrichment let us credit Meigs, who saw to it that Thomas was hired. And it is not simply quality that counts, it is the sheer abundance.

Acanthus leaf and grape relief in the center of a saucer dome. (Day)

Opposite: View of a House corridor. (Day)

A deer's head on the center panel of the arch. (Day)

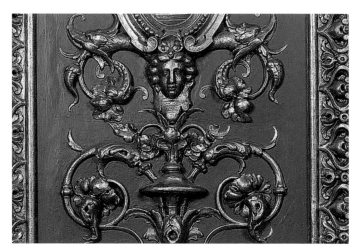

A female mask at the center of the relief on a wall panel. (Day)

*Corn, snakes, flowers, and leaves on the upper part
of a wall panel. (Day)*

*A pair of dolphins and an animal mask at the bottom of the
relief of the center arch. (Day)*

Opposite: Underside of an arch in a House corridor (note relief on center panel). (Day)

APPENDIX

Identifications

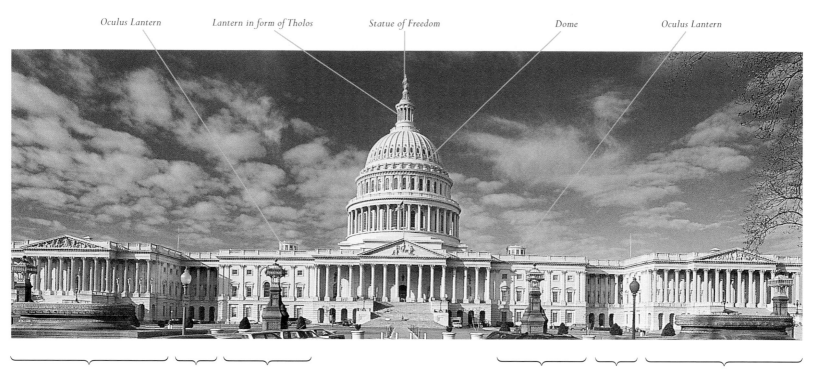

Oculus Lantern   Lantern in form of Tholos   Statue of Freedom   Dome   Oculus Lantern

New House Wing   Corridor   Old House Wing   **UNITED STATES CAPITOL** / **EAST ELEVATION**   Old Senate Wing   Corridor   New Senate Wing

Pediment

Balustrade

Entablature

Corinthian Colonnade

Balustrade

Cheekblocks

PORTICO AND STEPS OF THE SENATE (NORTH) WING

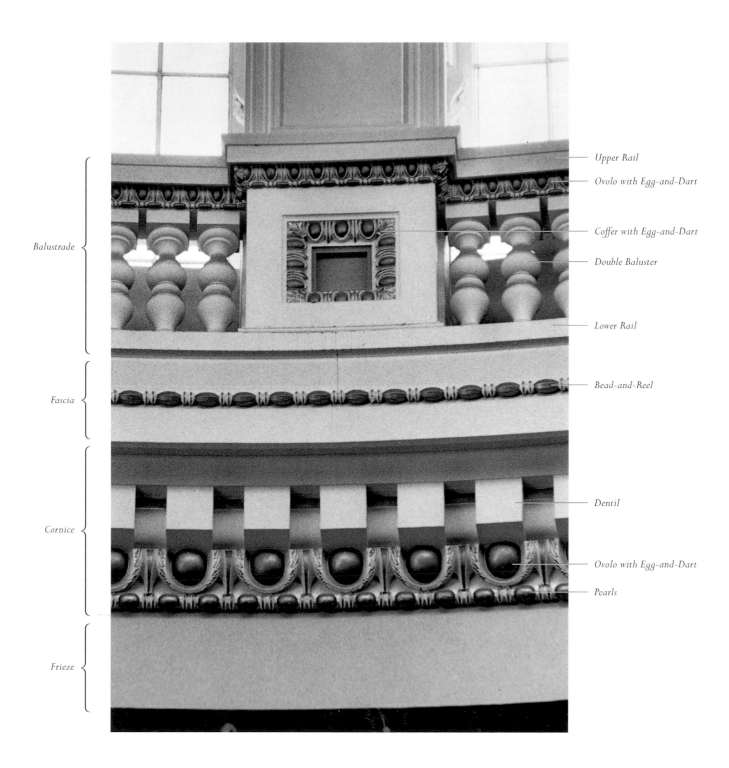

Balustrade

Fascia

Cornice

Frieze

Upper Rail

Ovolo with Egg-and-Dart

Coffer with Egg-and-Dart

Double Baluster

Lower Rail

Bead-and-Reel

Dentil

Ovolo with Egg-and-Dart

Pearls

CAST-IRON CORNICE AND BALUSTRADE WITH DOUBLE BALUSTERS
AT THE BASE OF THE DRUM IN THE DOME

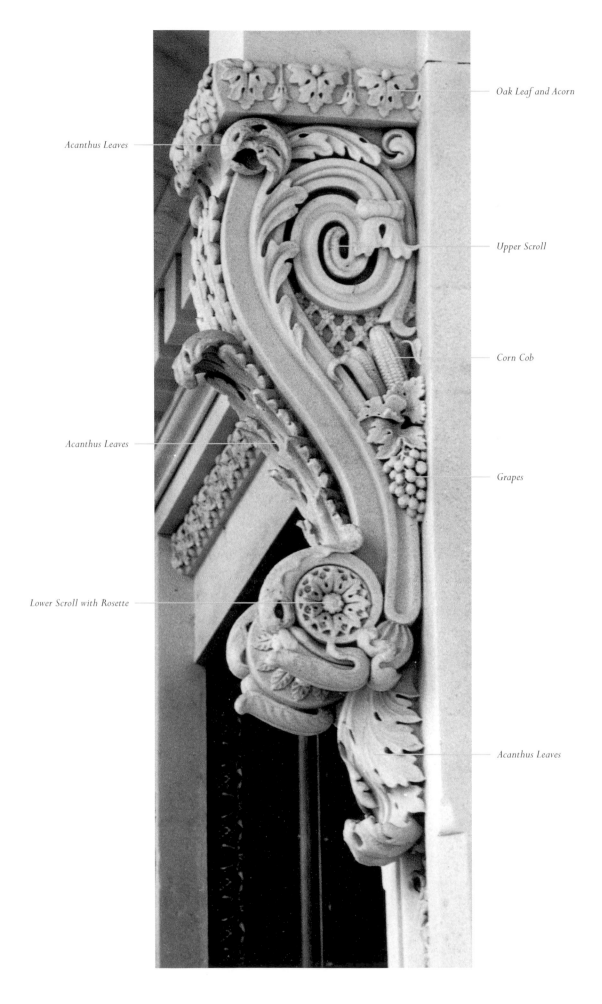

Oak Leaf and Acorn

Acanthus Leaves

Upper Scroll

Corn Cob

Acanthus Leaves

Grapes

Lower Scroll with Rosette

Acanthus Leaves

ANCONE OF BRACKET AT THE DOORWAY OF THE SENATE (NORTH) WING

APPENDIX

Bracket with Three Scrolls

Scroll, or Volute

Acanthus Leaf

Astragal

Gadroon

Astragal

Acanthus Leaves

Acorn in Acanthus Cup

Leaf-and-Dart

Imbricated Bay Leaves

LANTERN BRACKET IN THE SENATE RECEPTION ROOM

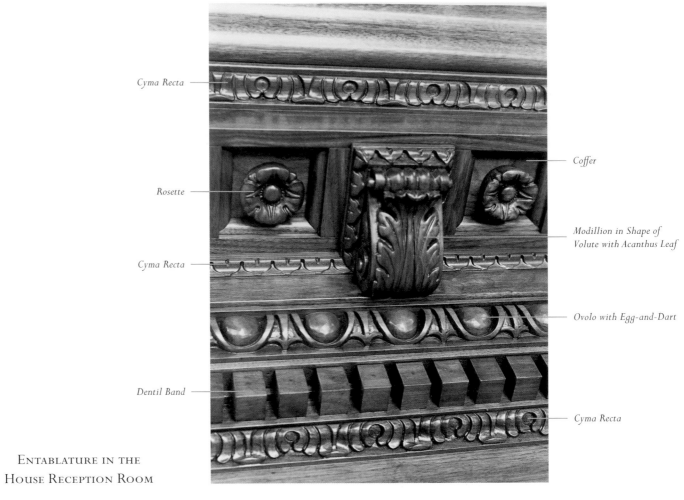

Cyma Recta

Rosette

Cyma Recta

Dentil Band

Coffer

Modillion in Shape of
Volute with Acanthus Leaf

Ovolo with Egg-and-Dart

Cyma Recta

ENTABLATURE IN THE
HOUSE RECEPTION ROOM

Flowers

Rinceau

Bayleaf and Bayberry Garland

Tendril

Acanthus Leaves

Basket

Rinceau

Tendril in Rinceau

Vine Leaves

CANEPHORE IN THE
MAIN BRUMIDI CORRIDOR

ABACUS. The slab that forms the top of the capital. *See* ORDERS OF ARCHITECTURE.

ABUTMENT. A masonry mass that takes the weight and thrust of an arch, vault, or truss. *See* ARCH.

ACANTHUS. A Mediterranean plant (*Acanthus mollis* and *Acanthus spinous*) whose deeply serrated leaf was stylized by the Greeks and the Romans to become one of the principal ornaments of classical architecture. It identifies a Corinthian capital.

Acanthus spinosus

Acanthus

AEDICULE. A small house or templed frame.

ANCONE. A scroll-shaped bracket, customarily found in pairs, that supports a cornice over a door or a window. *See* BRACKET.

ANTHEMION (ANTHEMIA, pl.). An ornament based on the honeysuckle or palm leaf. Also a Palmette.

APPLIQUÉ. *See* SCONCE.

ARABESQUE. An intricate decorative pattern joining plant, animal, and sometimes human forms.

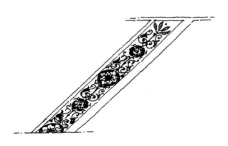

ARCH. A curved construction used to span an opening or recess.

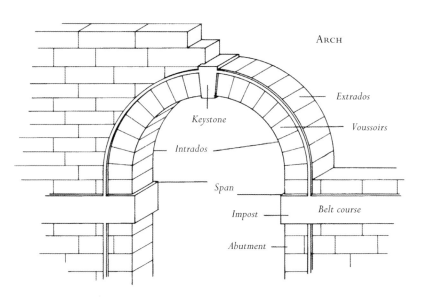

ARCH

Extrados

Keystone

Voussoirs

Intrados

Span

Impost

Belt course

Abutment

ARCHITRAVE. The bottom third of the entablature, the part resting on the column or pilaster and supporting a frieze. It is often divided into fascia. *See* ORDERS OF ARCHITECTURE.

ASTRAGAL. A small half round to be seen on a capital. *See* ORDERS OF ARCHITECTURE and MOLDINGS. Also a molded strip applied to one side of a door leaf where the two leaves meet. It is designed to project over the adjoining leaf when the door is closed.

ATTIC. A story built above the cornice of a building.

BALUSTER. An upright support in a variety of turned shapes, customarily swelling toward the base. When one shape is inverted and superimposed on its model, it is called a double baluster. Used in a series and supporting a rail, it forms part of a balustrade.

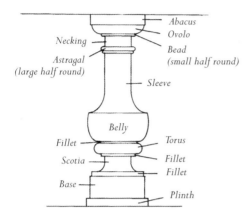

BARREL VAULT. A ceiling or roof construction as an extended arch over a space. Customarily semicylindrical in shape. *See* VAULTING.

BASE. The bottom part, made up of moldings, of the column and the pilaster, or of any architectural of decorative sign. *See* ORDERS OF ARCHITECTURE.

BASEBOARD. A flat projection at the floor level of an interior wall. *See* DADO.

BATTER. An incline given the face of a wall.

BAY, BAY LEAF, BAYBERRY. A stylized leaf and berry of the bay tree, by laurel or sweet bay (*Laurus nobilis*) often imbricated as in a wreath, in a swag, or in the enrichment of a torus.

BEAD, BEAD MOLDING. A small half round. *See* MOLDINGS.

BEAD-AND-REEL. A molding made up of elongated beads and disks.

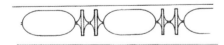

BEADS. *See* PEARLS.

BED MOLD. The molding on which a cornice rests. *See* ORDERS OF ARCHITECTURE.

BEL ÉTAGE. The principal floor, customarily above the ground floor, reserved for reception rooms. Also Piano nobile.

BELT COURSE. A horizontal band of masonry extending across the facade of a building. Also String course. *See* ARCH.

BEZANT. A coin-shaped ornament.

BRACKET. A support for a projection, such as a cornice, usually scroll-shaped, as in a console bracket.

BUCRANE. An ox skull. An ornamental device often used with garlands, festoons, and ribbons.

BRACKET

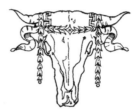

CABUCHON. A round or ovoid device with a convex surface, often elaborately framed. Also found in jewelry.

CAISSON. A sunken panel in a vault or a dome. *See* COFFER.

CAPITAL. The crowning member of a column or a pilaster. *See* ORDERS OF ARCHITECTURE.

CARTOUCHE. A shield or ovoid form often bearing inscriptions and devices in relief, frequently set in an elaborate scroll frame and bordered with ornament.

CAVETTO. A concave molding with the profile of a quarter round or close to it. *See* MOLDINGS.

CHAIN BAND. A series of circles joined by paired hyphens, often with rosettes in the circles. When bordered by acanthus, it is known as a foliated chain band.

CHAIN BAND

COFFER. A sunken panel in a ceiling, vault, or dome, or the underside of an arch. The great example of a coffering is to be found in the Pantheon in Rome.

COLUMN. A round, vertical support, consisting of a base, shaft, and capital, usually upholding an entablature. *See* ORDERS OF ARCHITECTURE.

CONSOLE. A decorative bracket in the form of a scroll supporting a balcony, a table, or an overhanging wall.

CORINTHIAN COLUMN. One of the five orders of columns, mainly distinguished by its capital of acanthus leaves and volutes. It was the favorite order of the Romans. *See* ORDERS OF ARCHITECTURE.

CORNICE. The projecting top section of an entablature. *See* ORDERS OF ARCHITECTURE.

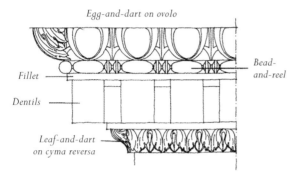

Egg-and-dart on ovolo

Fillet

Dentils

Bead-and-reel

Leaf-and-dart on cyma reversa

CORNUCOPIA. Also known as a horn of plenty, it is a goat's horn overflowing with fruit, grain, ears of corn, and similar items.

CORONA. The flat part of a cornice between the cymatium above and the bed mold below. *See* ORDERS OF ARCHITECTURE.

COURSE. A horizontal layer of masonry.

COVE. A concave surface connecting a ceiling and a wall.

CROSSETTE. Also Greek ear. A lateral extension of the architrave moldings at the top of a door or window frame.

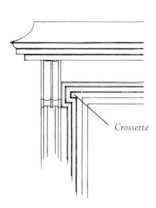

Crossette

CYMA RECTA. A molding with an S-shaped curve, concave over convex. *See* MOLDINGS.

CYMATIUM. The uppermost molding of a cornice, usually in the shape of a cyma recta. *See* ORDERS OF ARCHITECTURE.

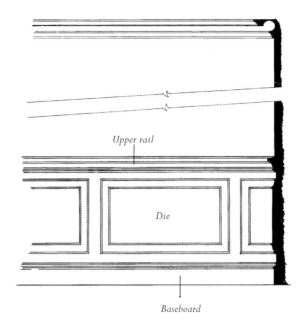

Upper rail

Die

Baseboard

DADO. A continuous wall pedestal or wainscot consisting of a base or baseboard, a die, and an upper rail or cap molding.

DENTIL. A small projecting block used in rows, called a dentil band or course, forming part of a cornice. Dentils resemble teeth. *Denticulated* or *Denticular* means enriched with dentils. *See* CORNICE.

DOME. A convex roof or ceiling, hemispherical, semiovoidal, or saucer-shaped, built over a square, octagonal, or circular space.

DORIC COLUMN. One of the five orders of columns, with a simple capital consisting mainly of an abacus and echinus. *See* ORDERS OF ARCHITECTURE.

ECHINUS. An ovolo or quarter-round molding that is part of a capital. *See* ORDERS OF ARCHITECTURE.

EGG-AND-DART. A familiar convex molding, an ovolo in profile enriched with eggs and arrowhead. *See* CORNICE.

ENTABLATURE. The upper part of an order, supported by columns. Made up of three major horizontal members: architrave, frieze, and cornice. *See* ORDERS OF ARCHITECTURE.

ENTASIS. An almost imperceptible swelling added to the tapering of the column shaft. It is a necessary refinement to correct the optical illusion of concavity that results if the column is straight.

ENTASIS

EXTRADOS. The outside surface of an arch. *See* ARCH.

FASCIA. The plain horizontal band or bands, often combined with moldings, that make up the architrave, the lowest, third part of the entablature. *See* ORDERS OF ARCHITECTURE.

FESTOON. A garland made of fruits, flowers, leaves, or husks, and hanging in a curve. Alternative term: Swag. *See also* GARLAND.

FILLET. A raised, narrow flat band between the flutes of a column. Also a raised or sunken band when combined with other elements. *See* MOLDINGS.

FLEURON. A small flower-shaped ornament usually found on the abacus of a Corinthian column. *See* ORDERS OF ARCHITECTURE, CORINTHIAN.

FLUTE. A concave groove or channel running vertically on a column or pilaster shaft. Also found in enriched moldings. Collectively called fluting.

FLUTTERING RIBBON. (*See* illustration.)

FRET. A geometrical meandering pattern of horizontal and vertical straight lines making a band. Also called Greek key.

FRIEZE. The middle horizontal member of an entablature above the architrave and below the comic. *See* ORDERS OF ARCHITECTURE.

GADROON. Old spelling: Godroon. A convex rounded ornament, always in a set; for that reason, most often called gadroons. The gadroon is round at the upper end and tapering to a point at the other.

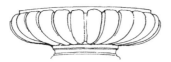

GARLAND. An intertwining of fruits, leaves, flowers, or husks.

GROIN. The ridge at the intersection of two vaults. A groined vault. *See* VAULTING.

GUILLOCHE. An ornament composed of continuous interlaced curving lines. When there are two linked patterns, it is known as a double guilloche.

Single guilloche

Double guilloche

GUTTAE. A series of cone-shaped or cylindrical pendants on the underside of a triglyph. *See* ORDERS OF ARCHITECTURE.

HELIX. The volutes, or scrolls, of a Corinthian capital. *See* ORDERS OF ARCHITECTURE; CORINTHIAN.

IMBRICATED. A pattern of overlapping leaves or scales, usually of bay leaves, oak leaves, or bezants. *Imbrication:* a band of the same.

IMPOST. A cornice-like bracket from which an arch springs. Also called impost block. *See* ARCH.

IONIC. One of the five orders of columns, recognized by its capital of volutes, or helixes. *See* ORDERS OF ARCHITECTURE.

IMBRICATED

JIB DOOR. A door made to look indistinguishable from the wall in which it stands.

KEYSTONE. The wedged top stone of an arch. *See* ARCH.

LEAF-AND-DART. A repetitive band made up of a stylized leaf and a dart. Sometimes called water leaf, a term invented by an eighteeth-century archaeologist.

LINTEL. A horizontal member spanning an opening in a door or a window.

LUNETTE. A semicircular wall inside an arch. Often applied to a painting that fills the same.

MEANDER. *See* FRET.

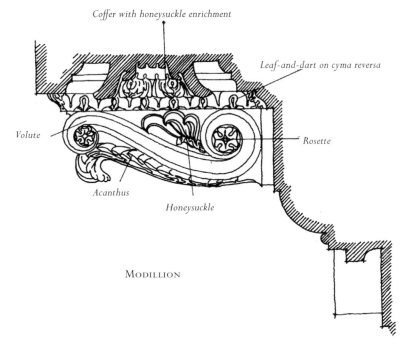

Coffer with honeysuckle enrichment

Leaf-and-dart on cyma reversa

Volute

Rosette

Acanthus

Honeysuckle

MODILLION

ORDERS OF ARCHITECTURE (FIVE ORDERS). An order consists of a column with base (except in the Greek Doric), shaft, and capital and its entablature. Each order has its own formalized ornament. The orders are the basis of architectural design in the classical tradition, providing lessons in proportion, scale, and the uses of ornament. The five orders are Tuscan, Doric, Ionic, Corinthian, and Composite. *See* illustrations comparing the orders on the next page.

OVOLO. A convex molding, either elliptical or quarter-round. *See* MOLDINGS.

PATERA (PATERAE, pl.). An ornament, usually in the form of a rosette, to be found in coffers.

PALMETTE. *See* ANTHEMION.

PEARLS. A small molding resembling a string of pearls. Also known as beads.

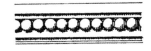

1. Raised fillet

2. Sunken fillet

3. Bead
Called an Astragal when found on a shaft

4. Cavetto

5. Ovolo

6. Cyma recta

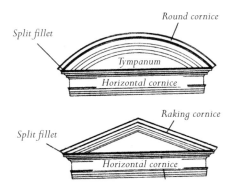

METOPE. A square panel between triglyphs on a Doric frieze. Often decorated with a relief. *See* ORDERS OF ARCHITECTURE; DORIC.

MODILLION. A small bracket used in rows under the corona of a cornice and extending from the bed mold. It frequently takes the shape of an ornamental double volute.

MOLDINGS. Plain or decorated profiles either rectangular or curved and either above or below the surface. Their purpose is to provide a transition or to produce light and shade.

MONOLITH. The shaft of a column consisting of a single block of stone. Also monolithic.

NECKING. Also known as collarino, a wide surface at the top of a Tuscan, Doric, or Ionic column. *See* ORDERS OF ARCHITECTURE.

NICHE. A recess in a wall, usually with a semidome, designed as a place for a statue.

PEDESTAL. A base for a column, pilaster, or statue. Also a post in a balustrade. *See* BALUSTRADE.

PEDIMENT. A triangular gable with a wall, called a tympanum, framed by a cornice. Originating with the Greek temple, it is found today crowning an entablature, a door, or a window. When it has a round cornice instead of two sides of a triangle, it is known as a round or segmental pediment.

Round cornice

Split fillet

Tympanum

Horizontal cornice

Raking cornice

Split fillet

Horizontal cornice

PENDENTIVE. A triangular curved surface between two arches and beneath a dome.

PIANO NOBILE. *See* BEL ÉTAGE.

PIER. A heavy vertical mass of masonry used for support with none of the details of a column.

7. Cyma reversa

8. Scotia

9. Torus

MOLDINGS

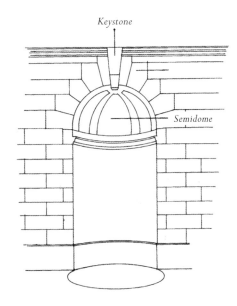

Keystone

Semidome

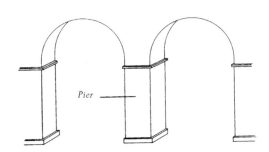

Pier

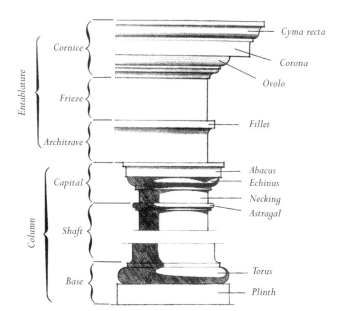

Entablature
- Cornice
  - Cyma recta
  - Corona
  - Ovolo
- Frieze
- Architrave
  - Fillet

Column
- Capital
  - Abacus
  - Echinus
  - Necking
  - Astragal
- Shaft
- Base
  - Torus
  - Plinth

TUSCAN

ORDERS OF ARCHITECTURE
(Five Orders)

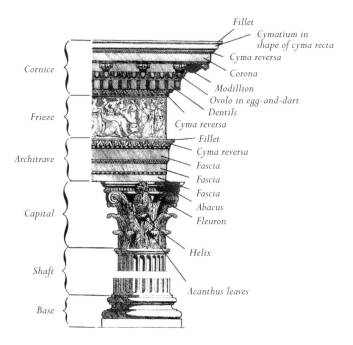

- Cornice
  - Fillet
  - Cymatium in shape of cyma recta
  - Cyma reversa
  - Corona
  - Modillion
  - Ovolo in egg-and-dart
  - Dentils
- Frieze
  - Cyma reversa
  - Fillet
- Architrave
  - Cyma reversa
  - Fascia
  - Fascia
  - Fascia
- Capital
  - Abacus
  - Fleuron
- Shaft
  - Helix
  - Acanthus leaves
- Base

CORINTHIAN

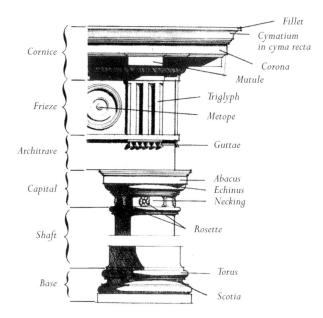

- Cornice
  - Fillet
  - Cymatium in cyma recta
  - Corona
  - Mutule
- Frieze
  - Triglyph
  - Metope
- Architrave
  - Guttae
- Capital
  - Abacus
  - Echinus
  - Necking
  - Rosette
- Shaft
- Base
  - Torus
  - Scotia

DORIC

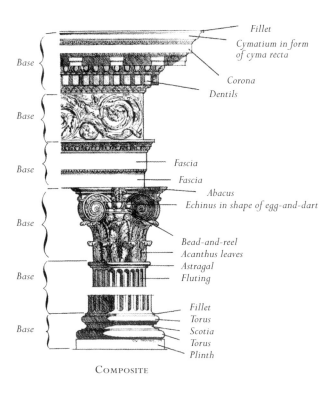

- Base
  - Fillet
  - Cymatium in form of cyma recta
  - Corona
  - Dentils
- Base
- Base
  - Fascia
  - Fascia
  - Abacus
  - Echinus in shape of egg-and-dart
- Base
  - Bead-and-reel
  - Acanthus leaves
  - Astragal
  - Fluting
- Base
  - Fillet
  - Torus
  - Scotia
  - Torus
  - Plinth

COMPOSITE

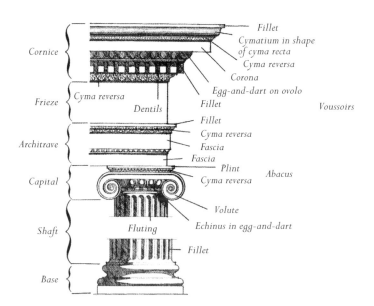

- Cornice
  - Fillet
  - Cymatium in shape of cyma recta
  - Cyma reversa
  - Corona
  - Egg-and-dart on ovolo
  - Fillet
- Frieze
  - Cyma reversa
  - Dentils
  - Fillet
- Architrave
  - Cyma reversa
  - Fascia
  - Fascia
  - Plint
  - Cyma reversa
- Capital
  - Abacus
  - Volute
  - Echinus in egg-and-dart
- Shaft
  - Fluting
  - Fillet
- Base

Voussoirs

IONIC

ROSETTE. A floral motive, usually round. Paterae in coffers are most often in the shape of rosettes.

PILASTER. A vertical rectangular projection from a wall, treated like a column with base, shaft, and capital.

PLINTH. An additional base beneath the base of a column, or pilaster, or baluster. A plinth course is a continuous plinth serving as base to a number of columns, pilasters, or balusters (balustrade).

POST. An upright supporting member.

PULVINATED. Pillow-shaped, as in the curved profile of a frieze, such as in a pulvinated frieze. It is also found in rustication, where the stones are given a pillow shape.

ROSTRUM (ROSTRA, pl.). The prow of a Greek or Roman warship used as a ram in battle. Stone imitations of them are part of the grammar or classical ornament and are customarily found in columns. Captured rostra were placed at the foot of the speaker's podium in the Roman Forum; for that reason such a podium is called a rostrum.

RUSTICATION, RUSTICATED. The same for cut stone in a wall that is channeled with grooves. The purpose is to convey an impression of solidity and strength and to give visual relief to the wall surface.

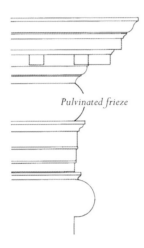

Pulvinated frieze

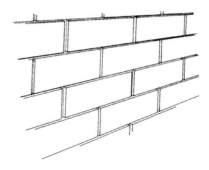

SAUCER DOME. A low concave ceiling, with the shape of an inverted saucer.

SCONCE. A bracket, secured to a wall, with a candlestick or several candlesticks, or imitations of same, or with arms holding lights. Also known as Appliqué.

SCROLL. A spiral found in the form of volutes of a capital or in the frame of a cartouche.

SCROLL FRAME. A frame adorned with scrolls that looks as if it were made of thick boiled leather.

RAKING CORNICE. Sloping cornice of the two sides of a pediment. *See* PEDIMENT.

REED. A bead or beaded molding, i.e., a small half round. When used in clusters, it is called reading.

REVEAL. The section of the wall framing a window or a door, customarily when the wall is thick.

RIBBON. An ornament in imitation of a cloth ribbon.

RINCEAU (RINCEAUX, pl.). A symmetrical swirling ornament of leaves, customarily those of the acanthus.

SEGMENTAL. The portion of a circle, less than a semicircle, defining the shape of an arch or vault.

SHAFT. The trunk or the longest part of a column between the base and the capital. *See* ORDERS OF ARCHITECTURE.

SHELL VAULTING. Vaulting used solely as decoration serving no structural purpose. It is made of plaster bonded by lath and held in place by struts attached to the beams. The Romans were the first to adopt the vault as a decorative device. With its value as an ornament, it evolved from being structural to being chiefly decorative. *See* VAULTING.

SOFFIT. The underside of an arch, a beam, or any spanning members. *See* ARCH.

SPANDREL. The triangular space bounded by the curve of an arch, a horizontal line through its top, and a vertical line rising from the impost or springing of the arch.

SPLAY. A sloped surface, usually in the arch of a door or window where one side is larger than the other.

SPLIT FILLET. A fillet found on the horizontal and raking cornices of a pediment, termed split because it divides at an angle where the two cornices meet. *See* PEDIMENT.

STEREOTOMY. The science and art of stonecutting. Also stereotomic.

STOPPED FLUTING. Where the flutes or channels of a column or pilaster, or any grooves, have been filled with rods or rods topped by acanthus.

STRAPWORK. A form of ornamentation consisting of folding and interlacing bands.

STRING COURSE OR BELT COURSE. A horizontal band across a facade. It can be flush or projecting, and given a variety of surfaces.

SWAG. *See* FESTOON.

TAENIA. The fillet at the top of a Doric architrave. *See* ORDERS OF ARCHITECTURE; DORIC.

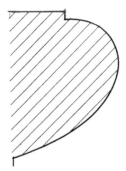

THUMB MOLDING. Also known as a quirked molding. In profile, it is part round and part elliptical.

TRIGLYPH. A projecting block with three channels forming part of a Doric frieze. *See* ORDERS OF ARCHITECTURE; DORIC.

VAULT. An arched ceiling. Prior to the coming of the steel beam, the vault of brick or stone was adopted instead of wood beams to cover a space. In the nineteenth century, a space would often be covered by several vaults supported on cast-iron beams. The illustration above shows a vault of brick and cast iron concealed by a flat plaster ceiling.

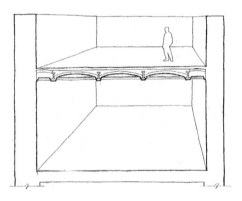

VAULTING. A method of covering space with masonry following the principle of the arch. Its great advantage prior to the use of steel and concrete was its being fire-retardant and long-lasting. Shell vaulting often replaced vaults of masonry. For instance, a stucco shell could be suspended by struts from beams.

VESTIBULE. An anteroom, entrance hall, or foyer.

VOLUTE. A spiral scroll as on an Ionic, Corinthian, or Composite capital, or any special ornament. Also known as Helix. *See* ORDERS OF ARCHITECTURE.

The glossary is based on *The American Vignola* by William R. Ware. For help in the definitions, the author is indebted to Dr. Richard H. Howland; to James Parker of the Metropolitan Museum of Art, and to Alvin Holm, president of the Philadelphia chapter of Classical America. The drawings were executed by Alvin Holm, Cameron MacTavish, Harvey Heiser, David R. Kulick, Steven W. Semes, Michael Javelos, Stephen Wright, and Stephen Piersanti.

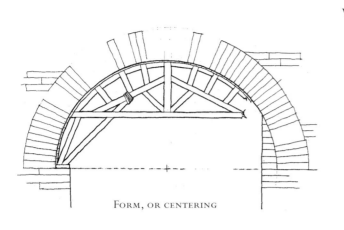

Form, or centering

Vaulting

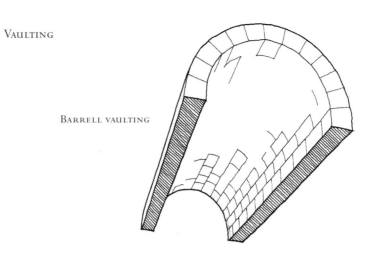

Barrell vaulting

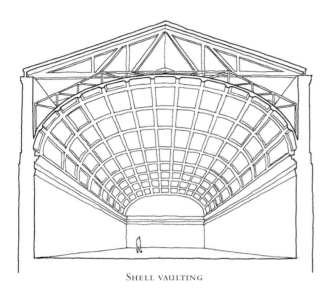

Shell vaulting

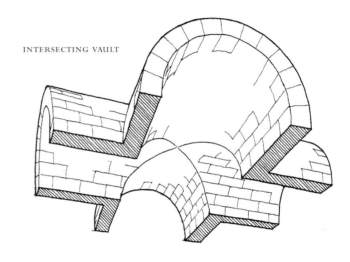

intersecting vault

Arcade

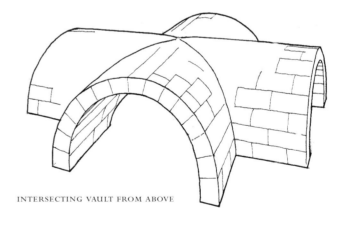

intersecting vault from above

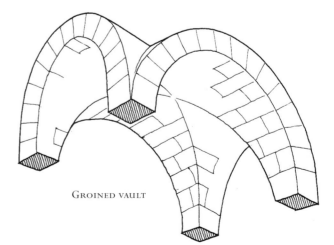

Groined vault

Louis Amateis, sculptor, 1855–1913. A native of Turin, Italy, he attended the Royal Academy in that city. After a year in Paris in 1882, he traveled to New York and then to Washington, where he had a studio. In 1892 he founded the School of Architecture and Fine Arts at George Washington University. His best-known work is the monument to the defenders of The Alamo in San Antonio, Texas. He died in Washington.

Giovanni Andrei, sculptor, 1770–1824. Born in Carrara, Italy, he evidently did his apprenticeship in the marble yards of that famous center of stonecarving. As a result of an invitation extended to him through Philip Mazzei, Jefferson's Italian correspondent and friend, he came to Washington in 1806. His first work, capitals for the House Chamber, was destroyed in the 1814 fire. A year later, he was sent to Italy to recruit sculptors and to have Corinthian capitals carved for the rebuilt House Chamber. The sculptors he retained were Carlo Franzoni, younger brother of Giuseppe Franzoni, and Francisco Iardella. He also did work for a chapel in Baltimore. He died in Washington.

Paul Wayland Bartlett, sculptor, 1865–1925. The son of a sculptor who was for many years an instructor at the Massachusetts Institute of Technology, he was born in New Haven. His father, not wanting him educated in this country, sent him with his mother to Paris. He blossomed early, displaying a bust in the Paris Salon of 1879 when he was only fourteen. He was a student of Pierre-Jules Cavalier and of Emanuel Frémiet, along with other Americans. In 1896 he contributed two bronze statues to the Rotunda of the Library of Congress, those of Michelangelo and Columbus. He did six figures that stand in front of the center attic of the New York Public Library. His most famous statue is the equestrian Lafayette formerly in the courtyard of the Louvre in Paris. (It was recently moved to make way for a grotesque glass pyramid.) Like a number of American artists, he lived and worked in Paris and there he died. The central figure and the Agriculture figures (on the right) of the House pediment he executed in Paris, the Industry figures (on the left) he modeled in 1914 in Washington. His models were carved in marble by a crew of journeyman sculptors in Washington.

George Blagden, stonemason, died 1826. English-born and English-trained, this skilled mason came to this country probably in the 1780s. In 1794 he was put in charge of the Aquia Creek sandstone quarries on the Potomac southeast of Washington as well as the stonework at the Capitol. When Benjamin Latrobe became Capitol Architect in 1803, it was Blagden who gave him "the only existing drawing of the Capitol"—that is, the one based on Thornton's design. He was to work for all the architects from Thornton to Bulfinch. Successful in business, he was also active in government and church matters, serving on the city council and as a member of the vestry of Christ Church, Georgetown. He was killed by the collapse of an embankment at the Capitol.

Constantino Brumidi, painter and sculptor, 1805–1881, was born in Rome, the son of Stauro (Stavros) Brumidi from Philiatra on the west coast of the Peloponnesus, Greece, and Maria Bianchini, a Roman. His father had a café on the Via Tor de' Conti, a street now bordering on the east side of the Forum of Augustus. Nearby was, and is, the Church of St. Quirico and St. Giuletta, where he was baptized and which was to be his church as long as he lived in Rome. (In all probability the café was on the site of the present Hotel Forum.)

His first recorded commission was designing the sculpture for the Weld-Clifford Chapel in the crypt of San Marcello al Corso. (Thomas Cardinal Weld was the first Englishman to wear the red hat after the Reformation. A very religious man, he had welcomed the Royalist refugees during the French Revolution and given property to the Society of Jesus, notably the land for Stonyhurst College, a famous Jesuit school. A widower, he renounced his estate to his brother and became a priest. Not long after, he was made a bishop, and eventually, in 1830, he was named cardinal. The Clifford buried with him was his daughter.)

Subsequent commissions stemmed from Brumidi's membership in a corps of painters serving the Vatican. He restored several large maps in fresco in the Loggia della Cosmografia in the Vatican Palace, and he did ten portraits in oil for the *Chronology of the Popes* in the Basilica of St. Paul's-Outside-the-Walls, executed in mosaic. (The paintings still exist, stored in the warehouse forming part of St. Peter's.) His last religious commission was the vault of Santa Maria dell'Archetto, a tiny prayer chapel behind San Marcello al Corso.

The same corps of artists was called on to decorate the palace and villa of Prince Alessandro Torlonia. The art of nineteenth-century Rome is usually passed over because it can hardly stand comparison with that of prior times. The city of 170,000 around 1840 had barely recovered from the era of the French Revolution and the Napoleonic Wars. During the turmoil, only those with business acumen had prospered, chief of these being the Torlonia family. Descended from a Frenchman from Auvergne who had settled in Rome in the eighteenth century and turned to banking, they became the bankers to the Holy See and the Roman aristocracy. Such was their affluence that they intermarried and joined the city's princely class. Part of this had to do with their being Maecenases in the grand tradition. Prince Alessandro, grandson of the Frenchman, became the best known; he restored the interior of the Gesù, the great Jesuit church of Rome.

Prince Torlonia built himself a palace, a new palace, in what is today a traffic maelstrom, the Piazza Venezia. To Brumidi fell the commission to execute figurative panels for the Gothic chapel. The palace was torn down in the 1890s to make way for the piazza and the Victor Emanuel Monument. In addition, Brumidi did panels for the foyer of the theater forming part of the Villa Torlonia on the Via Nomentana, now a municipal park. The buildings, inaccessible, are undergoing restoration.

Résumé of Brumidi's Roman work:

1837	The Weld-Clifford Chapel in the crypt of San Marcello al Corso, Piazza San Marcello 5
1838–43	Panels in the chapel of the Torlonia Palace, Piazza Venezia; destroyed in the 1890s
1840–42	Restored panels in the Loggia della Cosmografia in the Vatican Palace
1842, 1845	Panels in the foyer of the theater at the Villa Torlonia, Via Nomentana
1847	Ten portraits in oil for the Chronology of the Popes in the Basilica of St. Paul's-Outside-the-Walls, stored in St. Peter's
1851	Vault of Santa Maria dell'Archetto off the Via di San Marcello

In addition, he executed portraits. His commissions being irregular, he had another source of income: the family café. He made enough money to lend to relatives and others, as well as to have a studio at one time in the Palazzo Barberini.

Brumidi married and had two children, only one of whom lived to adulthood. His status was that of a family man in a small business who ran a café and worked as a professional artist, but he served Rome's best clients: the Church and the House of Torlonia.

For that reason it is difficult to explain why he became an active supporter of the Roman Republic of 1849. We have to remind ourselves that in Italy at the time, artists were not part of the community of "free spirits" we call "bohemia," the independent world of artists and writers with its own code and outlook. That was still confined to Paris; in Rome the native artist was part of an informal guild based on craft. The political concept of revolution had yet to be applied to the arts, nor was there the antibourgeois prejudice so often associated with bohemia. If Brumidi knew little or nothing of this last, then why was he for the Roman Republic? This can only be explained by the presence of nationalism among the class of modest lawyers, small businessmen, and shopkeepers known as the *piccola borghesia*, the petty bourgeoisie whose incipient patriotism was tinged with anticlericalism. They were, in the 1840s, caught up in the movement for the unification of Italy, an Italy with Rome as its capital, and they saw in the papacy with its Papal States a major obstacle.

Brumidi's role would have passed unnoticed had he not participated, as a captain in the Civic Guard, in a raid in May 1849 on a monastery of the Olivetans (a branch of the Benedictine order), San Francesca Romana (also known as Santa Maria Nova), at the southeastern end of the Forum near the Arch of Titus. The episode was like something out of a comic opera. The raiders expected to find money that the monks had collected to further the beatification of their founder. They thought the treasure was concealed in the building, and in searching for it they damaged walls and floors. Not finding the money, they instead took chairs, a large tablecloth, tableware, and other objects. Brumidi had deposited the pictures found there in the Lateran Palace as required by the republican authorities. On the return of the Papal forces with French support, his fellow republicans returned the stolen property and even repaired the damages they had done.

The matter would appear to have been settled, but as it turned out, the monks were satisfied but not the law. In February 1851 the raiders, including Brumidi, the "*Pittore e Caffetiere*," were put in prison. In court Brumidi had many defenders testifying to his piety, to the respectable operation of his café, to his having prevented the sacking of a Jesuit residence, to his loyalty to the Pope, etc., and to the fact that he was only in the Civic Guard as a family man and a café owner. The favorable testimony had no influence in court; he was sentenced to thirty-three months in prison. Fortunately, he was pardoned after serving thirteen months, much of which had been spent in pretrial detention.

Far more important in his release was the role of two Americans then in Rome. One was the New Yorker John Norris, a Jesuit studying in Rome who had befriended Brumidi. It was he who brought Brumidi's situation to the attention of the great Bishop John Hughes of New York. Hughes, in Rome in the spring of 1851 to receive the pallium (the ring of wool bestowed on those elevated to archbishop), evidently petitioned the papal court to free the artist. In June 1851 Brumidi asked the court, as had been agreed, to allow him to leave for the United States. The aim of his going was to execute pictures for the decoration of churches. Permission granted, he left the Papal States, probably by way of Leghorn, to arrive in New York in September 1852.

Other than receiving a copy of the King James Version of the Bible from the American Bible Society, he was given an Anglicized version of his first name by the immigration authorities. He who in Rome had the name Costantino was now Constantino, with another "n."

Religious commissions were not immediately forthcoming. There is mention of work in Mexico City where he is supposed to have painted a picture for the cathedral, yet there is no record of it. He executed a number of portraits, such as the one of Father Norris that is still in the possession of the family. One of his commissions at the time was the large picture of St. Aloysius Gonzaga for the church of the same name which is on North Capitol Street, a few blocks north of the Capitol. It shows the young Aloysius receiving his first communion from St. Charles Borromeo. It and two neighboring circular pictures he owed to Father Benedict Sestini, the church's architect. It is pleasant to record that Archbishop Hughes, who had rescued him years before, officiated at the church's consecration in 1859.

Little is known of his family. His wife did not accompany him in 1852 but came later. She died in 1859. He married again a year later and had a son, Lawrence, in 1861. He continued to do church work on and off. There are some panels in St. Dominic's in Washington. In 1871 he did a crucifixion for St. Stephen's in New York. Another was *The Apparition of Our Lord to Sister Marguerite Mary* for the chapel of the Visitation Convent, formerly on Massachusetts Avenue in Washington. When the convent moved to Bethesda, Maryland, it went to Trinity Church, Georgetown. Painted over in the course of a redecoration, it remained there until some Brumidi admirers of Greek extraction removed it; it is now in Chicago.

A chronological list of Brumidi's work at the Capitol follows:

Subject and Location	Date
Agriculture and portraits in H-144, former House Agricultural Committee Room, now the House Appropriations Committee Room	1855–56
Cornwallis Sues for Cessation of Hostilities under the Flag of Truce, formerly in the House Chamber, now in the House Dining Room	1857
Ocean deities, marine and military symbols, battle scenes, portraits in s-127, s-128, and s-129, former Army and Navy Senate Committee Rooms, now the Senate Appropriation Committee Rooms	1858, 1871

Figures symbolizing commerce, the laying of the Atlantic Cable, in s-211, former Senate District of Columbia Committee Room, now the Lyndon Baines Johnson Room	*1858, 1867*
Symbolic figures and portraits in s-216, the President's Room	*1859*
Decorations and portraits in the Brumidi Corridor	*1859 onward*
The Apotheosis of Washington in the Great Rotunda	*1864–65*
Medallion portraits in s-118, Democratic Policy Committee Room (Senate), former Senate Committee on Foreign Relations Room	*1872, 1874*
Symbolic figures and decorations in s-213, Senate Reception Room	*1871–74*
Inventors and ornament in the Patent Corridor	*1873*
Symbolic figures and decoration in s-212, Vice President's Office	*1876*
Lunette, Signing the First Treaty of Peace with Great Britain, in North Brumidi Corridor	*1874*
Portrait of Robert R. Livingston in main Brumidi Corridor	*1878*
Lunette, Cession of Louisiana, in North Brumidi Corridor	*1875*
Lunette, Bellona, Goddess of War, in West Brumidi Corridor	*1875*
Historical panels in the Rotunda Frieze	*1877–80*

As mentioned elsewhere, Brumidi was still at work in 1879 at the Capitol when he had a serious accident. Painting the frieze that bears his name, he would be hoisted to the platform some sixty feet above the Rotunda floor in a wooden cage. It was one of the city's sights to see the seventy-four-year-old artist being raised around 10:30 in the morning to the platform and then, at 3 P.M., being lowered to the floor. In October he lost his balance and fell, only to catch hold of a ladder, which broke his fall. Rescued by a guard, he left, never to return. He died on February 19, 1880, and lies buried in Washington's Glenwood Cemetery.

A note of explanation about his end. As he lay dying in his house at 921 G Street, he sent for Father Sestini, but the priest, who was out of town, arrived after his death. The funeral, with the Reverend J. A. Walter reading the burial service, took place at No. 921. No mass was held, and he was buried in Glenwood Cemetery among Protestants. The assumption is that, with his American marriage, he had married outside the Church and therefore could not be buried in a Catholic cemetery. Further, for all his religious work, he was not a regular communicant.

CHARLES BULFINCH, 1763–1844, America's first native-born professional architect, was from Boston. His family, particularly on his mother's side, was wealthy, with close links to the old country. As a proper Bostonian, he went to Boston Latin School and to Harvard

College, class of 1778. At college he took an interest in architecture and became familiar with the books of the ancient Roman Vitruvius and the Italian architect Palladio, as well as books on English architecture. In the Harvard College Library he discovered such key texts as James Stuart and Nicholas Revett's *Antiquities of Athens* (volume 1, 1762).

In 1785 the young Bulfinch was sent to Europe for two years. Like the painter John Trumbull, he stayed in Paris with our minister to France, Thomas Jefferson, and he was able to travel as far as Rome. Still, it was London that made the greatest impression on him, especially the recent buildings of Robert Adam and Sir William Chambers, two Scottish architects. Both had produced handsome books of their work. Interestingly enough, eighteenth-century English architecture was to have a greater influence on him than on the English-born Latrobe, who looked more to the ancient Greeks.

Not long after his return home, he married a cousin, thereby strengthening the Boston link. It is not surprising to find among his clients such names as Amory, Coolidge, Otis, Paine, and Perkins.

His first commission, executed in 1790, was the first monument in the country to be erected to the War of Independence. A Doric column topped by an eagle, it stood atop Beacon Hill. Removed with the construction of the Massachusetts State House, it was later reconstructed in what is today a parking lot east of the building. The principal inscription at its base is worth repeating:

Americans. While from this eminence Scenes of Luxuriant fertility, of flourishing commerce, and the abodes of social happiness meet your view, Forget not those who by their exertions Have secured to you these blessings.

His career may be said to have been well launched when he was invited to design the Hartford State House in 1792. (One source of evidence of his role in the building comes from a letter of the painter Trumbull.) The inspiration is presumed to have been the Liverpool Town Hall.

What followed seems unusual for one so careful in the way he conducted his life. The project—it would be called a speculative development today—was the Tontine Crescent in Boston, a too rare example of monumental civic design. The residential row, for such it was, failed, and both Bulfinch and his wife lost everything.

Still, fortune smiled on him. The architect was invited to design the Massachusetts State House on which his fame rests; it was built from 1795 to 1797. Although its gold dome no longer commands the skyline, it remains one of the best examples of public buildings of the era. Interestingly, in keeping with his leaning toward things English, Bulfinch turned to London's Somerset House by Chambers for his model. He also rebuilt and enlarged Faneuil Hall, the "cradle of liberty" in the American Revolution. Another work was University Hall, which houses Harvard University's administration.

Despite his success, the Tontine disaster forced him to work outside the field of architecture. In 1799 he was chosen chairman of Boston's Board of Selectmen, which was tantamount to being a city manager, and he held the job until 1817. It did not prevent him from being buffeted about by financial difficulties, one of which was serious enough to land him briefly in debtors' prison. Prominent architects in the first half of the last century appeared to have had more than their share of money troubles.

In the summer of 1817 President Monroe came to Boston and it devolved on Bulfinch, as chairman of the Board of Selectmen, to escort him around the city. Monroe easily recognized his worth and evidently was no less impressed by his tact. With Latrobe's departure later in the year, the President appointed Bulfinch Capitol Architect at a salary of $2,500 in January 1818.

Outside the Capitol, the architect had few commissions in Washington, one being the Unitarian church, long since demolished. Oddly enough, sandstone gatehouses that he had placed around the Capitol still survive, but elsewhere in the city, two being on Constitution Avenue near the Ellipse.

After President Jackson abolished the office of Architect of the Capitol, Bulfinch went into virtual retirement. At least he was rewarded with one important job: the Maine State House in Augusta, built from 1829 to 1832. With it to his credit, he could boast of three state capitols. Only one other architect matched him in numbers: Cass Gilbert, architect of the United States Supreme Court, along with the capitols of Minnesota, Arkansas, and West Virginia.

Bulfinch died in 1844. He lies buried, like many another proper Bostonian, in Mount Auburn Cemetery in Cambridge.

ANTONIO CAPELLANO, Italian sculptor, dates unknown. He was in New York in 1815 and then went to Baltimore, where he executed the relief for the Battle Monument. In the 1820s he was at the Capitol and subsequently returned to Italy.

EMERICH A. CARSTENS, painter, 1823–1902. Born in Germany, he was among the many Germans who came to this country after the revolution of 1848. He first worked in New York, and around 1851 he came to Washington to decorate the Capitol, serving as foreman of a painting crew. In that position he impinged on Brumidi's authority. There were differences between the two and he left. Carstens had a successful career decorating public buildings, churches, and residences in the Washington area, and he was to return to the Capitol to do restoration work.

ENRICO CAUSICI, sculptor, died 1832. A native of Verona, Italy, he came to this country in 1822. He executed the reliefs *The Landing of the Pilgrims* and *Daniel Boone and the Indians* in the Great Rotunda in 1825. He also did the *Liberty* and the *Eagle* in Statuary Hall. His most famous work is the colossal statue of George Washington atop the Washington Monument in Baltimore. He died in Havana, Cuba.

JOHN GABSBY CHAPMAN, painter, 1808–1889. Born in Alexandria, Virginia, he attended the Pennsylvania Academy of the Fine Arts in Philadelphia and, from there, proceeded to Rome and Florence. In 1831 he returned to this country and settled in New York. He made his reputation as a prolific illustrator; one project was a popular Bible with 1,400 illustrations. *The Baptism of Pocahontas* was painted in a studio in Washington. In 1848 he returned to Rome, where he remained until near the end of his life, at which point he came back to this country to die on Staten Island, New York.

HOWARD CHANDLER CHRISTY, painter, 1873–1952. Born in Ohio, he studied at the National Academy of Design and the Art Students League and with the painter William Merritt Chase in New York. He became a most successful magazine and book illustrator, famous for his magazine covers. In addition to *The Signing of the Constitution of the United States*, he did a number of portraits of congressmen.

EDWARD CLARK, architect, 1822–1902. Born in Philadelphia, he studied drawing with his architect father and engineering at an engineering firm. A student and then draftsman of Thomas Ustick

Walter's, he was in charge of construction at the General Post Office and the Patent Office extensions and he was assistant to Walter at the Capitol. Upon Walter's resignation in 1865, he became Architect of the Capitol and saw to the completion of the porticoes, the enlargement of the main entrance in the center portico, the transformation of the Old House of Representatives to Statuary Hall, and the building of the present marble terraces and the replanning of the grounds between 1873 and 1893 by Frederick Law Olmsted and Thomas Wisedell. He supervised the installation of elevators in the building in 1874 and the replacement of gas by electricity, completed in 1897. He was among those who pressed for the Library of Congress to have its own building on account of its expanding collections. Clark's last responsibility was overseeing the construction of new offices in the space vacated by the Library of Congress.

ARTHUR SCHMALZ CONRAD, painter, 1907–1975. A graduate of the Yale School of Fine Arts, 1931, he was a successful mural decorator and portraitist.

FILIPPO COSTAGGINI, painter, 1837–1904. A student at the Accademia di San Luca in Rome, he came to this country in 1870. His work is found in churches in New York, Philadelphia, and Baltimore, and he also executed portraits. He executed a portion of the Brumidi Frieze in the Great Rotunda.

ALLYN COX, painter, 1896–1983, was born in New York, the son of the mural painter Kenyon Cox, whose work is to be seen in the Library of Congress. He attended the National Academy of Design and the Art Students League, both in New York. In 1916 he won the Rome Prize at the American Academy of Art in Rome and was in Italy for five years. Like his father, he embarked on mural work. Among his commissions are murals in the William A. Clark, Jr., Library of the University of California in Los Angeles, the Law Building of the University of Virginia, the Cosmopolitan Club in New York, and the George Washington Masonic Memorial in Alexandria, Virginia. At the Capitol, he completed the Brumidi Frieze in the Great Rotunda and executed the portrait of Henry Clay in the Senate Reception Room and the decorations of the first-floor corridors in the House wing.

THOMAS CRAWFORD, sculptor, 1813–1857, was born in New York, the son of immigrants from the North of Ireland. As a boy, he would neglect his studies in order to draw and sketch. His parents, bowing to his interest, apprenticed him at sixteen to a wood-carver. Three years later, he was in the studio of John Frazee and Robert E. Launitz, stonecarvers and sculptors. When he could, he studied drawing and read much of the literature and history of ancient Greece and Rome. A youth of such energy and evident skill was destined to make the voyage to Italy, and in 1835 he arrived in Rome with a letter of introduction to no less a figure than Bertel Thorvaldsen. The first American sculptor to settle in the Holy City, he was to study with the Danish sculptor and with Vincenzo Camuccini, director of the Accademia di San Luca. He was among those who frequented the French Academy in Rome, very much a center for younger artists, where they drew models as well as the antique.

In the American colony in Rome at the time were Robert W. Weir and John G. Chapman, who were to paint pictures for the Great Rotunda.

Crawford did not have to worry about commissions. Orders for

St. Isaac's Cathedral, 30, 31, *31*, 36, 45, 47-48, *48, 80*
St. John's Church, 22
St. Matthew's Cathedral, 89
St. Paul's Cathedral, 4, 15, *15, 32, 48, 80*
St. Paul's Outside-the-Walls, *25*
  Basilica of, *24*
St. Petersburg, 3, 30, *31*
St. Peter's Cathedral, 16, *18, 26, 32, 36, 38, 48, 80*
Sammons, Richard, *29*
San Andrea della Valle, 86
San Francisco City Hall, 38, *39, 75, 80, 85*
San Marcello al Corso, *24*
Sargent, John Singer, 165
Savannah, siege of, 4
Saÿen, Henry Lyman, 169
Scheffer, Ary, 132
Schmidt, Charles, 120
Schmolzé, Carl Herman, 86
Schoenborn, August, *29,* 30, 49
Sewall, Jonathan, 133
Seydl, Jon L., *24*
Sherman, William Tecumseh, 106
Shrady, Henry Merwin, 34, 142
Simmons, Franklin, 142
Sir Walter Raleigh, Explorer of Virginia (Gevelot), *81*
Sistine Chapel, 63, 80, *124*
Sixtus I, Pope, *25*
S. Knipp & Company, 166, *167*
Smith, John, *79*
Smithsonian Institution, 20, 22, 94-95, 138, 141
Soldiers and Sailors Monument (Brooklyn), 37
Speaker Thomas Brackett Reed (Sargent), 166
Stadt Huys, 137
Stanton, Elizabeth Cady, 89

Stanza della Segnatura, 156, *156*
Statue of Liberty, 34, 41, 89
Stevens, Thaddeus, 130
Stewart, J. George, 139
Stone, Horatio, 89
Strickland, William, 13
Strieby, George W., *25,* 119
Stuart, Gilbert, 132, 166
Stuart, James, 90-91, *92, 95,* 98, *100*
Sullivan, Francis P., 128
Sullivan, Jeremiah, 72
Sumner, Charles, 103, 128
Supreme Court, U.S., 33, 44
Surrender of General Bourgoyne at Saratoga, New York, October 17, 1777 (Trumball), 75, 77, 79, 80-81
Surrender of Lord Cornwallis at Yorktown, Virginia, October 19, 1781 (Trumball), 75, 76, 79, 89

Taft, Robert A., 34, 126, 130
Taney, Roger B., *55,* 106
Telegraph, 160
Tennessee State Capitol, 13
Thayer, Sylvanus, 21
Thomas, Charles F., 86
Thomas, Ernest, 126, 171
Thornton, William, *5, 6, 7, 7, 8,* 10, 12, 19, 35, *52, 52, 53-54, 53,* 63, 120, 123, 130-31, 138-39, 142, 169, 171
Tonelli, Francesco, 65
Tower of Winds, 91, *92*
Tracy and Swartwout, 36, 37
Traité théorique et pratique de l'art de bâtir (Rondelet), 21
Traquair, James, 93
Treatise on the Decorative Part of Civil Architecture, A (Chambers), 54, *55,* 110
Trollope, Frances, *75,* 95

Truman, Harry, 121, 168
Trumbull, John, 4-5, 10-11, 75-76, 79, 80, 89, 109, 137
Trumbull, Jonathan, 75, 97
Tulip Hill, 5
Turner, Charles Y., 36

Udine, Giovanni da, 115
Union Station, 104, 140-41, 153
United States Botanic Garden, 34, 142
United States Capitol Historical Society, 136
United States Department of State, 61

Vanderlyn, John, 12, 76, 132
Vatican Palace, 63, 80, 116
Vermont Marble Company, 72
Vespucci, Amerigo, 155-56
Villa Medici, 115, *116*
Virginia State Capitol, 89
Volpato, *116*

Walter, Thomas Ustick, 8, 13-20, *14, 16, 19, 20,* 22-23, 25-31, *29,* 33-36, 45, 47, 49-51, *52,* 57, 60, 61-65, *62, 63,* 67, *68,* 73, 85, 88, 97-98, 103, 105, 110-12, 114, 119, 123-24, 128-29, *131,* 134-38, *137,* 142, 145, 147, 151, 158-61, 163, 165, *165, 166,* 171
War (Persico), 11, 126
Ward, J. Q. A., 34
Warren, Joseph, *116,* 119
Washington, D.C., 3, *3,* 7, 31, 33, 61, 67, 86, 89, 140
Washington, George, 2-5, 7-8, 10-11, 23, 35, 65, 67, 86, 88-89, 91, 101, 109, 120, *125,* 126, 130, 133, 153, 156, 162-63, 166
Washington Aqueduct, 22
Washington at Valley Forge, 1778, 151

Washington Crossing the Delaware (Leutze), 133
Washington Monument, 34, 97, 112, 138
Washington's Farewell to His Officers, New York, December 4, 1783 (Crawford and Rinehart), 69
Washington State Capitol, 37, *37*
Washington's Tomb, 97
Webster, Daniel, 18, 51, 67, 94, 97, 99, 102-3, 107, 112, 126, 132
Weinman, Adolph A., 36
Weir, Robert W., 12, 21, 77
Weld Chapel, 24
Wemyss-Smith, S., 38
West Point, United States Military Academy at, 21, 23
West Virginia Capitol, 37, *37*
Westward the Course of Empire Takes Its Way (Leutze), 133, *133*
Wharton, Edith, 50, 67, 124
White House, 4, 7-8, 20
Whitman, Thomas Jefferson, 26-27
Whitman, Walt, 26-27, 49
Wilder and White, 37, *37*
William Penn's Treaty with the Indians, 1682 (Gevelot), 80
Wilson, John, 89, *90*
Wilson, Woodrow, 104, 133
Wisconsin (French), 36
Wisconsin State Capitol, 36, *36, 37, 85,* 89
Wisedell, Thomas, 33, 138-39, 142
Woolworth Building, 37
World's Columbian Exposition, 34
Wren, Sir Christopher, 4, 15
Wright, Orville and Wilbur, 81

Yale University Art gallery, 75
Young, Cliff, 115, 134